Legislature California

Testimony in considering Assembly bill no. 10, concerning the regulation of railroads

1884

Legislature California

Testimony in considering Assembly bill no. 10, concerning the regulation of railroads
1884

ISBN/EAN: 9783337221706

Printed in Europe, USA, Canada, Australia, Japan

Cover: Foto ©Andreas Hilbeck / pixelio.de

More available books at **www.hansebooks.com**

TESTIMONY

TAKEN BEFORE THE

Judiciary Committee of the Senate

OF CALIFORNIA,

IN CONSIDERING

Assembly Bill No. 10, concerning the Regulation of Railroads,

(Generally known as the Barry Bill.)

Twenty-fifth (Extra) Session of the Legislature of California, April, 1884.

PRINTED BY ORDER OF THE SENATE.

SACRAMENTO:

STATE OFFICE, ... JAMES J. AYERS, SUPT. STATE PRINTING.

1884.

REPORT.

On the fourth day of April, A. D. 1884, the Senate of California referred to the Judiciary Committee of the Senate, the following bill, which had passed the Assembly :

AN ACT TO PREVENT DISCRIMINATIONS AND ABUSES BY RAILROAD CORPORATIONS.

The People of the State of California, represented in Senate and Assembly, do enact as follows:

SECTION 1. All railroads built or owned by corporations organized under the laws of the State are public highways, over which all persons are entitled to transportation for persons and property on equal and impartial terms. All roadway and right of way acquired by such companies is for public use. All persons and companies engaged in operating any such road, or in transporting freight or passengers over the same, or which shall hereafter operate or engage as aforesaid, shall forward, move, and carry impartially for all persons offering freight to be transported or moved, without discrimination, preference, or favor to one over another, in price, dispatch, speed, or accommodation of any kind, except as herein provided. All freight shall be dispatched and forwarded in the order in which it is received or tendered for transportation (except that a preference may be given to perishable articles and to express matter and fast freights), and equal and similar facilities, not 'inferior to any in use January first, eighteen hundred and eighty-four, shall be extended on like terms to all connecting transportation lines, whether by land or water, in the receipt and delivery of goods, exchanging cars, making connections by rail, and all other arrangements for expediting and facilitating the receipt, transfer, transportation, and delivery of freight.

SEC. 2. All persons and companies mentioned in the first section of this Act shall at all times keep posted in a conspicuous place, accessible to the public, at each of their stations and offices, a printed table or schedule, of all rates of freight and charge in force for transportation between all points and stations to or from which they carry, and shall furnish (for examination) a printed copy of such table or schedule to all persons demanding the same. Such rates shall be equally available to all persons demanding transportation for person or property over said road, or any part thereof, without discrimination or favor to any, as provided in section one hereof. All discounts, rebates, special contracts, special rates, and other devices for charging more or less than such published rates, are forbidden ; *provided,* that a uniform discount (to be established and published as aforesaid) for payment in advance, or for prompt payment, may be made, and different rates may be charged for express matter, fast and slow freights, and for carload lots, and lots under a carload ; all such rates and discounts to be available to all applicants on equal terms.

SEC. 3. All railroad corporations must at all times maintain all their track and other structures in good and sufficient repair and in a state of complete efficiency for the purposes for which they were constructed or adopted. Any such track or structure, decayed, destroyed, or removed must be diligently replaced or restored to as good or better condition of usefulness and efficiency as before such decay or removal.

SEC. 4. No railroad corporation organized under the laws of this State is permitted to accept any charter or corporate franchise from any other Government, State, or sovereignty ; and no corporation organized under the laws of any other Government, State, or sovereignty is permitted to operate any railroad or carry by rail within this State.

SEC. 5. Section four hundred and one of the Civil Code does not apply to railroad corporations formed by the consolidation of two or more companies previously existing : but the term of the existence of corporations so formed shall not extend beyond that of any of the corporations entering into the consolidation.

SEC. 6. On the expiration or forfeiture of the charter of any railroad corporation, its road and appurtenances and right of way acquired by it, remain vested in the people of the State for public use. Its other property shall be sold, and the proceeds, after payment of its debts and liabilities, divided among its stockholders.

SEC. 7. Any railroad corporation violating the provisions of sections one, three, or four of this Act, shall forfeit its charter and corporate privileges, and shall be adjudged to have incurred such forfeiture and to be dissolved, in an action on behalf of the people of this State, to be instituted by the Attorney-General. Any officer, agent, or servant of any railroad company, who shall take part in the making, carrying out, or enforcing of any contract or agreement for railroad transportation in violation of the provisions of this Act, or in collecting charges, or paying, or allowing discounts or rebates forbidden thereby, or who shall directly or indirectly enter into any agreement or undertaking, or give any orders or directions for, or consent or ratification to the carrying of freight on terms in any respect different from those prescribed in this Act, or further making of any discount or rebate hereby forbidden, or for violating the provisions of this Act in any particular, shall be deemed guilty of a misdemeanor, and shall be punished by imprisonment for not less than thirty days nor more than six months.

SEC. 8. Rates of freight or fare adopted by the Board of Railroad Commissioners, if not put in force and complied with by the railroad companies affected, may be enforced by writ of mandate on behalf of the people, to be sued out by the Attorney-General. Any company failing or refusing to comply with a peremptory mandate issued in such action, shall forfeit its charter and be dissolved. On appeal from judgment awarding a peremptory mandate, in such cases there shall be no stay of proceedings on appeal.

The Senate Judiciary Committee, having said bill under consideration, passed the following resolution:

Resolved, That producers, shippers, and merchants be invited to appear before this committee and make any statements of facts pertinent to the matters involved in said bill, and that any member of the committee may furnish to the clerk of the committee names of any persons whom he may desire to have appear before the committee.

Notices were sent to such witnesses in the following form:

ROOM OF JUDICIARY COMMITTEE, STATE CAPITOL, CAL. }
—— ——:   Sacramento, ——, 1884.   }

DEAR SIR: By request of the Judiciary Committee of the Senate of California, you are hereby invited to appear before said committee, at your earliest convenience, to make statements to the committee concerning the matters involved in the Barry Bill (so called), now pending before said committee. Very respectfully,

SUMNER T. DIBBLE, Secretary.

By order: C. W. CROSS, Chairman.

All witnesses who appeared for examination were examined by the committee, each Senator being permitted to ask questions. The evidence was taken down by a shorthand reporter, and, by resolution of the Senate, duly passed April 14, was printed.

The evidence taken was as follows:

STATEMENT OF MR. HARRISON,

Of the firm of Richards & Harrison, San Francisco, before the Judiciary Committee of the Senate of the State of California.

MR. CHAIRMAN AND GENTLEMEN: I am really unprepared for this opportunity, of which, with a little preparation, I should have been very happy to have availed myself; yet the worthy Senator from San Francisco having introduced me, if I am allowed to show you the action of the special contract system, and how it has affected the merchants of our State, if that is germane to the subject, I should like to make a few remarks, inasmuch as our firm have been personal sufferers, and we have been endeavoring through the Railroad Commission to obtain relief from the oppression of the special contract system. I suppose you are aware that there are four provisions, which, stripped of their verbiage, may be expressed in a few words.

The special contract system, such as the Central Pacific Railroad and the Southern Pacific Railroad have adopted, exacts that the signer shall not patronize sailing vessels or steamers, nor import their goods into this State in that manner. That he shall not buy from or sell to a man who is not a contractor. That they shall have the right to examine our goods and see that the classification of all the goods is conformed to. That they shall have the right to examine our books, and if necessary break into our safe and examine it to see that we do not buy from or sell any freight to a man who is not a contractor. Now, gentlemen, I admired the Chairman of this committee to-day when he offered a resolution indorsing the action of our Minister to Berlin; because he made a fine and a strong effort to prevent the German Empire from discriminating against the American hog. Gentlemen, you needn't go to Germany to make your discriminative fight. Your discriminative fight is with the railroad company, as discriminating against the merchants, and if our Ministers are to be extolled for protecting the American hog, the California merchants will thank the Legislature for protecting the American merchants. Now this bill of Mr. Barry's, as far as it is apparent, is intended, and it occurs to me to say, that the desire of our community is that this discriminative action should be abolished, and in order to do that it will be necessary to adopt the extreme measures of penalty as they appear in the bill.

The railroad has affected everything. We have from day to day submitted our case to the Railroad Commission, and have been met with the information that they have no authority and no power to reach this matter; that it is beyond their jurisdiction. What is the use of referring anything to the Railroad Commission if they have no jurisdiction and claim none? Although members of the legal profession say that they have jurisdiction, they turn round and say that they have not, and the result is that the matter is thrown back into your teeth, and I can see no help for it now but to pass a specific law that will reach it. As far as its being a party measure, I think it ought to be put down as one of the few measures outside of party. I may be put down as one of the few merchants that have contended with the railroad. The result of this discrimination has so enslaved our community that they will not appear before you. Our Board of Trade and our Chamber of Commerce have railroad agents in their bodies and there is not a man that dare put his head up without being marked. The Central Pacific Railroad Company do what the United States Government do not dare to do. In the Custom House the Republican and the Democrat, the Chinaman and the Greek, are all classed alike—every man knows his tariff. The grade is gradual, and there is no distinction and no discrimination. Now, I do not pretend to be a lawyer; I do not pretend to be able to qualify this bill with any legal aspect; but as far as its spirit is concerned, it appears to us as the proper expression. We have got to have relief. We must have relief. Discrimination cannot exist in any civilized community. You do not dare to do it in your own family, nor to discriminate against one of your children, without seeing how quick he will take offense. You must prevent it and give us relief, and this bill, as I understand it, will do so. Unless you make the penalty severe they will escape it again as they have continued to escape others.

Beyond this I have nothing to say. If you are desirous of knowing about the system the railroad has adopted with the merchants, I am here to answer any questions. Few merchants dare to do so, because they have become their slaves. If you shut out our shipping vessels and steamers, you might as well shut up the Golden Gate as far as the merchant doing business in San Francisco is concerned. He might as well be in the heart of Arizona. The same contract extends to other places besides San Francisco, and they import their goods in the interior towns. What would New York do without protection from things of that kind? Here we have the opening of the Pacific closed up. Do you suppose that the merchants went voluntarily into this system of serfdom? No, sir; the first man was beguiled through Stubbs and Vining, their oily agents. They beguiled the first few; intimidated some, and coerced the balance. We are now fighting for the beautiful harbor of San Francisco. We are no better off than the merchants of Arizona. With the Golden Gate closed up we might just as well emigrate. What is California without the Golden Gate and the bay? Nothing. We are closed up with our fine harbor and our facilities. I will be very happy to answer any questions.

MR. SULLIVAN—What is the ground upon which the Railroad Commission stated its opinion that they had no jurisdiction in your case? Answer—They claimed that these contracts had been made mainly in Omaha, some two thousand miles from here, by Mr. Vining, the agent of the Union Pacific Railroad Company, and that they had no control over such contracts made out of this State. In other words, that the merchants of San Francisco are bound by a contract made two thousand miles from San Francisco, alongside of the Missouri River, where they had never seen a ship.

Q. Out of the proceeds received from freight, what is the percentage of the Central Pacific Railroad? A. They get forty-six per cent, and the Union Pacific Railroad gets fifty-four, and, although the counsel for the railroad admitted that they were responsible only for what was collected in this State, that proportion belonging to the Central Pacific Railroad Company, our worthy Railroad Commissioners claimed that they had no jurisdiction over that either, and that they had no jurisdiction at all.

Q. Upon the ground that the contract was made outside of this State? A. Yes, sir.

Q. That they could not segregate it? A. They could not segregate it. It was segregated and admitted in Court that they had segregated it, and that they had collected forty-six per cent—that, it was claimed, was the portion of the Central Pacific Railroad Company. They took the ground that no more contracts should be made with the Union Pacific Railroad Company. That, they knew would break up the special contract system.

Q. Do I understand you that they discriminated against your firm, in favor of merchants in San Francisco? A. They have open rates, and contract rates. By signing a contract they get contract rates; if you don't you have to pay open rates. We were the largest importers in our line of goods—do more than all the rest—and we saw that we could not do justice to our business, our customers, and ourselves, and sign a special contract, and the rates on the goods compelled us to get our goods around the Horn, by sea. We had to sign a contract, by the custom of the road, or pay open rates, and as soon as they made us do that we commenced suit against them.

Q. What is the difference between the contract and the open rates? A. From fifteen to fifty per cent.

Q. Did they take the position that there was no discrimination because these were open contracts that everybody could sign? A. We had the privilege of signing them.

Q. Did not two of the Commissioners say that it was not discrimination within the purview of the Constitution? A. They said that we could sign the contract just as we could in the retail business. That it was just the same thing.

Q. What would be the effect of the Barry bill upon this discrimination that you speak of? A. As I understand it here, merchants against whom discrimination was had might appeal to the Attorney-General to have the charter of the road forfeited.

Q. How could you prove that they discriminated? A. It is merely a matter requiring evidence. Their admissions are on file, and a special contract is easily obtained, and the open rates can be easily obtained; so that any one can see that there is a plain discrimination. A matter of figures between fifteen and fifty per cent.

Q. Is there any truth in what is said about the railroad company, that they charge according to the value of the material? A. Yes, they do. In one case that I will quote: Ruled paper pays sixty per cent more than unruled paper. The ruling alone making a difference of sixty per cent. In plain English, they take the oyster and leave the merchant the shell.

Q. Do you know of any instance where they have examined the books of the merchant for the purpose of finding out whether he has stood by the special contract made with the railroad? A. Yes, sir; I presume they have nullified contracts, and the parties have commenced suits for damages where they had a special contract, where a man dared to buy goods from a party who carried them around the Horn. They have a system of rebate by which they exact open rates, and they remain for a period of from one to three months, and then repay the difference between the open and the special rates, thus always keeping the merchant in debt and slavery.

Q. What is meant by the term "expense bill?" A. It means a freight bill where the amount is intended to be refunded, notifying the agent to collect and to pay the difference within a period of two or three months.

Q. You mean to say that they charge the open contract rate, and then return it? A. They used to do that, but I understand that they found that it was not necessary, and they discontinued it, and now they collect their contract rates.

Q. What is the position of the merchants of San Francisco in regard to this railroad company, if they were called upon by this committee to give testimony here? Will they testify in regard to these matters? Will they dare tell the truth here? A. I never knew them to tell the truth yet.

Q. Are you acquainted with the mercantile community of San Francisco? A. Yes, sir.

Q. How long have you resided in San Francisco and been engaged in business there? A. Fifteen or sixteen years.

Q. Do you know the most of the importing houses there? A. I do, sir. I believe I have collected from the wholesale houses of San Francisco for the last fifteen years, twice a month regularly.

Q. You have a large personal acquaintance? A. Yes, sir, and with the Board of Trade.

Q. Have you talked with the merchants there sufficiently to speak advisedly as to whether or not they would be willing to come here and give testimony concerning any discrimination that might be made against them, or concerning the question of discrimination at all? A. I have talked with them frequently. When I subpœnaed them in my case to testify they came to me with tears in their eyes and begged off.

Q. What was their excuse? A. That their business pursuits were so closely allied to the railroad business that they didn't dare to go; that their contracts might be broken again, as they had been, upon that pretense.

Q. They all wished you success? A. Certainly; they pat me on the back behind-hand, and tell me I am the champion.

Mr. Brooks—Do I understand you that you have no fault to find with any other company than the Central Pacific Railroad? A. And the Southern Pacific Railroad Company.

Q. They do not allow you to buy from parties that ship around the Horn? A. No, sir.

Mr. Cross—Have you ever found a lawyer who advised you that a special contract that limited you to whom you should buy from was not valid in law? A. I have heard them say it all along, but it is a very difficult thing to prove without consulting with the merchants.

Q. I would like to know whether the importers, as a class, are dissatisfied with the present system? A. I can tell you as a fact, that out of the hundred and odd merchants in San Francisco, there are five who approve of the special contract system.

Q. Could you give us an idea as to whether or not that system increases the cost of goods in the general markets of this State? A. It does.

Q. Could you give us some idea as to what per cent? A. The fact is just this: Certain goods will come around the Horn by sailing vessels—heavy goods—hardware, nails, and things of that class, and certain other goods come by steamer, and certain other things of finer quality, changing, by nature of the fashions, or, are of great value, would naturally come by rail. Now, if we had these importations by three channels, we would have every class of goods bearing its natural and proper burden of freight. As it is now, they make a certain reduction upon heavy goods, and make it up on other classes of goods. That is what we should have from the opportunities that the seaboard naturally gives us, but as the thing stands now, nearly every merchant of San Francisco has been coerced. or beguiled into this special contract, and the balance have been compelled to go out of business. We import a certain class of goods around the Horn, not having any special contract, that would only come in vessels, and if that is taken away, there will be no independence any more among our merchants, and there is no such thing as profit any more in California since it has been done; that has been taken from us.

Mr. Reddy—Is it not a well known fact that the merchant, if he does not enter into this special contract with the road, will have to pay advance rates; that is, that the freight on his goods will cost him a great deal more? A. Yes, sir; I should say from fifteen to fifty per cent, according to the exactions of the railroad.

Q. Whether that contract is legal or not cuts no figure? A. It cuts no figure.

Q. From fifteen to fifty per cent is sufficient to make almost any device legal if he will suffer that by not entering into it? A. Yes, sir; if he wants to keep in business.

Q. And the railroad company have so managed that business as to get nearly all the merchants into the system? A. Yes, sir.

Q. And each one that fails to abide by these contracts is compelled to pay extra freight? A. Exactly.

Q. And further ostracised by not being permitted to buy from any other merchants who do not enter into the system? A. He cannot buy from them.

Q. And the result is that he might not only be injured by the extra charge, but his business may be broken up entirely? A. Yes, sir.

Q. Do you know of any instances of discrimination in the matter of forwarding freights outside of the advance in charges; do you know of any discrimination in the forwarding and delivery of freights? A. In our special case, when they found out that we had the temerity to contend with the Central Pacific Railroad Company, they stopped our freight entirely. They said that we must pay our freight in advance. We were paying more than anybody else, and for that reason must pay in advance; and by corresponding with the traffic manager he said: "If you sign our special contract you can have it delivered, and needn't pay before you deliver it." And in our case our goods were stopped on the road, and we had to send a check forward twenty days before the goods got here in consequence of the instructions given by the Central Pacific Railroad Company that any freight coming for Richards, Harrison & Co. must have the freight paid in advance. That is how we are situated. Perhaps that is not discrimination.

Q. Do you know of any other merchants who have been treated in the same manner? A. I do not, Senator. I know one that had his contract taken away from him and the man ruined in the business, and he commenced suit against them for damages.

Q. Do you know whether or not he made application to the Railroad Commissioners for redress? A. No, I do not.

Q. I understood you to say that you formally made application to the company for redress? A. We did.

Q. And the answer was that they had no power and no jurisdiction? A. No jurisdiction. That we had the power to sign the contract as well as anybody else, and we did not sign it.

Q. It was suggested to you by the railroad company that you had better sign the contract. Was that the idea? A. Exactly.

SENATOR SPENCER—It is only the same class of goods that you are prohibited from buying from people that ship around the Horn? A. Any kind of goods.

Q. You don't mean to say that because they have a special contract with you that you cannot buy any other kind of goods which are shipped around the Horn? A. Any kind of goods.

Q. I thought that it was goods that you shipped by the railroad company? A. No, sir; any kind of goods.

Q. Supposing that there was a dispute between the railroad company and the consignee, as to freight, say about a matter of $500. Would you have any rule in regard to paying that? A. I would have to pay for it, and then duplicate it, and try to get it back from them.

Q. Senator Cross asked whether you had asked any lawyer whether that part of the contract which related to the prevention of your buying from any other parties than those with whom you had the special contract, was void as against public policy?

MR. CROSS—No; that was not exactly as I asked it.

A. That has been the general construction. I never saw a lawyer yet that did not say it was unlawful.

Q. That it was void? A. Yes, sir; void, illegal.

Q. Upon what terms did they forfeit this man's contract, and take it away from him? A. They did, added on increased rates of freight. The man had two carloads of goods arrive under his contract. He was connected with one of the oldest and most respected houses of San Francisco. It was some cooper stock, and they found out that this party had bought some lumber—heavy lumber—which came around the Horn; that this contractor had bought his goods from a house that did not have a special contract. When the first carload of his goods arrived they raised him up thirty-three per cent. He propounded the question to them: "Why do you charge me over the contract rates?" and the answer was, "For cause." Every officer that he went to, up to his royal highness, Mr. Stubbs, answered, "For cause."

Q. Do you know that there are people employed by the railroad company for the purpose of finding out whether a man is following out his contract? A. Yes, sir; they have spies. They have men on the wharf to take the marks of the goods, and to follow up the dray, and see where it goes, and to examine the tags, and see whom you sell to, and will ask for the key to your safe.

Q. That is what you stipulate for in the contract? A. Yes, sir.

Q. That is one of the reasons why you wouldn't sign the contract? A. Exactly.

Q. Have you a copy of one of those contracts? A. No, sir; but I can get you one. The Railroad Commission have one.

Q. What is the status of your case in Court? A. They are trying to keep it out of the Federal Courts, and in the State Courts. That is one reason why I like the Barry bill.

Q. You brought suit against them in the State Court, and they tried to remove it to the Federal Courts? A. Yes, sir; but they have not succeeded.

Q. You have the complaint filed, and have argued the matter as to jurisdiction? A. That is all, so far.

Q. Did I understand you to state that they declined to allow you to sign the special contract? A. No, sir.

Q. Has the discrimination on the part of the railroad company contributed to increase the price of any commodity in San Francisco? A. Yes, sir; I hold that it does. The rates are arbitrary. Certain goods would naturally come round the Horn, and by steamer as well as by rail, and be cheaper.

Q. What class of goods have you been dealing in that would have been received in this way? A. Beer, principally. I have been dealing in it a good many years.

Q. That is one of the largest imports? A. Yes, sir.

Q. What would be the difference in getting them over the two routes? A. A difference of fifty dollars to a carload.

Q. How many cases in a carload? A. Eighty barrels.

Q. About seventy cents to a case? A. Yes, sir; enough to keep us out of business.

Q. Could you sell these so much less a case if you had the benefit of these contracts? A. Yes, sir.

SENATOR WHITNEY—Everybody, I understand, has the right to enter into these contracts if they choose. There is no discrimination as far as that is concerned? A. Generally they do, but they have refused to give them to some people that I know of.

Q. Do you know of any person who has declined the privilege of entering into these contracts? A. I do. The way that we have managed our business, we send our goods ten thousand miles; by rail from Milwaukee to New York, and then around the Horn; some thousands of miles by water by sailing vessels, and a voyage takes about six months. We import our goods for one half of the contract price on the railroad.

Q. So really you make money out of that? A. Yes, sir.

Q. So really there is no great hardship about it after all, only you do not get goods so quick? A. We are ostracised in business, and that is an outrage.

Q. By sending to New York you get them for one half the price? A. In this special instance, yes.

Q. The difference in the price would make more than you lose in interest? A. Yes, sir.

Q. So, actually, by going to New York, and getting goods round the Horn, you get goods cheaper, and every other merchant could do the same if he chose? A. Exactly; but they have got to get certain classes by rail.

Q. The special contract works a benefit to you rather than an injury? A. No; I don't think it does. I think I would go out of business by it. We have a good deal of business, but our firm can't fight them alone. We have refused a hundred agencies. We can't do American business. We can't afford to pay fifty-three per cent and expect to exact that from the public.

Q. You could send these other goods to New York, and send them around the Horn the same as beer? A. And pay additional for the goods to be sent by rail? No, sir; you can't do that. The railroads are built for the people.

Q. Why couldn't you do it? A. Because certain classes of goods pay ninety dollars a ton to New York.

Q. Why, can't you send other classes of goods around the Horn the same as you do beer? A. No; the railroads have the odds on goods where the goods are light and expensive.

Q. Could you get them as quick? There are classes which it is necessary to get in time that you are kept out of by not being able to ship them when wanted? A. Certainly; if the goods are valuable, you can afford to pay railroad freight.

SENATOR BROOKS—You can't do American business, you say? A. No, sir; on account of the discrimination we are not able to get a certain class of goods around the Horn.

Q. Your complaint is not so much about that as it is that it deprives you of American trade? A. Yes, sir.

SENATOR SULLIVAN—Does it not require a large capital to do business where you send goods around the Horn, much more than it would if you could get those goods in a few weeks? A. Yes, sir.

SENATOR CROSS—It would throw the business into the large importing houses? A. Yes, sir. Merchants should have the privilege of importing goods by rail or by water, and they should all be allowed to ship at the same price. We have got to have it, or the country cannot prosper.

SENATOR SULLIVAN—Supposing that all the merchants of San Francisco should enter into this special contract system, if ships came out here wouldn't they have to come out in ballast if they wanted any particular freight from this coast, such as wheat, for instance? A. If all signed the contracts no ships would come here at all.

Q. If they did come for shipping wheat or grain, wouldn't they have to come out in ballast? A. I would think so; they might bring coal; I don't believe that the railroad company have a special rate on coal; they must have overlooked that.

MR. WHITNEY—Does it make one or two dollars difference in the price of coal, whether they have to bring it for ballast? A. I don't know as they would lose any money on coal.

SENATOR SULLIVAN—Would it not be better for the farming interests if a great part of the freight were brought here in ships, so that they could have freight both coming and going? A. Precisely. The freight of the farmer would be a great deal less; we should have some encouragement for ships to come here, and on some goods we can give them reasonable freights for coming, and ships are not coming here unless they get freight from the farmer; that is plain enough, and I see that it has been talked about that our railroads are trying to keep our ships away from here entirely, and if they can't bring coal here, the farmer will be compelled to ship his wheat by rail.

Q. If we could encourage the building of ships in the harbor of San Francisco, wouldn't that give us some relief? A. Only by taxes, or something of that sort.

Q. It is stated in one of these documents that the port charges are higher in San Francisco than in any other of the American cities? A. Dockage is cheaper in San Francisco than in any other city.

Q. I understand you to say that if the merchant deals with those who do not have a contract with the railroad company, they are tabooed? A. Yes, sir: there is a provision put into the contract for that purpose, that if it could be arranged by two merchants, one shipping around the Horn and the other by rail, that by transferring carloads of goods, one to the other, so as to suit the requirements of their trade, they might do so, and this is put in there to prevent any goods being sent by water at all. I suppose they are afraid that a merchant could come into our store and buy five or ten packages of goods, and so they have regarded that as a reason to cancel their agreement, and if I were to buy a carload of goods from a contractor, and it was known, it would vitiate that man's contract, and they would decline to bring his goods at contract rates, and ruin him in business.

Q. I want to ask you whether the railroad discriminates against you in Colorado, Montana, Idaho, and Utah? A. They do. They shut out all the freights on goods that we import. We import from Milwaukee, around the Horn, by sailing vessels, and they ship the same goods and shut us out of the Montana markets, and still they charge them double rates.

SENATOR VROOMAN—That has been remedied by competition? A. Yes, sir.

Q. If we could encourage them to come here we would have the same benefit, would we not? A. Yes, sir. Would you expect an opposition bank to come here and start an opposition banking business? There is no room for another road. These railroads have every merchant's freight. Who are they to get patronage from?

Q. After a time they would get freight? A. No other railroad would come here unless they would sign a special contract to patronize them.

SENATOR CROSS—How long do these special contracts last? A. From year to year. They generally keep a little balance due about that time.

Q. Hasn't there been an attempt made to break through this special contract system by the North Pacific Railroad Company? A. I had an agreement with the traffic manager of the road, and I called him down to the office and explained to him that he would have to keep aloof from this special contract system regarding freights, and that if he would do so I would agree to give him one hundred thousand tons of freight within ten days. He agreed to that, and went away up north, and within ten days I telegraphed to him the names of the parties in every kind of business—one hundred thousand tons of freight—and it was agreed that he would keep aloof from the special contract system. These merchants were willing to patronize the road and take the goods down here by steamer from Oregon in order to get their freedom; and the Northern Pacific Railroad Company agreed to deliver the goods in San Francisco, without a special contract system, at the same rates or as cheap as they were delivered by the special contract system, still leaving the consignees the privilege of shipping such goods as they chose by water.

SENATOR DEL VALLE—You say that the contracts between the railroad and the contractors extend over one year? A. Yes, sir.

Q. Is there not a proviso in the contract that the railroad company shall, at any time for cause, cancel it? A. It affects those four provisions.

Q. They are the sole judges of that matter? A. Yes, sir; they have canceled them repeatedly.

SENATOR BROOKS—Who do I understand you to say that you had this agreement with in regard to the Northern Pacific Railroad Company? A. Mr. Muir, the Traffic Manager of the road. I don't know that they had any Secretary.

Q. Are you satisfied that the Central Pacific Railroad Company and the Southern Pacific are the same? Is there any lively competition between them? A. I don't think so.

Q. Have you any reliable information on that? A. The very depreciation of the stock from one hundred to fifty would be sufficient; all that was the bearing of the stock.

SENATOR CROSS—Do I understand you to say that the merchants in other places than San Francisco, in California, can have the benefit of the same special contract system? Can the Sacramento merchants have their freights at the same rates from the East as the San Francisco people? A. Yes, sir; at the terminal points.

Q. How many of them? A. I think some four. The original contracts were only made to San Francisco, and the merchants signed it under the idea that they were to have some protection, but since that they have increased the places and taken in Stockton, Los Angeles, and I am not sure whether Marysville or not—I know Stockton, Los Angeles and Sacramento. We have lost our southern trade, and the merchants in Sacramento and Stockton import directly from the East.

Q. That is to say, that the Stockton, Los Angeles, Marysville, and Sacramento merchants derive a profit which you would derive if it were not for such a system? A. They import them directly because there is no toll. They have to pay no San Francisco toll.

Q. Does that benefit those terminal points other than San Francisco? A. I don't know that it does. San Francisco ought to be the same as New York. It ought to be the distributing point for the Pacific Coast, and we merchants should get goods some by rail and some by water, and we should have all the principal trade.

Q. That would give you a monopoly of the business? A. Certainly it would give us a monopoly. A seaport is entitled to a monopoly. That is what has made San Francisco.

SENATOR REDDY—Do you mean that you are entitled to the advantages which a seaport naturally gets? A. Yes, sir.

Q. You are entitled to a monopoly of the carriage by water? A. Yes, sir.

Q. That is a monopoly that God Almighty created? A. Yes, sir; under his own hand.

SENATOR WHITNEY—Are not these people who live at Sacramento, and Los Angeles, and those other places, entitled to the advantages which a railroad gives to them? A. Not at the expense of San Francisco.

SENATOR McCLURE—Don't the San Francisco people complain that the railroad gives these special contracts to the small importers in the interior towns at the same rates? A. Yes, sir; they complain that the contracts are extended into the interior at the same rates.

Q. They refused to discriminate between a large importer and a small one, and the importer on Front Street complained? A. Yes, sir, merchants like to make money. It is a matter of whether they buy in New York or buy in San Francisco, with the extra freight added. It is so all over the world. San Francisco will command the trade, the business of the State; you can't take it away from her, although the Central Pacific Railroad has tried hard to do it.

Q. Then they have tried to distribute the wholesale business all over the State? A. No, sir.

MR. WHITNEY—Does not the opening of roads have that effect generally upon seaports? A. No, sir; simply moved the freights from the distributing points.

MR. CROSS—Is freight cheaper now than it was before the railroad was built? A. Freight by sailing vessels is about the same; by rail it is higher; because it is higher than a sailing vessel or steamer.

Q. Are sailing vessels and steamers in competition against railroads? A. No, sir.

Q. If they were permitted to come in and go out freely, would not there be a certain amount of competition between the ship and the railroad company? A. Certainly, there would be a natural competition.

Q. Do you think it would be beneficial to shut off shipping by entering into this special contract system? A. Be the ruination of the State. If the railroad company can make all this trouble importing, what would they do with exporting? The company would own everything. Excuse me, but what in the devil would there be left?

SENATOR REDDY—Do you see anything in the Barry bill which would operate injuriously to any one there? A. No, sir.

Q. It would permit certain classes of goods to come to the State by water? A. It throws the field open alike to everybody.

Q. Now you are compelled to bring all classes of goods by rail or else pay extra rates? A. Yes, sir, or they shut you out of business.

Q. Then the matter brought up by Senator McClure, that the present contract system allows the poor man to be on the same footing as the large merchant, would be precisely the same? A. Exactly; there is no special difference in it that I can see.

SENATOR KELLOGG—If the goods were all landed in San Francisco in the first instance and dealt out to interior merchants, how would that change affect them? A. I think it would be the natural protection of them. I think that large houses extend protection to small dealers in the natural growth of trade; it is so recognized all over the world. The large dealers in London deal all over the world. In New York they have branch houses even in Chicago and elsewhere, and it is natural that the seaport is where the natural gravitation of commerce comes, and in this case it ought to be left in San Francisco.

Q. That is to say, that large importers might establish branch houses in Marysville and monoplize the business? A. No; no.

SENATOR REDDY—If they allowed a fair rate to San Francisco, and from there to other points, it would be all right? A. Yes, sir.

Q. This present system is not of much advantage to the country merchants? A. No, sir; nothing more than it has made bad feeling between the former merchant and his patron. There are certain agricultural implements that should come by sailing vessels. We can import them for one half.

SENATOR SULLIVAN—I understand that all these other towns would have the benefit by allowing the merchants of San Francisco to bring their goods by sea? A. It would be open to all if it were not for this special contract system.

SENATOR CROSS—Would there be any wholesale business of imported goods in these towns of Stockton, San José, Sacramento, Marysville, and Los Angeles, do you think, if it were not for this special contract system? Does not the special contract system tend to build up the wholesale business in those cities? A. I don't see that they are any better off for it. I don't think there is a house on the northern part here that is any stronger than it used to be in these places. It is a matter of whether they buy in New York, with the extra rate added, or in San Francisco. It is so all over the world. San Francisco will command the business of the State. You can't take it from her, although the Central Pacific Railroad has tried to do it.

Q. Then they have tried to distribute the wholesale business all over the State? A. Yes, sir.

SENATOR WHITNEY—Does not the opening of roads generally have that effect upon seaports? A. No, sir; simply moves the freights from the distributing points.

Q. Is it not an indication of an increase of commerce? A. No, sir.

Q. I have heard it said that there was more goods pass over than passed under bridges on the Mississippi River; would you be inclined to think that was true? A. That may be the case. Now, to get our goods round the Horn ought not to be a disadvantage to San Francisco, when we have to pay an average of from forty to one hundred by rail. With San Francisco as a distributing point we could get our goods at nine dollars a ton and distribute them a good deal cheaper.

Q. Railroads do make new distributing points? A. Yes.

Q. The building of railroads about Chicago has made it a great city? A. Yes, sir.

Q. And it would not have been without? A. Certainly, the completion of railroads has made Chicago. Not one railroad, any more than it would San Francisco. Competition is what we want here, and whether we get it or not we do not want the special contract system.

SENATOR REDDY—Do you know of any reason why railroad management requires the merchant to enter into this contract not to bring freight by water? A. Because they want to control the entire carrying trade of the Pacific Coast.

Q. Is it not a fact that they get the merchant to enter into this contract so as to prevent the carrying by ships? Exactly.

Q. And so that they may get higher rates than they had before? A. Yes, sir.

SENATOR SPENCER—I understood you to say that you telegraphed the names of several gentlemen from San Francisco who were dissatisfied with the special contract system and were willing to ship by the Northern Pacific Railroad. A. I telegraphed one hundred thousand tons. I think there were thirty or forty names.

Q. How many of them were in the special contract system? A. No contractors except two.

Q. Do you feel that you would violate any confidence by giving those names? A. I should first like to have the privilege. Our merchants are very cowardly. I don't like to interfere with their business, and I have never done so, but if you want to examine my letter book I would be happy to allow you to do so.

Q. The action of these parties was partially prevented by Gould and Huntington getting control of the Northern Pacific Railroad? A. Yes, sir.

Q. And Muir did not abide by his contract? A. No, sir. He wrote to me that he was willing, and that the Directors were also, to take it at fifty dollars a ton.

Q. Who controls the Pacific Mail Steamship Company? A. They control it. They have a contract or pay so much to them for fixing the rates.

Q. Will the Barry bill affect that? A. In the Barry bill or under it they cannot afford it. If they can't control them what do they want to make the rates for.

STATEMENT OF H. M. YERRINGTON.

MR. CHAIRMAN AND GENTLEMEN: I am here representing the Carson and Colorado Railroad. It commences in Nevada and runs a distance of eighty-six miles in the State of Nevada to the State line of California, and then extends one hundred and seven miles in this State. I came down here with the view of going before the Board of Equalization in regard to taxes, but am very glad to meet you here in regard to matters which I understand are coming up in relation

2ᵇ

to railroads and railroad matters in our section of the State. I do not understand what it is that you particularly desire, but if you have any questions I will be very happy to answer.

SENATOR REDDY—Have you read what is known as the Barry bill? Answer. Yes, sir; a portion of it.

Q. What objections are there from a railroad standpoint to any section of that bill? A. That is rather difficult for me to answer in reading it over so hastily. There are a great many points, of course, that I might overlook. The only thing that I notice is the classification of the rates of passenger fares.

Q. That would not come into the Barry bill. Have you noticed section one, on page two, where it reads: "All freight shall be dispatched and forwarded in the order in which it is received or tendered for transportation (except that a preference may be given to perishable articles and to express matter and fast freights). Do you see any objection to that? A. No, I do not, excepting in the matter of transferring from a narrow gauge to a wide gauge. It is possible that we might make a carload in less quantity. They might deliver to us one of fifteen tons, and we might use two cars instead of one. I don't know as that would be an injury, so long as we did not injure the goods.

Q. Now, I will call your attention to section two, which reads, "All persons and companies, mentioned in the first section of this Act, shall at all times keep posted in a conspicuous place, accessible to the public, at each of their stations and offices, a printed table or schedule of all rates of freights and charges in force for transportation between all points and stations, to or from which they carry, and shall furnish (for examination) a printed copy of such table or schedule to all persons demanding the same." Do you see any particular hardship in that? A. No, sir, I do not; I would suggest one thing that it might be well to insert: that the agent be allowed to write in any changes that might be made, that would be needed in the freight that might come to the agent's office. You can see the reason for that.

Q. I see; a new class of freight might come along, and by being allowed to put it in, he would avoid the violation of the law? A. Exactly.

Q. Have you any objections to the bill as a whole? A. Well, I understand that the whole bill covers the proposition of operating roads.

Q. To prevent and punish discriminations. Now, that being carried out according to its spirit and letter, with a view to preventing discrimination, and not for the purpose of hurting any one who wants to obey the law and to prevent discrimination and protect the public, can you see any sound objection to that bill? A. We have had cases on our road where we had opposition from other roads, and the result was that we had to deliver goods, say at some certain point on our road, at less rates than we would deliver them at another point. If that would be discriminating, it would be a good thing for the parties. We could run against the other railroad. In other words, the lack of discrimination would destroy competition, and in that case the people would suffer, but aside from that, I do not see anything objectionable—I don't see any reason why we could not run under this bill.

Q. There are a great many points where there is not competition? A. There are in Nevada, we have the Nevada Central road, and it extends within sixty or eighty miles of us, and that is where, if we cannot discriminate, we cannot compete, if both rates of freights and fares were the same.

Q. Would you be in as good a position as the other road—you would have the same advantages? A. That is true.

Q. So that things would probably equalize themselves? A. We admit that.

Q. So that you would not regard this bill as being severe upon the parties who recognized that they must not discriminate? A. No, I do not, except where this thing is, if we see fit to run the road cheaper than the other. In that case the question would be, whether we would be allowed to do so under the law.

Q. If the same general rule were applied, you would be in as good position as the others? A. No doubt about that.

Q. The other fellow might want to take advantage of you as well as you of him, but if the law did not allow you to do so, it would be all right? A. It would be, so far as the road is concerned, but the customer would suffer in that case because he could not get the lower rates.

Q. Every rule will work a disadvantage to somebody? A. True.

Q. And in determining a general rule, in order to prevent discrimination, we cannot of course be guided by a particular instance where it would benefit, even though it did injure a single individual? A. Certainly.

SENATOR VROOMAN—Will you please read the bill, commencing with the word "All," on line five of page one, down to the close of the section, and see what you think in regard to that matter. Now, under the reading of that section you would be compelled to transport all freights, regardless of its character, over the whole road, between the same points, in the same direction, at the same price? A. Do you mean to say that that would not allow us to classify our goods?

Q. Yes, sir.

SENATOR CROSS—That is, lines twelve and thirteen, on page two, "except perishable articles and fast freight."

[Discussion omitted.]

Q. I will ask you to read line nine, and ask how you construe that? A. I construe it that we would have no right to classify our goods.

Q. If you were to insert after the word "another," on line nine, "of the same class of freight," or "of the same kind of freight," or "the same classes of freight," wouldn't the bill, with that amendment, prevent discrimination, and at the same time allow you to classify your freight? A. I think so.

Q. Now turn to line eleven, on page two. How long is your road? A. Nearly three hundred miles.

Q. Through what kind of a country is it operated? A. Through a mountainous country, principally.

Q. What is the general character of your business? A. Ores, machinery, borax, soda, and lumber.

Q. Do you ever have large amounts of wheat or grain? A. We are hauling considerable wood, but not much grain.

Q. Do you ever have a large amount of any kind of freight, more than you have facilities for transportation at the same time; I mean nothing more than you could move in a few days? A. No, sir, unfortunately not.

Q. Do you transport much live stock? A. Very little. The road runs through a small section of country; Owen Lake Valley, about sixty miles. It is very light. Our business is principally through a mountainous country, and for mines.

Q. I will now direct your attention to line five in section two; how do you construe that portion which reads, "And shall furnish a printed copy of all such tables or schedules to all persons demanding the same." Under the wording of that line, would you or would you not hold that you would have to furnish a patron of your road with a copy of the schedule all the way to San Francisco? A. No, sir; that ought to apply only to points on our road.

Q. Would it not be well to amend that in some respects, so as to make it clear? A. The difficulty would be to get the same rates; the rates being on different roads, it is difficult for us to tell; we would have to ascertain what we could do beyond where our road commenced.

Q. You mean, then, that there is no objection to keeping posted in your offices and stations a printed schedule of the fares and freights from that station to other points along your own road within the State? A. I see no objection to that. I would like, though, to suggest to you the same thing that I did to Mr. Reddy, and that is, that the agent should be allowed to interline or write in any changes that might be made in the schedule, the printed schedules.

Q. If you had a printed schedule, and subsequently a new industry should spring up along the line of your road that was entirely new, you would wish to interline that in the schedule? A. That is the idea.

Q. You could have it so that it might be interlined, so that the new rates might be put upon the schedule? A. The rates constantly change in freighting.

Q. How long is your road? A. About three hundred miles.

Q. And through a sparsely settled country? A. Yes, sir.

Q. How many trains do you run every day over your road? A. Two mixed trains. The passenger and freight are all on one train; one each way each day.

Q. About how many cars do you run? A. From three to eight.

Q. You have a small road, doing a limited amount of business? A. Yes, sir, we have.

Q. With that small road, and doing that limited amount of business, how many times during the year do you change your freight schedule? A. We probably would not change our freight schedule more than once.

Q. How many times do you have occasion to change it by adding to it and taking from it? A. Almost every day. Our freight agent does that by writing a note to the agent at the station that it is going from or going to, explaining what he is going to do about making the change. But we have a law in the State of Nevada that we have to give five days' notice that we propose making a change, and consequently you will understand where the trouble comes in about this sort of thing. It is a very necessary thing for him to do.

Q. Assuming that you had a long road and were running a great many freight trains a day over it, of course upon the same proposition you would change your schedule very often, that is in the way of adding to it and taking from it? A. Yes, sir.

SENATOR BROOKS—On page two, of line four, what is your opinion in reference to that provision, "All railroad corporations must at all times keep their tracks and other structures in good and sufficient repair," etc.? A. Well, of course that refers to bridges and things of that kind, naturally taking in the bed of the road and the ties. If the road is properly managed and it is necessary to keep those things in good order, there would be no objection to that. If they are destroyed, of course they would have to be repaired. If they are removed, there must be some good reason if they are not put back there again. I don't understand the necessity of that word "remove" in there.

Q. You would suggest, then, that the word "remove" be stricken out? A. Entirely. I don't see any sense in it.

Q. In section seven, line five, "Any agent, officer, or servant of the company, who shall take part," etc., what effect would that have? A. My impression is that it would be very difficult to find out how it was done or when it was done.

Q. Would it be hard upon the agents or employés of the road? A. It would be, if carried out strictly. The chances are that we would not have agents. That is a section that I have not read before.

SENATOR DEL VALLE—I want to ask you again about your construction of line five of section one, "All persons and companies engaged in operating any such road, or in transporting freight or passengers over the same, or which shall hereafter operate or charge as aforesaid, shall forward, move, and carry impartially for all persons offering freight to be transported or moved, without discrimination, preference, or favor to one over another," etc. Does not that refer to persons and not to things? A. I don't think so. I think under that, if a man came in to-day with a carload of silks, and another with a carload of potatoes, and the fellow who had the silks would say, "I want you to ship this at the same rate that you ship the potatoes at," you would have to do it. (Reading it again.) It seems to me that it is very plain.

Q. That it means that the prices should be the same for all kinds of freight? A. Yes, sir.

Q. You don't mean that if one had a carload of potatoes, and another a carload of something else, that you should charge one fifty dollars and the other seventy-five dollars? A. No, sir. It means that all should be entered at the same price; but it seems to me that if you would put in "of the same class, or character," or something of that kind, that would avoid it.

Q. In regard to this difference in prices, why do you say that there should be a difference in price? A. It says here, "no preference over another in price."

Q. Over another what? A. Over another shipper.

Q. It does not read *freight*, does it? A. No, sir.

SENATOR SPENCER, of Napa—Reading page two, beginning at line eleven, and down to line fourteen: "All discounts, rebates, special contracts, special rates, and other devices for charging more or less than such published rates, are forbidden; provided, that a uniform discount (to be established and published as aforesaid for payment in advance, or for prompt payment) may be made, and different rates may be charged for express matter, fast and slow freights, and for carload lots and lots under a carload, all such rates and discounts to be available to all applicants on equal terms." Is there-any objection against that sentence? A. I don't see that there is. I suppose that it means that it shall be shipped as it is received.

Q. That is the general rule with reference to other business, is it not—"first come, first served?" "All freight shall be dispatched in the order in which it is received or tendered for transportation, except that a preference may be given to perishable articles, and to express matter, and fast freight." Is that proper, in your judgment? A. Yes, sir.

Q. Supposing that I bring a load of fruit, and Mr. Del Valle brings another load of oranges, and another Senator brings another load—all perishable. Supposing I bring mine to-day, Mr. Del Valle brings his to-morrow, and Senator Brooks the next day; do you think it would be fair for you to take up Senator Brooks' car, that came last, and send it first? A. If I followed the law in the first place, his would not be there when the other came.

Q. If an amendment be put in there that articles of freight shall be carried in the order in which they are received, "of the same class or kind," does not that take it out of the rule that all freight shall be carried in the order in which it is received. And don't that give to the railroad company the perishable articles which they receive first to carry first? A. As between shippers?

Q. Yes, sir. Don't that obviate the very necessity that is apparently intended to be cured by the bill? A. I will explain that. Taking our mixed freights, our trains are made up of fast freight, slow freight, express, and passenger. Now, supposing that one had a lot of machinery, and another a lot of oranges, and one a lot of perishable fruit, and a lot of express, and all that. Under this bill it says that they shall be dispatched in the order in which they are received; without it we would have the right to leave the machinery and take the oranges or the melons, and leave the machinery till the next train could come and take them. That would be an answer to you, it would seem to me. This bill says that each carload, as it comes in, no matter to whom it belongs, should be sent forward immediately. If another carload comes that day, the one that comes to you first should be sent first. That is what I understand this law means, does it not?

Q. Do you mean to say that if I bring you a carload of potatoes, or a carload of wheat, and another person at the same time brings you a carload of perishable fruit, that this bill does not give the carload of fruit the preference? A. That is the way I read it.

Q. Don't this expressly give the railroad company the right to discriminate between persons that ship perishable articles? Don't it read so that it cannot discriminate in that freight? To cut it short—that there shall be no discrimination between persons as to classes of goods? Do you see the point? A. I see the point; yes, sir.

Q. Is it nothing more than fair that the railroad company should serve first the man who comes first? A. Not at all.

Q. Especially perishable fruit; the man who brings perishable fruit first should have it sent first? A. Yes, sir.

SENATOR SULLIVAN—You say that this road runs between Nevada and California? A. Yes, sir.

Q. In what States has it been incorporated? A. It runs from the Mountain House down, about half way from Carson, to Virginia City, in a southwesterly direction one hundred and fifty-eight miles, and then runs about thirty-five miles to the State line of the State of California. To the junction, the first portion of the road, is incorporated in the State of Nevada as the Nevada and California road; and from the junction to the State line, the Carson and Colorado section, the second division. Then we come to the State line of California and run one hundred and seven miles. That is the terminus of our road. We call that the Carson and Colorado, third division, and that is incorporated in the State of California.

Q. Your road is a narrow gauge road? A. Yes, sir.

Q. A standard narrow gauge? A. Yes, sir.

Q. Similar to the gauge of the South and the North Pacific Coast roads? A. Yes, sir.

SENATOR —— —Supposing that you should have occasion to remove a depot permanently because the travel did not warrant you in retaining it, or supposing that it should be destroyed by fire and you should desire to replace it at some other point on the line that you thought would be more convenient for a depot than the one where it had originally stood, wouldn't you, under the last clause of section three, be compelled to replace it exactly where it originally stood, or very near to it? A. Yes, sir; I think so. It would look that way. I was looking at this before. In speaking about this I had reference to tracks and bridges, but not to buildings. I supposed that structures meant bridges, and I said that a company should keep the road in good order, so as to be open at all times. "They must at all times maintain all their track and other structures in good and sufficient repair and in a state of complete efficiency for the purposes for which they were constructed or adopted. Any such structure decayed, destroyed, or removed, must be diligently replaced or restored to as good or better condition of usefulness and efficiency as before such decay or removal." Then that would be buildings.

That would prevent us from removing a station to any distance from where it was at the time it was destroyed.

Q. If the section read that you were to keep open and in good repair a continuous track, you would have no objection to it? A. That is the idea.

SENATOR REDDY—Would you not consider that under this bill you would have to rebuild a depot in the same position where it had hitherto been, even though both the interest of the traveling public as well as the interest of the railroad company would not be damaged by discontinuing it entirely, or by putting it in another place? A. I will tell you what I would do: If I wanted to remove a station on our road, I would go and do it, and if any one came to me and said, "You are to put this where it originally stood," I would say, "I will replace it," simply, unless the term "replacing" would mean putting back where it originally stood.

Q. Supposing that the conditions of your business were such that it would not justify you, as a business proposition, to replace it; suppose (as was suggested by Senator Whitney) that it was a mining camp that was worked out and all the people had gone away, would not you consider that, under this section, you would have to replace it? A. I should think I would have to.

. Q. Would you not think that would work a hardship to the company without any corresponding benefits to the traveling public? A. It would be.

SENATOR JOHNSON—In your judgment, as a railroad man, would the words "perishable articles" include live stock? A. That would depend upon circumstances. If I had live stock to send, and they were at a station where they could not get water, or where I could not take them out and feed them, I would feel obliged to forward them as soon as possible as against any other ordinary freight.

SENATOR VROOMAN—And if you could get water and feed? A. If I could, then I would take oranges, or fruit, or provisions in preference.

Q. Then live stock, with plenty of feed and water, would be classified with coal and iron and wood, and that kind of freight? A. No; not exactly. I would put them ahead.

Q. How could you, if you are to be governed by the doctrine of perishable and non-perishable articles under this bill? A. The question is, if an ox had plenty of feed and water, how long would it take him to perish?

Q. But he would eat his head off? Now direct your mind to this proposition: does this bill provide for any more than two classes of freight, non-perishable and perishable? A. That is all, of course.

Q. Then live stock, I understand you, if they had plenty of food and water, would not be considered perishable? A. No, sir.

Q. Then if you had a carload of ores to transport, and a man came along with a few head of cattle, which would have the preference under this bill? A. The cattle.

Q. How? A. They are more perishable than ore.

Q. But it does not seem to make any distinction in the bill? A.

That would have to be one of the cases that would have to be left to the railroad company, of course.

Q. This bill does not propose to leave anything to the railroad. It says you must not make any distinction except in regard to perishable goods? A. It would have to be left to the railroad company, as I understand it.

Q. As to non-perishable articles, it does not make any distinction? A. No, it does not.

SENATOR WHITNEY—Is it not frequently the case that the railroad companies have to exercise a discretion in such matters as cattle. Suppose a family of immigrants were coming along with their household goods, and that you had two or three hundred tons of ore to transport, don't you feel as though it would be your duty to transport the household goods? A. Yes, sir.

Q. And yet there is nothing mentioned about that in this bill? A. My judgment about that is that the bill is possibly intended for people who have not got any souls or hearts, or anything of the kind, and in that case I would make it as binding on them as possible. I want to do business so that if a poor man comes along with his goods we would try to let him get them on, and let the perishable stock hold over. And if we have a man that we don't like, we do it quicker for him than for anybody else, to show that there is nothing mean about our people. That is the way that we do business.

Q. Now, I want to know what you understand that word "accommodation" to mean? A. There might be, for instance, express freight which ought to go over the road quicker.

Q. Does that have reference to the cars or the accommodation furnished? A. I don't know that that term, as used here, would have a particular meaning.

Q. It don't mean anything? A. That is about it.

Q. Does not that mean by box cars, or flat cars, or things of that sort? A. The railroad company might possibly know about such things. A man might not want his goods to go on a flat car. I would not want a party to ship goods on a flat car if he had to take any chances on rain, or something of that kind; but I don't understand exactly. If we shipped the goods as they arrived, that is all we could do. I don't know any other accommodations that we could give.

Q. You don't know what the word "accommodation" does mean there? A. No, sir; I don't know what it means.

SENATOR KELLOGG—In connection with the question asked you by the gentleman in regard to household goods, I understood you to say that if the law was fixed in that way that you would not pay much attention to it? A. No; because we do those things without law asking us to do it.

Q. But if this bill was in force you would not be allowed to do it, or you would lose your charter? A. That refers to something else brought up here.

SENATOR REDDY—That is a legal question, that if he fails to obey he would lose his charter? A. I think there would be no doubt about that.

Q. I understand that that would be your idea in regard to the bill?
A. Yes, sir.

SENATOR BALDWIN—Don't you think it would be complying with the spirit of the law if you were to forward the band of cattle before you did the ore? A. As I said, I should feel very much like doing that. It is the humane way of doing.

Q. Don't you think it would be a compliance with the spirit of the law? A. Well, I presume that would be the result.

Q. If you complied with the spirit of the law, would not you be following the law? A. I don't find any fault, and I don't think if I did so, that I could be sued in any Court in the country and they could get a verdict from any Judge and jury.

SENATOR VROOMAN—I call your attention again to the words "or accommodations," as suggested by Senator Whitney, and ask: Supposing that Mr. A brings a ton of ore, and you put it on a box car, or on a flat car, and Mr. B brings a ton of flour, and you put it in a box car; would not A, under the reading of this bill, say, "You are discriminating against me; you have got the ore in a box car, and the flour on a box car, and I don't like it?" A. The railroad company have to handle the goods, and if they injure any, they are liable for the damage. But this bill describes the method, and says price, dispatch, speed, or accommodation. Now, of course the words are to be given some meaning in law, if possible. I say, as I said to this gentleman, I don't understand the words "or accommodations," and I don't understand why it was put in.

Q. It has a technical meaning, and is presumed to be used in the law in a technical sense? A. Supposing the man with the potatoes says, "Here, I want you to accommodate me," and the man with the flour says, "I want you to accommodate me." Now, I ship the flour in a box car, and the potatoes on a flat car, and I say, "I have accommodated you."

Q. Wouldn't that be governed by the word "dispatch?" A. No, "dispatch" means forwarding freight.

Q. Does not the word "speed" cover that. Does not the word "dispatch" govern the starting of freight? A. That is what I mean.

Q. Don't the word "speed" mean (reading the section), first, that you shall forward it in the order in which it is received; second, transport it on the same time one with another; and, third, that you shall afford to every shipper the same kind of accommodations as to character of car, without reference to the class of freight. Now, are not those ideas embodied there? A. As a general proposition, that is true, although I may say this, that on the Virginia and Truckee Railroad we are hauling ore on a steep grade, and we have cars purposely for those ores, and if a man should come to me and say, "I want you to put this ore in some different car," if we were acting under this bill, I should refuse to do so.

Q. Do you then give him the same accommodations? A. I would give him the same cars that I did his neighbor.

Q. In other words, you would give the same kind of accommodations to people having the same kind of freight to transport? A. Yes, sir.

Q. Then you would not give him the same accommodations as you would others, as to the character of the car? A. No, sir.

SENATOR REDDY—Would you put flour on a flat car and wood in a box car? A. No, sir.

Q. Flour being a perishable article if exposed to the action of the elements? A. I don't know but what I might, possibly, provided that I had no other cars in the yard at all but those two.

Q. Both parties arriving at the same time, could A, under the provisions of this Act, demand that his car should be forwarded first? A. It would look very much that way.

Q. Couldn't the railroad company excuse discrimination in favor of one over another in that way or by that means? A. I think so, although if perishable articles are to go first, I suppose as far as flour is concerned, that it would be considered a perishable article.

Q. I believe that it was intimated, by the Senator from Alameda, that you could not forward any freight, under this bill, till the schedule had been printed. Do you find anything there that prohibits the forwarding of freight before the schedule is printed? A. No.

Q. Supposing that it merely says that you shall furnish people, for examination, a schedule, and that some new, unclassified freight should arrive for which no rates had been fixed; now, being required to print, you know, as a business man, do you not, that when a man is required to do a given thing, that the law always allows him a reasonable time to do it in, unless the time is mentioned; consequently I assume that you would do so as a business man in endeavoring to comply with the law; and being permitted to interline or put down the rate in writing, would you not have a reasonable time to classify and fix the rate, in your judgment; would you act upon that principle, as a business man, if the law did not make any absolute prohibition of any kind? A. I suppose not.

Q. Would you not consider yourself following the law by taking a reasonable time to comply with it? A. Certainly not.

Q. You are willing to abide by the law in the management of that railroad? A. Exactly.

Q. As a business man, do you see anything in this bill that would prevent you from operating your road, or which would seriously embarrass you in the management of your road—I mean within the spirit of the law, acting under the proposition that there is to be no discrimination in the forwarding of freight or the dispatch of it; and without taking a hypercritical or technical view of the bill, but looking at the whole face of it, would you say, as a business man, that you would be embarrassed in the operating and management of your road by that bill; that is to say, would you be prevented from discriminating, and would that be a hardship, or would it create any serious obstacle? A. I don't discover anything of that kind.

Q. Of course you see a great many things that you would like to alter? A. Excepting some of these matters regarding what I have read here to-day, I believe the wording of the bill in some places is a little dark. Section one, line five, that you "shall forward, move, and carry."

Q. That is what you are doing, and really you could do a good deal more than you are doing? A. Yes, sir.

Q. You forward it as fast as any reasonable man would desire? A. Yes, sir.

Q. The probabilities are that you will do that for all of it? A. Yes, sir.

Q. You have no apprehension that you will be crowded by cattle, or ores, or coal, or anything that you are likely to get? A. No doubt of that.

Q. I ask you, as a railroad man, if it is not the desire of all railroad companies that their business shall increase? A. Always.

Q. Would it not be a prudent railroad man's business to say that he is ready to forward all freight? A. Yes, sir.

Q. And should he not do it? Does he not owe that duty to the public? A. Yes, sir.

Q. Do you find anything on that branch in it that would prevent you from operating your road and forwarding freight as it comes? A. No, sir.

Q. Have you heard any complaint against your company because they would not take and forward all freight? A. No, not to my knowledge.

Q. The railroads are not oppressed there by cattle or swine, or in a general way by live stock or any other kind of freight. The trouble is that they cannot get enough? A. That is the trouble.

Q. Do you apprehend any great trouble in the future on the part of the railroads accommodating the people with their freight? A. No, sir; I do not.

Q. There is nothing to apprehend on that score, in your judgment? A. That seems to be the case.

Q. You shall "forward, move, and carry, impartially." If all persons offering freight to be transported can be accommodated, there can be no trouble there? A. No; not at all.

Q. They might like to discriminate, because almost every man likes to serve his friend first, but not being permitted by the law, it might hurt some of your friends, and might not. That would not bother the railroad company at all? A. Not at all.

Q. It would only bother those people who are friends of the railroad? A. That is all.

Q. You would not be allowed to discriminate? A. Except in this instance we will be able to discriminate: the company could as against a poor man, because it would enable him to ship his goods and get back freight.

Q. You assume that in some cases the railroad company should be permitted to discriminate? A. Yes, sir.

Q. But it would not prevent any company from operating their road if it denied them that right? A. Not at all.

Q. Is it not an awful power to be placed in the control of the railroad company to be allowed to discriminate between persons. Does it not put it in their power to destroy any individual in the community where the people are all served by one road? A. Well, that is true.

Q. It is an awful power, isn't it? A. Yes, sir; but I don't think the railroads want to destroy any one.

Q. Don't they destroy communities? A. No, sir.

Q. But if they take a notion to do so they can injure them seriously? A. Yes, sir; but it is against the interest of any railroad company to do it.

Q. Then it would not do them any harm to deny them that right? A. No.

Q. It would do them no harm from being prevented from doing what they do not want to do? A. That is so.

Q. "Discrimination, preference, or favor to one over another," that we have already treated; the whole business? A. Yes, sir.

Q. "In price." You are not charging one man more than another in price for the same services? A. That is correct.

Q. That is the way that men ought to be served. Will that embarrass your railroad? A. Not at all.

Q. The next is, "dispatch and speed." That is to say, that you will not give one man a superior right over another in the matter of time. That won't hurt the railroad? A. No, sir.

Q. "Or accommodation of any kind." That means, as I understand it, that all shall be treated alike or about alike? A. The whole thing being assumed that no accident is going to occur on the road.

Q. By washouts, or snow, or anything of that kind. That does not cut any figure here? A. No.

Q. Of course everybody served on that trip would have to stand the washouts, "except as hereinafter provided." "All freight shall be dispatched and forwarded in the order in which it is received or tendered for transportation." There is no harm there in a general way? A. None at all.

Q. "Except that a preference may be given to perishable articles." That rule is already observed by railroad companies? A. Yes, sir.

Q. And they will not have any greater burden imposed upon them if this bill passes than they have now, in that respect? A. The same.

Q. "And to express matter and fast freights." If anybody has any matter that he is in a hurry to send, of some character, and he don't want it to go by slow freight, all he has to do is to pay the fast freight? A. That is it.

Q. All persons who want to send goods by the fast freight can have the same accommodations upon the same terms? A. Yes, sir.

Q. That is upon an existing railroad principle? A. Yes, sir.

Q. That would not embarrass the railroad company in any way? A. No, sir.

Q. "And equal and similar facilities, not inferior to any in use January 1, 1884, shall be extended on like terms to all connecting transportation lines, whether by land or water." That can't hurt you. Railroad people do not expect to retrograde. That is not likely, is it? A. No, sir.

Q. Now, you have stated your only objection to section one, and that was as to printing the schedule; and I see no difficulty there, if the law was amended (looking at it in a business manner) so that if you are required to print a schedule, you would have a reasonable time to do it in; and there being no prohibition there to forwarding freight, and no prohibition to writing in the schedule, you can do it if the law does not prohibit it? A. Yes, sir.

Q. If a man comes with a new class of freight, there is nothing in this bill to prevent you from writing in there whatever you want to. This bill needs no amendments as far as that is concerned? A. That is not inserted, that you may be allowed to write in. When that is in that will do. That is not in.

Q. It is not prohibited? A. No, sir.

Q. We are now reading a penal statute (as this is in a measure), and what is not prohibited by penal statute, you may do. That is law? A. I presume that is law.

Q. If you can do it now, you can do it if this bill does not prohibit it. Do you not so understand it? A. I suppose if you say that is legal, it must be so.

Q. Well, not necessarily; but I thank you for the compliment. I feel very proud of it, but at the same time I submit it to your good judgment and sense, as a business man, wouldn't you so understand a penal statute which says you shall not do this, and if you do you shall be punished, and if in looking over that statute you found that that which is not prohibited you may do, would you so understand it if this were in the nature of a penal statute? A. If the law required that it should be printed, and I should write it in, I might be doing something contrary to the law.

Senator Reddy—Well, I will call your attention, Mr. Chairman, to the fact that the word "printing" includes writing, and that the word "writing" includes printing.

The Chairman—If I am to answer the question I would say that that is true as to the construction of contracts, but not as to the construction of statutes (reading Code). Writing includes printing, but it does not say that printing includes writing.

Q. There is no prohibition here in regard to forwarding freights. Now, what, to your mind, would be the result, say, if a person brought a band of peculiar animals—we will say camels—for which you have no classification. Would you allow the man to hold the camels at the railroad station, perhaps in want of food and at great expense, and you had no other freight to ship, until you would go to Carson and visit the printing shops and have it done? Would you say: "Gentlemen, you will have to wait till I can send to Carson and get my schedule altered before I can send your camels?" A. No.

Q. Why not? A. Because you would have absolute action.

Q. Would you credit lawyers (I won't say lawyers, because they might be credited with anything), but do you think that the Courts in this country would consider that you had injured anybody by acting in that absolute way without injuring anybody? A. No, sir.

Q. Then, as a business man, you would forward the camels and get your schedule printed as soon as you could? A. It is the same proposition that I gave you with reference to the poor man with his household goods. There are lots of things that would come into this bill that the Courts would never worry me about.

Q. If you forwarded my furniture—being a poor man—the same as you forwarded any other poor man's, you would not be discriminating, would you? A. No, sir.

Q. That law does not say that you shall discriminate to that extent, but that you shall treat everybody alike? A. Yes, sir.

Q. You have had a large railroad experience? A. Quite large; quite considerable.

Q. When you lay out a railroad, you are required to file a map in some public office in the State? A. Yes, sir.

Q. On that map what do you show? A. The line of the railroad.

Q. And you get a franchise then, and the power of the State is used to give you a right of way over that line? A. Yes, sir.

Q. And then towns are built up along the line of that road? A. Yes, sir.

Q. And the railroad generally goes by the town; in fact, the people generally invite them to build there? A. Very frequently.

Q. Do you know of an instance where a town site has been started, and a Court House built, and a whole community settled along the line of a road which has grown to be a thriving community? A. Yes, sir.

Q. The purpose for which a railroad is formed is stated in the articles of incorporation, is it not? A. Yes, sir.

Q. Now, do you claim that you have a right to change that, and to discriminate against one of those communities that has been built up on the strength of that? A. No, sir.

Q. Then if your depot should be burned down at the town of Hawthorne, would you claim that you would have a right to rebuild it five miles away from the town and leave it out entirely? A. No, sir.

Q. If that power were given to the corporation which has laid out the line of its road, and given notice to the world as to where it should run, and has invoked the power of the State to enable it to establish its route upon that line of route, and the people having built up a town, or started a town, and made a general depot for supplies and shipping, do you claim that it would be right for a railroad company to alter the accommodations and to remove its track and buildings from that town? A. It would be a very great hardship.

Q. Would it hurt any railroad to deny them that right, in your judgment? Can there be any objection to doing it, looking at it in the light of the railroad interests? A. I will tell you something that occurred a short time since. The Government of the United States gave us land enough to put up buildings. A party came in and put up a house for a hotel, and we never for a moment supposed that he was trying to get control. He had asked us if he could build a house on it, but the first thing we knew he came in and says, "I have got a title from the United States, and I own all these buildings," and he was going to sell town lots, and so on. We thought it was rather rough, and we proposed to remove our station about five miles from there, and let him keep his buildings. Now, there was a case in which, if I had the power to do things, I should have probably done it.

Q. Supposing that you had any station established on the line of the road, and it turned out that the title thereto was in the State, and the laws of the State had been used to remove you from it, do you think you would forfeit your charter if the State itself removed you from that station?

SENATOR ——We submit that that is a legal proposition.

THE CHAIRMAN—This raises the question whether, if any Senator objects to a question, upon any ground, the Chair shall rule upon the objection. My idea would be that such a course would be proper, but I would like to have the sense of the committee upon it.

[Ordered that such course be pursued.]

Q. I understood you that it would not interfere with their rights to compel the railroad company to keep up all their bridges and so on, and keep them in repair "for the purposes for which they were constructed." If they desire to do that, then they are not injured if the right is taken from, are they? A. No, sir.

Q. (reading bill). "If it is restored to as good a condition as it was before, and serves the purposes for which it was intended," that is all that the bill demands, is it not? A. That is the way that it is here, although the question might be as to whether it was to be restored to the exact spot where it was before, from which it was originally taken.

Adjourned till two o'clock.

———

SENATOR VROOMAN—I understood you this morning, in your testimony, to state that you were addressing yourself principally to the moving of freight and carrying loads, and with reference to the effect of this bill upon the transportation. Was that it? A. That was the understanding; yes, sir.

Q. Have you anything to say in regard to moving freight in quantities less than a carload, and as to the effect that this bill would have upon it? A. In answering that question, I did not speak at that time of freight on things of that kind. In doing business, as a rule, we usually receive carloads of ore on our road at a particular station, although at some stations we have parts of carloads. We have, as our main business, straight carloads of lumber and wood, and ores and machinery, and that is what I had reference to.

Q. What would be the effect of the bill if you were to ship in less quantities? A. It would bother us considerably if we had to ship in quantities less than straight carloads.

Q. In what way? A. It might be that a half a dozen people would come with a carload, having a ton or a ton and a half apiece, and if we were obliged to make up a car and only take one ton we would be obliged to charge such a rate that a man could not afford to pay it, or else let it stay till we got a carload. And that is what we do. We ship it as quick as we possibly can. They cannot expect us to ship a part of a carload. If a man wishes us to ship a part of a carload we are obliged to charge for a full rate.

Q. Suppose that a quantity of wood is presented to you, such as will load all of your cars but one, and would furnish half a load as to that; and that a quantity of coal is presented at the same time. Do you ever put wood and coal in the same car? A. No sir; unless it is in sacks.

Q. If it was coal in bulk? A. Not in bulk.

Q. Under this bill, these being presented at the same time, and being of the same class of freight as to being non-perishable, what would you do, there being something here to prevent you from shipping freight except in the order received? A. If I could not arrange to put them both in the same car I would necessarily be compelled to hold them until I could get another, if I correctly understand it, or charge enough to send a half a car. That would be the only thing left open.

Q. You have no objection to section one of the bill as it now stands, so I understood you to state this morning? A. No, I did not intend that.

Q. What do you intend to be understood as saying upon that point? A. I wanted to answer that the freight when offered should be "of the same class or kind."

Q. How would you have the bill read? A. "All offered of the same class or kind."

Senator McClure—You would put after the word "another," "of the same kind or class" (reading it in that way).

Senator Vrooman—Generally, you would have that limited so discrimination would apply to persons, but would not apply to classes of freight. Have you anything to say in regard to line eleven, on page two? A. The same thing would apply all the way through, "of the same class or kind," because the same objection to that first section would prevail all the way through.

Q. Then it would be so drawn as to prevent personal discrimination and partiality? A. That would be the one that I would prefer. I exemplified that about the carload of silk and the potatoes in talking about this matter this morning. That was my view then, and it is now, although I don't know that I made myself understood.

Q. Have you anything further to say about section two, as to having a schedule printed as to how far that should go. Have you any suggestion to make, as a practical railroad man, with relation to the amendment of that section? A. In speaking about that matter, I suggested that there should be an opportunity left open for the agent to fill in in writing any changes to be made, so as to avoid the making of a new schedule every time a change was made, which might be every day, but, of course, my understanding was without very careful reading of the bill, that it applied only to stations within this State; for instance, we would not like to say as a matter of fact that we would deliver, or undertake to deliver, goods on our line beyond the junction of our stations or east of the particular point—at the end of it possibly.

Q. Will you give me the name of any particular station on your line? A. Virginia City.

Q. Supposing that this bill was in force in California, and your office in Virginia desired to ship freight to California, under this bill

3

as it now reads you would have to furnish a schedule from Virginia to every point on the whole route—an entire schedule? A. No, sir; I did not so understand it; I think it would be only necessary to show what the schedule was on that particular line of the road where he wished to ship.

Q. Line four, on page two, reads " between all points; " now, would not this bill be better by inserting, after the word " transportation," " from that particular station to all points and stations to or from which they carry over their routes in this State? " A. That, it seems to me, would be the fair thing; I don't see why they should ask for a schedule to go over all the routes outside of the State, because outside of the State we are getting into different lines; we have different rates and different tariffs; the law itself gives us a difference; we have a different one in Nevada from what we have in this State, and all the agent wants to know is what the freight is to this station—where the goods are to be shipped to—is; he has got to know that so as to know what to charge.

Q. Then if it were to read, " Transportation from that particular station to all points and stations to or from which they carry in this State," it would cover every possible case of accommodating the patron of the road? A. It seems to me so.

Q. Have you anything to say concerning section three, further than you said this morning? A. As I said this morning, in reading it over first I had the impression that it related to bridges, etc. But in the discussion afterwards between Mr. Reddy and another gentleman, the question of stations was brought in, and then the next thing that came up was about the proposition of the railroad taking away the stations, and removing them off some four or five miles into some other town. I took occasion at the time to say that it was wrong to do that. If that was the intention and design to destroy the town or community, it was bad business and ought not to be done, I don't care who did it. But if that is the object of this bill, to prevent that sort of thing, let it be inserted. If that is not the purpose, then it might operate to prevent the company from doing the things that it would be necessary for them to do. For instance, we have a station at a mining camp, and it goes all to pieces. We have one case like that to-day. In fact, we have taken away a station and closed the office, and taken away our telegraph operator. Now if we wanted to take that building down, and go and put it somewhere else, I understand that under this law you couldn't do it; but the presumption is that if we have built a branch from there to any of the mining camps, and we didn't keep that up, it would follow that, under the provisions of this bill, we would lose our charter, and I understand that is the intention of the bill.

Q. I suggest that the bill is very plain and expresses certain ideas. Whether it expresses the ideas intended I don't know. We are to presume that it means what it says upon its face; we pursue it upon that basis. I ask you if section three, assuming that it means what it says, would be in the interests of the people of the State who are engaged in railroad building? A. Certainly it would not, in that view.

Q. Speaking as a railroad man, after you had a charter to build a road (having in mind section three), say between Sacramento and Stockton, with branch lines, and say that you had constructed a branch line to some mining camp, and after operating it a year and found that it did not pay running expenses and was an accommodation and a benefit to no one, state whether or not you think you would have a right to take up that branch line and discontinue it without forfeiting your charter? A. I should hope so.

Q. Looking at this bill? A. Looking at this bill I don't know as I could.

Q. I will ask you now if you consider this bill, as a whole, in the interests of the productive—or would it be beneficial, if it became a law, to the productive and manufacturing interests of this State in the matter of transportation? A. It would place things in such a shape, so far as our company is concerned, that we could not carry out the projects which we have in view, and it would be injurious to a great deal of the business of the State.

Q. Injurious because of·the restrictions that it would place upon transportation? A. Not that only, but there is another thing I would like to say. I would like to ask you this question, after looking over section three: Suppose that a railroad was built under the laws of this State, and was found not to pay at all, and that it was running, say four trains a day, and came to the conclusion to run but one train a day, could a person insist that those trains should be put back again, and that it should be done immediately; or if the train had to be made up, and there was not sufficient for a train, and nothing to take as freight, and he then withdrew it, would he be subject to prosecution under this law?

Q. That is the way that I read the bill. It is perfectly plain in regard to those provisions. A. If that were the case, supposing that we concluded to shut our road down for six months.

Q. You would forfeit your charter. A. They might say that the business might come here again.

Q. "Equal and similar facilities, not inferior to any in use January 1, 1884," etc.; that is, if they were running ten trains a day on the first of January, 1884, they would always have to run that many, or at least that many trains, or forfeit their charter. A. Where is that? I want to say that I never saw this bill till I came before this committee. I looked at a bill which I understood to be brought up, but which was not the case. Of course I have answered all the questions which gentlemen asked me as well as I could.

SENATOR CROSS—You had the impression that the Barry bill was the one which fixed the freights and fares? A. Yes, sir. I was interested in the rates of freights and fares on roads, and I wanted to give the committee my views in regard to freights and fares.

SENATOR VROOMAN—Of course you are interested in the railroad enterprises? A. Yes, sir.

Q. If this bill were to become a law and go into force in this State, would you as a railroad man, or as a moneyed man, feel justified in investing your means in the construction of new railroads? A. No, sir.

SENATOR SULLIVAN—In reference to that point in section one, that the carrying should be of the "same class or kind," isn't that the point into which discrimination enters? For instance, here is a ton of ore which contains base metal, and here is another ton which is of a finer quality. Now, on one you might charge $10 a ton, and on the other you might charge $30 a ton. One would be class A, and the other would be class B. Now I take it, and I think you will bear me out, one does not take any more trouble or require any better service than the other, and the cost of carrying each ton is the same; the only difference is that one brings to the miner more than the other. Now, I take it that if these words were put in, "of the same class or kind," the provisions of the law with regard to discrimination would be defeated in regard to discrimination by considering the value of the ore? A. You are a miner and opening up your mine, and you have two or three classes of ore. You come to the railroad company and say, "What are your rates for transporting ore per ton to San Francisco?" He says, "Twenty dollars a ton to San Francisco." You say, "What will you haul my ore for?" I will say, "How much have you got? How long will you be able to ship with us? What is the ore worth?" You tell me that you have ore which is worth $500 a ton, but the great majority of it is low grade and not worth more than $30 a ton, and that you want to ship it all. I will say to you, "In order to enable you to do that, if you will give me all of this ore, I will take the low grade at almost cost, or probably at cost (we have done that several times), but I want you to give me a fair living rate on the ore which pays $500 a ton." That is the proposition that I make to you. Then you say, "What will your rates be?" and I will tell you. Probably the rate on the best ore would be ten dollars a ton more than on the other. My object in doing that would be this: In running your mine you would have supplies to take back and men at work, for which I would get freights and fares, and back freights, and if I aid you in getting your mine running, and in getting out several thousand tons of ore, I do something in getting it in, and in getting in supplies. That is the answer to that point.

Q. I have read that answer somewhere in the report of the Railroad Commissioners, and it does not seem to my mind a reason why you should charge such a great difference as I notice is charged. Now, there are three or four different classes. Instead of ore, we will take silk. There are three or four grades of silk. One grade is marked $1 a yard, another $5, and another $10. Now, if a railroad company is allowed to classify its freight "of the same kind" or character, it would make classes A, B, C, D. It would enter into the profits of the person who is the consignee. In other words, it would be charging according to the amount which the silk would bring in San Francisco. Do you understand that to be the meaning or the object of using the words "of the same class or kind?" A. I understand. Do you want to know the reason why that is done?

Q. I understand that is done, and that is one reason why the Barry bill is brought forward. A. Supposing a carload of silk was worth $10,000 and another carload was worth $5,000. There is such a thing as a smashup and a carload of silk being destroyed, and the railroad company would have to pay for it. And they are frequently destroyed by fire. A car may get off the track, and we might lose the profits of a year, and of course they want something to offset that.

Q. That is your idea of the reason for the difference in charges? A. There are various other things that enter into it. I am not so well posted in the silk business as I am in other business.

Q. Take for instance the question of chairs used for offices such as our Chairman has. Now, one man is charged two dollars and fifty cents in the market for an ordinary oak chair, and a walnut chair is worth two dollars and seventy-cents or three dollars. Now, we must assume that it is not on account of services, or of room that the chairs occupy in the car, for those are the same; but I understand that . there is a great difference in regard to the freight that is charged upon them. A. I don't know that there is.

Q. Don't you think that this change in the Barry bill from offering freight to be transported, to offering freight of the same class or kind, carries it right back to the present basis; that it gives the common carrier the rights which he has at present? Would it make any change in results between the common carrier and the consignor and consignee of goods? Wouldn't it leave the railroad companies in the same position that they are in to-day? A. I dare say that it would in·some respects.

Q. Would it not in all respects? A. No; because here it says that they are to take the various freights as they come in their order. There is no law of that kind now. It imports that it does. That is what I understand is the object of this bill. I don't understand that the object of this bill is to cut down freights.

Q. No, sir; it does not. A. That is what it amounts to. There is an awful range. Take ores that run from $30 up to $500 a ton, and that is just what we are doing. If we lost one of those carloads, we should have to pay for it. We had a smashup the other day of nineteen carloads of ore, dumped right into a ditch, and the company had to pay for it.

Q. Would you take that, then, to be the reason for the difference in charges, the difference in the kinds of ore, and the different kinds of freight and merchandise? A. You asked me the simple question in regard to ore because I am more familiar with that. We have got mines running which pay men $4 a day, and merchants selling their goods to them, and farmers selling their produce and horses and cattle for use in working these mines. We are helping the whole country. They would never do anything in Owen's Lake Valley unless we shipped these ores, and we could never ship these low grade ores unless we charged a good round price on ores of high grade, that will bear it, to enable us to carry ores that will not bear it. If we can't open these lines, we can't run our roads.

Q. Take the higher grade of ore—any quality which will pay not only the miner, but also the transporter or common carrier—and I believe it is a fact and you will acknowledge that there is a difference, a great difference, beyond what you charge as freight in regard to the grades of ore—you classify them as A, B, and C? A. We have a classification that covers almost everything. For instance, we will take ore that is worth $200 a ton and bring it over our road and make arrangements with the Central Pacific Railroad to deliver it in San Francisco at $11 a ton. Now the miner can take his carload of ore here and make an average on his low grade ore.

Q. Do I understand you to say that there is ore in Inyo and Mono Counties of such a character that the consignor cannot make anything in mining it? A. Certainly; lots of it.

Q. How does the common carrier make anything out of it? A. There is some, fortunately, that is higher grade, and, as I told you, the miner manages so that by taking the rich and the poor together that he can get such a rate that he can make fair pay, and we are satisfied to bring it down here and we all make a good living at satisfactory rates.

Q. Did I understand you to-day that, taking this bill as a whole, if you were out of the railroad business you would not go into it again? A. I most decidedly say so.

Q. What is the principal point of your objection? A. It would be one very good reason that you would not allow me to classify my freight under that bill, and you would not allow me to discriminate as to persons or as to places. If I could discriminate I could help persons every day, but unless I can do it it don't make any difference and it is no use talking about it.

Q. As I understand this bill, it is one that inflicts a penalty, and therefore must be liberally construed under the statute. Now, this penalty: I understood you to say that if this bill was in force, and these people did these things, they could bankrupt any road? A. Yes, sir. There might be an agent of the company that would go to work and break nearly every one of these laws, because he did not like the company, and then should the railroad company go by the board? The company should not suffer because of his act. But the bill says that the company shall lose its charter and the man go to jail. Now I think that the man should go to jail, but the company should not lose its charter. If I understand this rightly, it says that the act of the agent forfeits the charter (reading section seven).

SENATOR BALDWIN—That refers to sections one, two, and three.

SENATOR SULLIVAN—You say that ores are classified, and that one grade is $50, and another grade $30 ore, and some very much higher, and that there are, of course, grades of intermediate value? A. Yes, sir.

Q. Now, this classification is not based upon any particular difficulty in carrying these ores, because, I presume, it is just as easy to carry thousand dollar ore as it is ore that is worth thirty dollars. It must then be based upon the principle of insurance, and not upon the facility of carrying it? A. No, sir; that cuts but a small figure; not a very large one. That is why I said that, if a carload should be lost, or ruined in going over the road, that the company would have to pay for it.

Q. If it is not insurance, why make this classification, if it is just as easy to carry high as low grade ore? A. I explained that there were a great number of mines in the country over which this road of ours runs, and in fact the majority of the mines is low grade ore. The people who own those mines know that the price they can afford to pay us is a price that we cannot afford to take, provided it was the only business we had. A man of that kind comes to us and we say, "We will put this rate down low, at almost cost," and in some cases we do it at cost. If in the future he gets ore that is worth $500 a ton, we want an advanced freight. We want to get even, as near as we can, on the carrying of this low grade ore. The road is entitled to have that for carrying this freight, no matter what it is, and therefore the rate is higher. A man comes to us to carry low grade ore. He is able to get his supplies, to work his mine and keep his men at work and get grub for them, and the farmer sells him grain, and it makes a general business through the country. That is the reason why we want to grade these ores.

Q. That is all right. But you have a mine that has high and low and intermediate grades of ore. I don't suppose that a mine has all low grade ore, or that a neighboring mine is all high grade; but if I understand you, what the low grade ore will not stand you put on the high grade? A. Well, it would come to that to some extent. But if we carried the high grade ore only, there is many a mine that could not afford to ship at all.

Q. So that, as a matter of fact, this system of making one man pay transportation of another is absolutely necessary? A. Well, no; not absolutely necessary; but, recollect, that in one case the railroad helps the low grade mine. We ought to have some credit for that. In the other case, the high grade man helps us, and he ought to have some credit for that, and between us all, we keep things smooth and get along well. In this State there are more people, and they make more money, and things flourish; and if we did not do so, they would not flourish. We are like the bricks in a house.

Q. Why can't the same rule obtain in railroads as obtains in shipping? I understand that they take either in weight or by measure all of the same class, and pay the same amount of money for it. For instance, if they are shipping thirty-dollar ore, whatever the shipper carries that for, he will not charge any more for carrying fifty-dollar ore, or sixty or a hundred-dollar ore. It is so much a ton. The value of the goods cuts no figure? A. You do not mean to tell me that a ship will bring rails and pig iron at the same rate?

Q. Pig iron is pig iron and rails are rails. If steel rails were made of a particular fineness, and might cost a little more than any other, still they would both pay the same freight per ton, and the same for instance with silks—silks at $1 a yard and $5 a yard—and they would pay the same price per ton or by measure. That is my understanding of the shipping rule for ships.

Senator Cross—May I call your attention to the matter that the consignor is insured against loss by water, which is not the case by rail.

Q. If you say that this is an insurance business? A. A ship, as I understand it, is a common carrier just the same as a railroad, as far as that is concerned.

Senator Cross—No; they——

SENATOR —— —There are marine insurance companies for that purpose.

SENATOR SULLIVAN—Let us take it, then, that these extra charges are for insurance; then the thing will not work at all; the rate is too high, because you can, even if a train is wrecked——. Well, I am going off on an argument. One of your propositions is, that if a train is wrecked you would have to pay for it if it got ditched, and so on. Suppose that the ore is not lost, even if it is ditched. It is there and you can pick it up again? A. By the time it got down into one of those fills twelve or fifteen hundred feet, I don't think there would be much picking up to be done. We paid some fourteen or fifteen hundred dollars for the loss of the ore of which I just spoke.

Q. But that is not always the case? A. That is generally the case with those things. Those things generally happen in a bad place. If you have two horses and one of them dies, it is generally the best one, and that is about the case with railroads.

Q. Then a party might relieve the railroad company by insuring his own goods, and if he did, then this discrimination should cease? A. No; because, as I said before, this insurance cuts but a very small figure in the case.

Q. It is not a very material figure? A. It might in some special cases, say, such as this silk business. There it might be a factor. I think the chances are that the railroad company might carry that freight for less money if they were freed from responsibility. I don't see but any shipper would be willing to make a difference in the freight if he was freed from insurance. I don't think I would charge as much.

Q. You say that you want to help out everybody, and in order to take the low grade ore as well as the high grade, you discriminate a little and shift the profits around. Supposing that your road was running through a well settled country, and that there was business at both ends and all along the line, then that discrimination would not be necessary, would it? A. It depends upon what you would be shipping in that country.

Q. Supposing that it was all ore, and that you had to find out the cost of moving the whole of it at so much per ton; a certain profit on this is all that you would want? A. Yes, sir.

Q. Supposing that there was plenty of ore, then there would be no necessity of making these shifting valuations? A. No, sir.

Q. You would simply charge a fixed price per ton on ore the same as you would on wheat? A. I dare say that would be the proposition.

Q. There would be no necessity in that case for discrimination or for shipping at lower figures? A. If it could be fixed so as to be satisfactory to the shipper the railroad would have no trouble.

Q. The price or the value of the thing would not really enter into the matter as a material factor in fixing the rate of the freight? A. As a general proposition, no; but there are so many things connected with this that there is no man who wishes or wants us to do like that. It is a difficult thing to handle. I think that is the case with everybody that undertakes to do it. As far as our roads are concerned, we have three or four of them, and we stand in and help everybody, and want everybody to help us. We all want to live. We don't believe in trying to ask people any more than we think they are entitled to pay us. Nor do we think that we should work for the people for nothing. When a railroad goes into a country it makes great changes; it treads on somebody's toes. Other people get rich from it. We are surrounded with a great deal of difficulty. The proposition is that railroads want a fair rate of freight and means for handling the freight rapidly and satisfactorily to themselves and their patrons. I would like to suggest that a railroad company is something like a merchant. If a man comes into his store he will treat him civilly in selling his goods to him, and do the best he can with him, and he wants the man to pay him; and that is the way that we attempt to do business. The railroads have done a great deal of business in the country as a general thing, and I am satisfied that it would be a very poor section of country where we are if it were not for the railroads.

Q. Don't you think that the country has done well by the railroads, too? A. It has, in a great many respects. We always have noticed this: That whenever we have gone into the building of a railroad through a country, they come to us and say, "Build your road, for we want it, and it is just what we want." We come here, and by and by somebody commences to growl, and I find that it is generally some new man that has come in, who don't know anything about the troubles that they had before the railroad was built; and then perhaps another new man comes in from the East, and he is dissatisfied, and so that is the way that the thing goes. If we make a success, then we rob somebody; if we make a failure, they say that we were fools for ever having had anything to do with it. That is about the way that the thing goes. We have been in both of these boats, exactly, with our roads. My theory about this whole business is, that if the bill is to be introduced to keep us railroad people straight and to satisfy the people (and we always find the people pretty square sort of fellows in general, if you get at them right), it will stop railroading so that we can't do any work or any business, and do it satisfactorily.

SENATOR WHITNEY—As I understood you this morning, your idea was, that by discriminating in price between low and high grade ores, you would enable the country to fill up, and population to come in? A. Yes, sir.

Q. You thought that you would get a return from the high grade ore, and from return freights, for the community? A. Yes, sir.

Q. And you understand those are the reasons why discrimination should be practiced by the railroad company? A. Very frequently; most generally.

Q. If you understand the provisions of this law it will be binding at all times? A. Yes, sir.

Q. And not allow you any discrimination? A. I understood so this morning.

Q. I understood you to say this morning that if this law were carried out you could not carry on your business but that in the instances given you would not be afraid that a jury would convict you of an infraction of the law? A. The idea that I had was this: that arose from the question of taking this poor man's furniture, and I said that if I did I did not believe that, even if it were in the face of this law, no Judge and jury would convict me.

Q. But if you thought there would be a swift conviction in every such case, would.your view be that you could carry on railroad business? A. No, sir.

Q. You would have to rely on the discretion of the community who dispensed the law, or else you could not carry on business under it? A. Well, it would be almost that. I think that the people themselves, in a great many cases, would complain that it was injuring the road, and injuring everybody, and if there was nothing else to be done they would petition the next Legislature to vacate the bill.

SENATOR SPENCER—With reference to the risk in transporting freight by water and by railroad, do you know about what the difference is considered? Whether greater or less in comparison with the other, and which it is in favor of? Suppose you ship goods from New York by sea, or ship them overland to California, and that you went to an insurance office to get insurance upon them; would one be cheaper than the other? A. I think so.

Q. About what proportion? A. I don't know; it must be very great.

Q. This morning you stated that you thought that this bill was not in some respects a good bill? A. Portions of it.

Q. What are the prominent features of this bill which you consider would be inimical to the interests or interfere with the interests of the railroad company? A. I think that this section (number one) that is where I would want that inserted.

Q. Is it not a universal rule that railroad companies charge all that the goods will bear, so to speak? A. No; at the present time we are not charging all that the law allows us.

Q. I understood you to say that if you were shipping ore that was worth ten dollars a ton and other ore that was worth thirty dollars a ton, that you would make a difference? A. I do.

Q. That is based solely upon the question of risk? It don't cost any more to put in a ton of ore worth thirty dollars than one that is worth ten? A. Certainly not.

Q. It takes just as many men to handle it and just as much work to transport it? A. Yes, sir.

Q. Then the only factor that enters into that is the risk in the event of loss? A. No, sir.

Q. Isn't that the only factor that ought to be considered? A. No, sir. I told you the reason why we classified ore. I don't know that you were in here.

Q. Yes, sir; I heard you say it was to encourage other business? A. Mines have low grade ore which could not be shipped at all were it not for the rate which the high grade will bear. Now we are entitled to five cents per ton and ten cents for passengers. That is the limit in the State of California. We do not charge up to that limit even with this discrimination of ours that we were talking about; we don't work up to that. In Nevada we are entitled to twenty cents per ton per mile, and our average is not ten on our freights. Now, by this classification or discrimination in ores we enable these men to go and keep their properties at work. We extend to poor men in that country our tariff from time to time and from month to month on their low grade ore, but we hope some of these days to get rich ore. Now, if they could not dispose of those low grade ores to enable them to pay expenses, and that is what we are doing all over Inyo County—we have over seven hundred mines that have been recorded there, as well as a great many that are working that have never been recorded, and some with only small tunnels, etc. And now we have gone into Inyo with this road, and a great many of these places that have been abandoned as being too poor to pay for working have started up, and we are bringing out silver and lead and are enabling miners to work these low ores. In cases of that kind, when a man comes to us, we say, " We will take this ore at cost to us, or with very little profit, but if you have any high grade ore we will want you to pay a higher rate." And when he comes to us with $1,500 ore we ship it at a higher rate, say $10 a ton more than the other. By doing that the community exists and lives and moves, and we are able to go on with our road, and the more work we do of that kind of course the cheaper we can do our work. That is another thing that benefits the people, of course, and the whole of this proposition benefits them. We are taking the position that by and by, through the opening up of these mines which we believe to exist in that country, that the business will improve, and the business grow better, and we will do a larger business, and the whole country will be benefited. If that can't be done then we are losers, that is all there is about that.

Q. Then I understand you that as a business proposition that the rapid development of the country and the benefits to the people are the two grounds upon which you base the reasons for charging different rates upon the two grades of ore, and for discriminating between the rates. About what difference do you make in the two grades? A. We would make perhaps twelve and a half or thirteen dollars.

Q. And you say, as a business proposition, that that forwards the development of the country? A. That is the ground that I take.

Q. Outside of that special instance, as regards ore, upon what principle is a railroad man justified in charging that difference in goods, generally of the same class or of the same kind; take any other goods of the same kind or character, that require the same time, and are of the same bulk, and the same trouble in transportation, the same labor and the same capital? Outside of the risk, is there any other factor that enters into it? A. I can hardly answer that question.

Q. No, sir. Now that is your chief objection to this Barry bill. That is the fatal objection to it, is it not? A. That is one of them. As I said before, in looking it over, I think that the proposition should go into the whole bill, "of the same class or kind," wherever that occurs.

Q. Suppose that you had to point out one objection, would you consider that the fatal objection? A. It is a very strong objection. I don't know that it is the fatal objection.

Q. So far as the profits of the road and the developments of the country are concerned, that would be very objectionable? A. That would be very objectionable, would it not?

Q. Well, you are answering questions, and I am not? A. That is one of the principal objections, and another is as to posting a tariff at all stations.

Q. You want that changed so that you will not have to get the whole printed? A. Get a volume of a thousand pages, and you have got a lot of things that the public do not want to know.

Q. I understood you to say to Senator Brooks, that if the charge was to be upon goods to be shipped, say from Virginia City to some other point in the State, say one hundred miles away, you should be required to furnish a schedule only between the two points? A. That is the proposition.

Q. That is the only objection to that? A. And have it within the State.

Q. You would not have any objection, in case we had to ship through another State, to furnish a through schedule? A. If we went into another State we would have another law to operate under, and another rate of freights, and we might go to work and get a rate that we could not carry under by that law without loss. If the agent at Virginia City wanted to ship to San Francisco, and he didn't know what the rate was, he would have to say, "You will have to wait till I can ascertain and let you know."

Q. If you had an understanding with another company through or by which you ship this freight, you could get at it? A. It says that you must do it.

Q. Supposing that you wanted to ship it through that route, you could made a contract, couldn't you, with the consignor of the goods? A. Certainly; that is another thing.

Q. If you undertook to contract you would carry them at contract price, wouldn't you? A. Yes; but it might take time.

Q. You would not be contracting to take the goods to San Francisco unless you knew what you were to pay? A. There are cases occurring that we don't know what the rates to San Francisco are, as a matter of fact, and we ship copper bullion and lead and that sort of thing to New York, and the charges are constantly shifting. I think there is every reason in the world why the tariff should be confined to the State.

SENATOR SULLIVAN—About that printed schedule. Do you change your rates often? A. These rates are changed frequently; sometimes one or two or three a day. I dare say that the Central Pacific Railroad Company must change a dozen a day.

Q. How does that come? A. There are new kinds of freight offered to them.

Q. Those are additional? A. Different kinds and lots. A great many things of that kind are occurring every day.

Q. You would not change your schedule for staple articles every day? A. That would probably stand.

Q. Those are permanent? A. Of course a great many would stand.

Q. I suppose that any changes that would be made would not be necessary more than once in six months, simply to correct errors, or to add new goods that were not on the original schedule? A. Yes, sir.

Q. Would the cost of printing a schedule be a large item? A. Yes, sir; it would.

Q. The first cost would be much greater than any subsequent cost? A. I presume that is so, of course.

Q. It would cost almost as much to print fifty or sixty as to print a thousand? A. Of course not, after the type is set.

Q. The original cost is the principal cost? A. That is it.

Q. Then any duplicate of the schedule would not be much of a hardship upon the railroad company. I understand that you have no serious objection to section three (reading it)? A. No, sir; not the slightest, except to the latter part.

Q. What is your objection to the latter part of that section, if it is taken in connection with the whole section? A. The point is this, if there is a station closed and it is found well to have another one a few miles away, if the company attempted to remove the structure they would be going contrary to the law.

Q. That is your interpretation of it? A. That is what I understand this bill to be.

Q. That is your only objection to that? A. That is the only objection; and then if a track is once laid it can never be taken up again.

Q. That is your statement as a conclusion? A. That is what I understand this bill to be; and if that is done the company will lose its charter. Of course I have reference to the side tracks, running off on the outside to outside camps, and outside places where it might be found to the interest of the railroad company to take up that track, and under this law they could not do it.

Q. Now you have what objection to section seven (reading it)? You observe there that before any forfeiture can be had the railroad company can have its day in Court? A. I presume so, of course.

Q. There cannot be a forfeiture until there has been a regular adjudication of the matter before a competent tribunal—I am only reading down to the word "Attorney-General?" A. The presumption would be that if a person were operating a road under this bill, and there was an infraction, that the charter would be destroyed the moment that the Attorney-General commenced the suit. It would be a foregone conclusion that he would win his case or else he would not want to bring one.

Q. That is your idea of the capacity of the Attorney-General of this State? A. That is about it.

Senator Vrooman—I move that the remarks be taken down.

Q. That is your construction of that section? A. If I voted for that bill I would expect that to be the construction.

Q. (Reading same.) Do you understand by that that this is a

declaratory statute? A. I don't mean by that that a man is going to run his case before the rule commences. I don't want the rule to commence.

Q. You don't want the railroad tried for forfeiture at all? A. No; I don't take that ground, but that is one of the reasons.

Q. Do you not understand that a railroad is at all times entitled to a hearing in a Court of justice, and that there can be no forfeiture till there has been an adjudication? A. Of course I understand that, but I don't want to get into the Courts.

Q. (Reading balance of section.) Have you any objection if any of the employés of your railroad company disobey the order of the company to their being punished for a misdemeanor? A. None whatever.

Q. If the railroad company should authorize the violation of the statute, don't you think that they ought to be both punished? They would be *particeps criminis*, wouldn't they? A. Yes, sir.

Q. You do not understand that this last section operates any forfeiture of the charter at all? A. To the charter? If I understand the law rightly any officer of the road breaking the law is not personally criminal in the way that you speak of, but that as a consequence the railroad company would suffer for it, and that they would lose their charter. No doubt they are running these things, or else they could not lose their charter.

Q. Do you understand that the last part of this section has any reference to the company losing its charter in any sense of the word? A. Most unquestionably; because the moment you find that the people of the railroad had done this thing, the railroad must lose its charter.

Q. That is your construction of it? A. It is the agent of the company that does these things. The company itself can do nothing.

Q. Then if the company itself do these things is it not perfectly right that they should be punished, and if the punishment be that they shall forfeit their charter if they do the same, that it shall be forfeited? A. If the company authorizes their agent to do anything unlawful they ought to be punished.

Q. We agree on that then? A. Yes, sir.

Q. If the servants, or agents, or employés do it, they ought to be punished, and not the company? A. Yes, sir; we would not have any law for the company unless that was done.

Q. Do you insure any shipments of freight for transportation; I mean in the company's offices? A. We never insure at all.

Q. Will you tell me the reason of the rule why railroad companies as a general thing do not insure? A. They become their own insurers. It is on the same principle that the shipowner who has nine hundred ships does not insure. He can afford to lose three or four ships a year rather than to pay the insurance on the whole.

Q. Is not the reason this: that your loss in proportion to the shipments is very light in proportion to the goods you carry? A. I suppose that it is, yet the proportion of loss is not small. If the railroad company should lose a valuable train—and it is one of those things that very frequently happen to trains that pass over their roads—their loss would be very great.

Q. Your road has come into this State within the last year? A. Yes, sir.

Q. How far? A. One hundred and seven miles.

Q. What is the name of your road? A. The Carson and Colorado.

Q. How far is it constructed in the State of Nevada? A. About one hundred and ninety miles.

Q. What was the cost of running your road last year in the State of Nevada? A. I cannot tell you exactly.

Q. Do you know approximately? A. I think the net income is somewhere about three hundred thousand dollars.

SENATOR VROOMAN—I do not see the relevancy of this.

SENATOR —— —We put it upon the ground that it is a private and not a public matter.

SENATOR SPENCER—This bill, in some respects, is a bill to regulate freights and fares, and it seems to me that the earnings of the road would throw some light on that subject. I understand that it has not been in operation here long enough to tell anything about it. A. Only about six months, in this State. I will answer any question any gentleman asks, and come as near as I can to the true facts, in regard to all these matters, and I wish to say that I have been looking at my returns, that we have finished one hundred and seven miles in the State of California, from the State of Nevada, within the last year. I am making up a statement to put before the Board of Equalization to show what we are doing in this State.

Q. You are not prepared with figures to answer the question? A. No, I cannot; I thought this bill was a bill to regulate freights and fares.

Q. I understand that, as a railroad man engaged in the operation of railroads, your mind has undergone some changes, in reference to this bill, since you have examined it? A. Only in this first section. I said this morning that in the way of freight, I believed that freights ought to be classified. You will bear me out in that; and I wish to be understood that I think that proposition ought to be followed all the way through the bill. The next question that came up was in regard to quantities. If you remember a gentleman asked me this morning, in regard to carloads of oranges, and all those things, and I think my answers were on that proposition. I admitted that I had gone over these things very hastily, and of course I answered them very rapidly, and answered them off-hand, but I answered them entirely with reference to straight carloads, because that is the kind of business we are doing. But when a company has a great deal of freight that must be delivered in large places like San Francisco, then it would be very difficult for companies to handle those small lots in rotation. In other words, if they have straight carloads they can take them to whatever destination they are to go, and if they can take them in that way they can put a less rate on the freight of the public, but if they are to carry the same cars to fifteen or twenty men, it is divided up, and of course takes more time. That question of small lots was not brought up at all. We were talking of straight carloads, and we do our business principally in that manner. So far as framing a schedule is concerned, I overlooked the fact that it is not pertinent to places outside of the State. That is the only objection that I see to it; but between stations that is one thing that the station-master is for, in his office all the time.

Q. Your rule in this matter in the State of Nevada, is that you do not charge as much for taking goods twenty miles as you do for taking them one hundred miles? A. I said we did not charge much more.

THE CHAIRMAN—It is the same as ours? A. Yes, sir; in regard to that it is.

Q. Is your road a narrow gauge? A. The Carson and Colorado is a narrow gauge; the Virginia and Truckee is a wide gauge, and where we connect with the Central Pacific it is a wide gauge.

SENATOR SULLIVAN—I desire to know if, in your experience, any man or company has been wronged by discrimination in Inyo or Mono Counties, where this road of yours runs? A. No, sir; I don't know of any.

Q. As I understand you then the Barry bill, with these few changes that you have pointed out, is in your opinion a good bill? A. It would not be unsatisfactory.

Q. If this change were not made in section one, so as to put in "of the same class or kind," then it would be extremely unsatisfactory? A. We could not do business at all.

Q. That is, if you could not discriminate between different owners? A. That is it.

Q. As you understand it now it provides for no discrimination as regards persons? A. I understand that.

Q. To come down to the point, I want you to make it clear to my mind whether, in case low grade ore is offered at the same time that high grade ore is, you would send the high grade first and leave the low grade behind? Here, for instance, are two carloads—one of a fine quality of ore and the other a base ore—and you classify them as A and B. Now, if that change were made in section one it would appear to me (I don't know whether I am correct in this or not, and if not I would like to be) that it would be necessary for you to forward class A, and if another carload was there of the same class that you would have to send it on before you would send class B? A. Provided it was delivered first.

Q. Who is to judge of the classes under this law; the railroad or the shipper? A. I suppose they would have to do it together.

Q. Suppose that I was a shipper, a miner, and that in some way I had offended the Directors of the company of the Carson and Colorado road, and they said to me, "Mr. Sullivan, we don't want to have anything to do with you; you can go and ship your ore, if you please, by mules, or in any other way you please, no matter to us." I know they are discriminating against me, and they can charge me any price they please? A. They can't.

Q. Then, under this law, if they are allowed to discriminate as to a class, or kind, if it be passed, and they will be compelled to give me a show, and not to crush me entirely? A. I am not a lawyer, and I do not understand the laws of this State very well, and I never saw anybody that did. If this wrong was done you by the Carson Directors, it seems to me that you have got your redress under the law as it now stands, just as well as you would have it under this bill.

Q. Supposing that they would not carry for you at all, or charge you a very high price? A. They can't do that, because the law says that you shall only be charged five cents per ton per mile. You can't get over that.

Q. Assuming that you were charged five cents per ton per mile, you know very well that there is a great deal of ore that will not pay the shipper to ship at that rate? A. That is true; it would be a very bad business, but you can't compel the Directors, or anybody else connected with the railroads to do so, because somebody else would be the sufferer by it.

Q. Do you know anything about the special contracts of the Central Pacific Railroad with the merchants of San Francisco? A. I have heard of them; I don't know anything about them.

Q. You have no knowledge of any special contract system on your line, whereby you can discriminate in favor of one man and against another? A. We don't do that class of business.. If we have a quarrel with a man, we try to treat that man better than we do any other, so as to show him that we are not so bad as he thinks we are.

Q. Now as to section two; you would make such changes as would be needed by the agent only at points within the State? A. Yes, sir.

Q. Don't you think that a railroad corporation should be treated just the same as a natural person? A. Yes, sir.

Q. Upon the principle we were arguing just now? A. Yes.

Q. Then if a railroad company follows the principle invoked, and should commit an infraction of the law, don't you think that the corporation should suffer, just as a natural person would, for such infraction of the law? A. Yes, sir.

Q. But you think that if it does so, it ought not to lose its charter? A. No, sir; because an agent might be annoyed at the company and do these things purposely.

Senator Vrooman—Do you think that all persons should be treated alike, regardless of the kind of freight? A. No. The honorable Senator's question was as to the same kind of freight, of course.

Q. I did not understand him to say "the same kind of freight." A. You understood me in that way, did you not?

Q. Yes, sir.

Senator Vrooman—Upon this question of charging all that the traffic will bear, what would you charge for ore worth $500 a ton, between any two points on your railroad? A. It ranges from ten to fifteen dollars to San Francisco.

Q. About what grade is the ore for which you charge fifteen dollars? A. On two hundred dollar ore.

Q. How much more would you charge for ore that is worth $500? A. Not much.

Q. Just enough to make up for the risk? A. Yes, sir.

4 b

Q. In other words, there is a limit, and when you get to it you think you are getting a fair rate? A. That is it exactly.

Q. As a railroad man, and a man of business, do you consider the services which you render to a man whose ore is worth five hundred dollars worth any more than to the man whose ore is worth twenty dollars, aside from the benefit that you confer on him? A. No; I don't know that it is.

Q. Do you not think that it confers a greater benefit upon the man whose ore is worth ten dollars a ton, than upon the one whose ore is worth twenty dollars? A. Certainly.

Q. In fixing your rates do you take into consideration the value of the services that you may render to the man whose freight you transport? A. To some extent.

Q. Do you think, as a business man and a railroad man, that it would be possible to carry on the transportation business in this State by rail, with a uniform system for rates, unless the maximum was so high that it would practically be of no benefit—that is, if you had to charge alike for all the carrying business—without destroying many of the industries now going on? A. If the Legislature of this State allowed the railroad companies in some cases to charge fifty cents per ton per mile, it would be a good proposition for the people, or if they charged it per hundred pounds.

SENATOR SULLIVAN—It does not cost the railroad company any more to transport a ton of ore worth thirty dollars than it does one worth five hundred dollars, so that you do not charge according to the cost of the services, but according to the value of the article? A. A kind of ad valorem tax. I mentioned awhile ago that the proposition of freights and tariffs was a difficult one to handle. Take a road, for instance, only six miles long, and it would be one to a thousand that their different rates would not be arranged so as to be satisfactory to the people and also to the railroad company. The longer you haul the cheaper you can do it. The same thing applies to the United States mails, and everything else that is taken. I don't think that you would find from the business of the company that it paid the best where the most business was done—where is the bulk of the business. So many things come in that it is difficult to explain it.

Q. A man don't know where he is till he figures up at the end of the year? A. That is the general way.

SENATOR SPENCER—And he generally finds himself there? A. I don't know about that. I know a great many railroads in this State that it would be difficult to get the cost of.

SENATOR SULLIVAN—Isn't the true system to charge according to the value of the services rendered, and not according to the value of the article shipped; isn't that the true system of railroading? A. I think that they ought both be taken into consideration.

Q. I mean the cost of the services rendered? A. I think that the value of the articles handled and the amount of the work done by the railroad company should both be taken into consideration.

Q. Why should the value of the article be taken into consideration? A. For various reasons that we have been discussing here to-day. It is proper and natural to put the best property in the best kind of cars, expensive cars, and various matters of that kind come in.

Q. When the United States pays an ad valorem tax on things, it does not take into consideration the cost of those things, but simply pays it for the purpose of getting a revenue? A. They take into consideration the fact of whether a thing is a luxury or otherwise.

Q. They get in a certain amount of taxes. If you have the idea in your mind of getting in a certain amount of revenue, do you figure simply the cost of moving the articles and getting a fair profit upon them? A. If I understand you rightly, they consider both the cost and the value of them. They both come under the proposition, as I said before.

SENATOR SPENCER—Do railroad companies charge more for carrying ores that are worth a thousand dollars a ton than for those worth a hundred dollars a ton? A. Certainly.

Q. That is, on the basis of risk in case of loss? A. Yes, sir.

Q. Do they charge any more for shipping a small man than for a large one? A. No, sir; we don't ship men by the value, the same as we do horses; if we did some of them would not have any value.

SENATOR CROSS—It occurs sometimes in California that some men of great value have been carried for nothing? A. I have heard so.

SENATOR CROSS—Will you look at section seven, which provides that "any railroad corporation violating the provisions of sections one, three, and four of this Act shall forfeit its charter and corporate privileges;" and then look at section six, which reads: "On the expiration or forfeiture of the charter of any railroad corporation, its road, and appurtenances, and right of way acquired by it, remain vested in the people of the State, for public use, and its other property shall be sold, and the proceeds, after payment of its debts and liabilities, divided among the stockholders." I desire now to ask you this question as leading up to some others: By whom, on behalf of a railroad company, is its business transacted at the various stations along its line? A. By agents.

Q. Now, look at section one, which provides that freight must be forwarded in the order in which it is received. Does it ever occur that those agents become hostile to the interests of the company? A. Very seldom; it sometimes happens.

Q. Supposing that under such circumstances the authorized agent of the railroad company should violate this provision of the law, and forward a carload of freight, which was received second in order, in preference to a carload received first; can a person do so if so minded? A. Certainly.

Q. Without any special direction from the Board of Directors? A. Certainly.

Q. Suppose that the agent of the company was furnished with all these printed forms, and that some man should apply to him, and that he refused to furnish one; do you think that might transpire under the provisions of this law? A. Yes, sir.

Q. What is the value of the rolling stock of your road? A. Probably $100,000.

Q. What is the total valuation of your road? A. About $3,000,000.

Q. Then, under this bill, if one of your agents became hostile to the interests of the company and forwarded a carload of freight out of its order, all of that three million dollars' worth of property would be forfeited except its rolling stock? A. That is the way I understand this bill.

Q. In your judgment, as a reasonable man, is that a reasonable law? A. No; I should call it pretty rough.

Q. Is there a bonded indebtedness upon your road? A. Yes, sir.

Q. How much? A. Four and a half millions.

Q. Have those creditors any control over the management of the railroad? A. Not at all.

Q. What do you say is the value of the rolling stock? A. In California and Nevada both, $200,000.

Q. And this station agent may do this act, which violates the law, and all the property except the rolling stock would be forfeited. What would become of all these bonds—the bonded indebtedness? A. It would be worthless.

Q. Where are those bonds held? A. In New York and San Francisco.

Q. What are the bonds worth in the market? A. Between three millions and three millions and a half.

Q. What would all those bonds be worth if the law provided that any agent of the company could forfeit all of this property except the rolling stock, to the State, by simply forwarding a car of freight out of its order? A. Would not be worth a dollar.

Q. Then the effect of this bill would be to place in the hands of any agent of this company the power to destroy the entire value of the bonds, which are now worth three to four million dollars? A. That would seem to be the effect.

Q. Would you consider that an objection to this bill? A. A very great one.

Q. You stated that the value of the road was about three millions of dollars; what would be its value if the law placed the power in the hands of an agent of that road to in a moment perpetrate an act which would turn over all that property to the State except its rolling stock? A. It would be worthless.

Q. Now, look as this next section, which provides that a printed schedule must be exhibited whenever demanded. Suppose that one of your agents became dissatisfied, and hostile to the interests of the company, and refused to deliver, when requested, that printed schedule, and that thereby the property was forfeited, could you give us an estimate of what the damage might be to the company by the simple failure to show a book when asked for? A. Be a loss of the whole property.

Q. Something like three millions of dollars? A. Yes.

Q. Then, under this law, if one of your agents should simply refuse to show a book when asked, the result would be to forfeit three millions of dollars? A. Yes, sir.

Q. Would you consider that feature a possibility under this bill? A. Yes, sir.

Q. Suppose that this bill were passed, by which an employé or agent, by simply refusing to show a book, could forfeit the entire property and could render entirely valueless the bonded indebtedness or other indebtedness, where is the man that would, under such a law, furnish capital to build railroads within the State of California? A. I don't know.

Q. Could you find him in the State? A. I don't think you could find him anywhere in the world.

Q. What is the name of your company? A. The Carson and Colorado.

Q. In how many States has that company charters? A. Two; California and Nevada.

Q. Built in both? A. Yes, sir.

Q. What would be the result if a law were passed which provided that if any road received a charter from another State it should forfeit its charter in this State? A. It would be very bad.

Q. Do you consider those dangerous features of this bill? A. I should say so.

Q. What do you think of the provision that three or four millions of dollars' worth of property should be sacrificed by the mere act of an agent? What do you think of that, as a business proposition? A. I don't think it would be a very good one. I don't think anybody would. I think that in speaking about this road I have been basing it as three hundred miles long. This Act, of course, does not apply to the State of Nevada. That would be our saving clause. There are one hundred and seven miles here.

Q. Have you ever known of such things as Conductors knocking down? A. I have heard of it.

Q. Supposing that a Conductor on your road, within the State of California, where you had a fixed rate of charges, had charged a passenger two cents more than the regular fare, and that you spoke to him about it; that he would either have to stop or quit the road; who would own the road then, you or the Conductor? A. The Conductor.

Q. He would have you in a position, where, if you said to him, "Either quit knocking down or leave the road," to bring a complaint before the Attorney-General and have your charter forfeited? A. This bill does not operate in that way.

Q. Does it not? It says that if one man is charged more than another, thereby the charter is forfeited. What do you think of these matters as a business proposition? A. I think, as I said before, that this is going to be a very bad business for the railroads in this State.

Q. Have you any idea of the amount of bonded indebtedness of the Central Pacific Railroad Company? A. No, sir.

Q. Do you know that about twenty-seven millions of them run to the Government of the United States? A. I don't know; I know very little about it.

Q. What would any railroad bonds be worth to their holders, if there were a law that a Conductor, or a station agent, might, in a moment, do an act which forfeited all its property except the rolling stock? A. Be very bad.

Q. Could you sell bonds under such circumstances? A. I think if the parties buying understood it, it would be very difficult. It would seem to me I would not want to buy the bonds of any road or anything else, if I was likely to lose them—if that was going to be the effect of the bill.

Q. This bill cuts a great deal deeper than you thought at first glance? A. Yes, sir; an examination shows that it cuts.

Q. The railroad business is necessarily conducted by local agents, is it not? A. Yes, sir.

Senator Spencer—Do you find any place in this bill where it says that an agent of a railroad company refusing to give you a book, thereby forfeits its charter (reading section seven)? That speaks of this in its corporate capacity, and you so understand it? A. I understand that if any of these people do these things——

Q. Do you understand that what a man does by an agent he is just as responsible for as if he does it himself? A. Yes, sir.

Q. Then, he must be authorized to do it? A. It does not necessarily follow.

Q. If he does it without the scope of his agency, it does not follow that his principal would know it; you know that as a business proposition? A. It may be as a legal one; I dare say it is legally correct.

Q. It does not say that if any station agent refuses to perform any of these acts, he will forfeit it? A. That is just the point we were discussing this afternoon. Sometimes we run all of our cars over the road, and we are short of cars, and it is a difficult thing to move freight in any manner; at other times we have a surplus. A party might feel very much aggrieved at not getting his freight off, but on account of the difficulties that the company had, it could not very well be avoided.

Q. You agree with me, that all men should be treated alike with regard to dispatch, speed, price, and accommodations furnished? A. Yes, sir.

Q. Should not all men be charged alike in regard to forwarding freights? Say a man brought his freight to you for shipment; isn't he entitled to the first privileges on that route, and should not that be shipped first—I mean in a large quantity? A. I don't know but it should to some extent.

Q. Isn't that an instance of the rule that all men should be treated alike with reference to dispatch and speed, etc.? Suppose that you bring a suit at law before your neighbor, and you are ready for trial; wouldn't you think it a great hardship if your neighbor should have your suit postponed till his was tried? A. True.

Q. Supposing that you were to go to a tailor and order a suit of clothes; don't you think it would be a hardship if Senator Sullivan could come after you and get his clothes made first? A. Yes, sir.

Q. Then, if there was to be a classification of freight, it would be but an assertion of the general rule? A. Yes, sir.

Q. You do not understand that this bill is to fix any rate of freights? A. Not at all.

Senator Johnson—I will ask you whether, in your opinion, all men ought to be charged alike in reference to freight? A. I do.

Q. And with reference to dispatch and speed? A. Yes, sir.

Q. And with reference to accommodations, and all that? A. Yes, sir.

Q. Then, if the meaning of this bill is to that effect, you would agree to it? A. Yes, sir; if that is the meaning.

Q. Turning over to page two, do you understand that portion of that section to refer entirely to the dispatch and forwarding of freight? A. Yes, sir; I believe that everything is to be left as it was on the first of last January, in that respect.

Q. Suppose that a given body of freight is to be moved; does it make any difference which portion of it moved first? A. That depends upon circumstances; it depends a good deal upon the class of freight.

Q. Suppose you had at a warehouse two hundred tons of wheat, and you go to the agent and say, "I want you to get your cars right in and take that away; I want you to arrange to put the cars right on," and you make the special arrangements to bring the cars up, and that then there was another man came in with a hundred tons of freight which he was anxious should also go right away? A. There might be some bother in getting the cars there, or something might occur; that might be one difficulty. If we had to take all of the first man's first, that would be rather bad for the second one, you know.

Statement of Wm. Johnston.

Senator Sullivan—Please look at that bill, and say what you think its effect would be upon the consignors of the State, and the people who are engaged in transporting goods over railways, as to whether it would be favorable or unfavorable? Answer. That part of it that refers to discriminations would, in my opinion, be favorable to shippers.

Q. Would it be unfavorable to railroads? A. I do not think that it could be. I am no railroad man; I never have run a railroad.

Q. Would you say that this is a bill which was equitable between man and man? A. Yes, sir.

Senator Cross—Where do you live? A. At Richland.

Q. That is a wheat producing place? A. Yes, sir.

Q. Has there been any complaint in your neighborhood that the railroad company do not forward freight in the order in which it is received? A. Not that I know of.

Q. Do you know of any person in that community ever having been charged more than any other man for the same services by the railroad? A. Richland is not a shipping point by rail; everything is shipped by water.

Q. Do you know of any cause of complaint by the agriculturists of the State that freight offered for shipment was not shipped in its order? A. Not of my own knowledge.

Q. Do you know of any case where one man has been charged, for shipping his products, more than another, for the same class of goods or produce by rail? A. Not of my own knowledge.

Q. From any source of information that you would consider reliable? A. I don't know that reports that a man gets on the streets or from newspaper articles are reliable things to bring before a committee of this kind.

Q. Have you any information on that subject that you would consider thoroughly reliable; if so, we would be glad to have it? A. Well, from persons who are shipping, I understand there is a special contract system adopted by the railroad company by which the parties who sign the contract can ship for less than those who do not.

Q. Do you know whether those relate to agricultural products, or whether they relate simply to merchandise? A. I do not know.

Q. Do you know whether or not the result of these contracts is that freight is delivered at Stockton, San José, Marysville, Los Angeles, and Sacramento, at the same prices that they are received in San Francisco? A. I never heard Marysville included in the list; the others, I understand, have the same price.

Q. If the result of the system was that freights were received at the same prices at these points that they are in San Francisco, do you think it would be favorable to the mercantile communities in those towns? A. Yes, sir.

Q. Did you hear the testimony of Mr. Harrison? A. Yes, sir.

Q. Do you agree with Mr. Harrison in his views that all the wholesale trade should be done in San Francisco? A. I do not.

Q. Do you think that there would be any impropriety in doing a wholesale business in those places? A. I do not.

Q. You stated that as far as the subject of discrimination was concerned you thought that the bill was good? A. Yes, sir.

Q. What do you say of the balance of the bill; is it, in your opinion, a just measure? A. I approve of it.

Q. You approve of all the balance of the bill except sections one and two? A. I don't know of anything in the bill, as far as my knowledge goes of railroading, that would be detrimental to the railroad company, and certainly it would be beneficial to the parties who reside and do business along the lines of the road now.

Q. You have examined the bill? A. I have examined the bill from a producer's standpoint.

Q. How in regard to a consumer's standpoint? A. Also in regard to a consumer's standpoint.

Q. And you think that the bill is a just bill? A. The exception that I want to make is from a railroad standpoint. Not being interested in or acquainted with railroads, I don't know what effect it would have upon them.

SENATOR CROSS—Do you know of anything amounting to an inconvenience or injury by the company not furnishing information as to the rates of freights and fares? A. No, sir.

SENATOR SULLIVAN—Do you know anything about the special contracts made by the merchants of San Francisco in regard to carrying merchandise over the Central Pacific Railroad? A. It is a matter that I do not know anything about.

Q. Have you ever seen one of these special contracts of the Central Pacific Railroad Company? A. Yes, sir.

Q. Do you know, as a matter of fact, that this special contract binds a shipper to send all his goods by rail? A. Yes, sir.

Q. You are a producer and a man who understands the benefits accruing to the State of California by this discrimination being done away with. What I desire from you is your opinion as to whether this special contract system is a good or a bad thing for the State? A. I think it not good for the State.

Q. Do you think that a merchant, or a producer like yourself, should desire to ship by water—say wheat or cereals of any kind—that it would be more beneficial to the State at large that he should be compelled to ship all of his grain or productions by rail? A. I think that a person ought to be allowed to ship by whatever route he received the most benefit.

SENATOR CROSS—Do you know whether those special contracts relate to outgoing commerce, or whether it relates simply to freights coming into the State? A. The contracts that I am acquainted with, or know anything about, are contracts relating to incoming freights.

Q. Contracts that in no manner affect the productions of California? A. The contracts that I know anything about do not.

Q. Have you ever known of any complaint, or cause of complaint, that any railroad company did not keep in a state of complete efficiency its track and other structures? A. No, sir.

Q. Have you ever known of any cause of complaint from the fact that any railroad company in this State hold charters from any other State? A. I want to modify that answer with regard to the Santa Monica wharf; I believe that they allowed that to go to destruction.

Q. They did worse than that, didn't they? A. All that I know is what I read and saw. It has gone to destruction; I don't know what destroyed it.

SENATOR KELLOGG—They took up the track, didn't they? A. I don't know.

SENATOR SULLIVAN—Do you know, as a fact, in the history of California, whether the Central Pacific Railroad Company, or the Southern Pacific Railroad Company, or any other railroad corporation, has ever removed its track, in order to injure any town or city which was disposed to hold to its rights? A. There has been a railroad removed in this county, I understand; I don't know who removed it. I understand that the Central Pacific had a road in this county, leading from Freeport to Franklin, that has been abandoned and removed, to the detriment of Freeport, in this county.

Q. You know that as a fact? A. Yes, sir; I know that as a fact.

SENATOR CROSS—This road from Freeport to Franklin; do you know whether that would pay the expenses of operating? A. I couldn't say that I know anything about it. I was not interested in the road, and don't know what the returns were. I believe that it did.

Q. You were asked a question, which was objected to, as to whether a road had been removed from where it was intended to be built? A. I had reference to the road from Freeport, which was removed after it had been built.

Q. In your judgment, should any railroad company be compelled to maintain a branch road after it ceased to be remunerative? A. That depends upon their charter; what they agreed to do.

SENATOR KELLOGG—Do you not know, that between Marysville and Knights Landing, they were compelled to remove a part of the road on account of the road being under water so much that they were not able to keep it open? A. I only know that by hearsay.

Q. You know it well enough as a matter of hearsay? A. I believe it to be so.

Q. Do you think it would have been right for the company to have been compelled to keep it open? A. That would depend again upon what the company agreed to.

Q. Would not the fact, that they were compelled to keep up an entire new line of road, be sufficient cause for abandoning that part after it had ceased to be of use to the public? A. I don't know; they should keep their contracts.

SENATOR KELLEY—Do you know whether or not, that railroad, spoken of by Senator Kellogg, was a subsidized road or not? A. I do not know.

Q. Do you know whether they received any bonds from the counties through there? A. I don't know what the conditions of the road were.

SENATOR VROOMAN—You think that the railroad company should stand by its contracts? A. Yes, sir.

Q. Like everybody else? A. Yes, sir.

Q. Would you think it right that a law should be passed imposing upon the company conditions other than those in its charter? A. No, sir.

Q. I understood you to state that the question of whether a company should have a right to remove its track depended upon its charter? A. Yes, sir.

Q. As a business man and a producer, do you think it would be right to impose upon the company anything in addition to what is found in its charter, as to its right to remove any of its structures? A. I do not believe in retroactive legislation.

SENATOR VROOMAN—Do you think that any rate of transportation is special which is open to every man in the community in like circumstances? A. It might be special, and yet be open to every man in the community. Any rate for a certain kind of transportation.

Q. Suppose that you had a special rate, or a rate peculiarly applicable to a certain class of goods? A. We pay a special rate on some kinds of goods that we ship out of the State.

Q. Suppose that there is a rate on wheat to be shipped from here to San Francisco, and that that rate is open to every man that has wheat to ship. Is that a special rate? A. It is special as to wheat.

Q. And that would be so as to every class of goods? A. That is my understanding.

Q. Then is it your understanding that there ought to be a uniform rate on all kinds of goods between certain points, irrespective of the character of the goods? A. No, sir.

Q. Well, it is true, is it not, that in the transportation business the rates on goods are classified? A. Yes, sir.

Q. And there is a rate for each class? A. Yes, sir.

Q. Would you call that a special rate? A. Only as to the class.

Q. Do you think that those rates should be prohibited? A. No, sir.

Q. Do you think that a contract that every man in the community has the privilege of signing, is a special contract? A. I do.

Q. Why? A. Because it is not open to all shippers who do not sign it.

Q. It is open to all shippers who desire to sign it? A. Then it is special.

Q. That is your idea of a special contract? A. Yes, sir.

Q. Supposing that it should appear in evidence that if the special contracts were not in force it would result in an increased rate of transportation, and in preventing these interior towns from being distributing points, what effect do you think it would have upon the business interests of the State? A. I think that anything that would prohibit the interior towns from being points of distribution would be detrimental.

Q. Do you not think that any system of transportation which opens innumerable distributing points, instead of being all at one point or place, is in the interest of both the producer and consumer? A. I do.

SENATOR SULLIVAN—Does not the special contract system discriminate against the shipping interests of our State? A. Yes, sir; I think it does.

Q. Does it not, in other words, discriminate against another merchant who desires to send his goods by sea? A. I think that Senator Vrooman misunderstood me; I did not know that there was any difference between San Francisco and the other points as to contracts.

Q. You do not know what the contracts in San Francisco are? A. If they are different, I do not know. If they are alike, I do know.

Q. You do know what the special contracts are in San Francisco, do you not? A. As I stated, there might be a difference between the contracts signed in San Francisco and the other places. If there is, I don't know of any difference. I know the contract system of Sacramento.

Q. Is it similar to that of San Francisco? A. I do not know.

Q. As far as you know about the contracts at Sacramento; do they not compel every man who signs them to send all his goods by rail? A. They do.

Q. Do they not compel every man who signs them to avoid having any business dealings with a man who ships his goods by water? A. Yes, sir.

Q. Is it not a fact that any injury done to the shipping interests of San Francisco, either directly or indirectly, by special contracts, or by any other system devised by the railroad managers, is an injury to the State at large, and that includes not only San Francisco, but Sacramento, Marysville, Los Angeles, and all those points known as terminal points? A. So far as it affects them.

Q. And also places that are not terminal points, such as Nevada, Placerville, and Quincy. In other words, any injuries done to the shipping interests of San Francisco are injuries to the State of California? A. Yes, sir.

Q. Is it not a fact that these special contracts of the Central Pacific Railroad do injure the shipping interests of San Francisco? A. I think they do.

Q. And that is as well to the State at large? A. To the State at large, I think they do.

Q. You live at San Francisco? A. Yes, sir.

SENATOR WHITNEY—What facts do you know to exist growing out of the special contract system which operates injuriously to the State? A. I know of a firm in San Francisco that is doing business here and selling a certain class of goods, and the business depreciated and almost ceased because they did not sign a contract, and they were obliged to sign it in order to continue their business, so that they could ship their goods from the East and compete with others who had the benefit of the special contract system.

Q. They were successful after they signed the contract? A. Yes, sir.

Q. Do you know whether they suffered any disadvantage after signing the contract? A. Yes, sir.

Q. In what particular? A. They were prohibited from shipping the article of wire, in which they were dealing largely, by water, and they were obliged to get it by rail, and they could have shipped it cheaper by water.

Q. Did that have the effect of injuring their business? A. The effect of lessening their profits.

Q. The railroad company can afford to do business at a less figure if they have a larger volume of business, can they not? A. Yes, sir.

Q. Is not the tendency of the special contract system to increase the volume of the railroad business? A. Yes, sir.

Q. On that account does it not enable them to contract business at a much less figure than they would be able to do without the special contract system? A. I should think it would.

Q. To that extent, then, would it not operate in favor of the consumer? A. No, sir.

Q. Why not? A. Because they do not do it.

Q. Because they do not decrease the freight correspondingly? A. No, sir.

SENATOR SULLIVAN—Is it not a fact that the Central Pacific Railroad Company desires to drive off competition by water, and for that purpose may lessen its rates of freight and passenger fare (to drive off the water craft from places like Sacramento and San Joaquin) for the time being? A. I don't think I can answer that question.

Q. The point I desire to make is this: that after having lowered the rates and driven off the water craft, they will then raise the rates? A. They cannot do that now; it is prohibited by the Constitution.

Q. I understand; but within the limits of the Constitution? A. They can't raise it at all. It is unconstitutional.

Q. Do you not think it would be better if the railroad and the water craft were allowed to compete, one with the other? A. I do.

Q. In that way would not the producer and the consumer reap a larger profit than they do now? A. Yes, sir.

Q. Do you know, as a matter of fact, in regard to wheat being shipped from stations along the line of the Sacramento River, that where the sloops and the water craft were driven away, the railroad company discriminates injuriously against those men who patronize water craft? A. I only know by hearsay.

SENATOR SPENCER—I understand that you have read this bill? A. Yes, sir.

Q. Do you see anything in the bill that is inimical to the interests of the producer? A. No, sir.

Q. You do not pretend to pass upon the legal aspects of this bill at all? A. No, sir.

Q. Therefore, in answering some of these hypothetical questions, you did so with no reference to your knowledge of law? A. Yes, sir.

Q. Let me ask you whether, as a business man, you believe that the mercantile interests of this State, as well as the farming interests, would be better subserved by the transportation companies serving all the people alike, irrespective of special contracts or any contracts excepting a general and uniform rate for transporting freight at a reasonable price for all persons? A. I do.

Q. You think that is the proper system, do you not? A. Yes, sir.

Q. You do not think that any contract should be entered into by a transportation company with any person where they imposed any limitations upon him or any penalties as to who he should deal with, or how he should transport any goods or class of goods that he transported with them, do you? A. I presume you do not mean by a special rate that there should be the same rates for a special carload that there was for a small quantity, do you?

Q. No; I do not mean that. A. Then I will answer your question in the affirmative.

Q. How long have you lived in this State? A. Thirty years.

Q. What is your business? A. Agriculture.

Q. What class of goods do you generally ship? A. Grain, fruit, poultry, and stock.

Q. You have a personal experience, outside of your general reading and knowledge of these subjects, in shipping grain, stock, and agricultural implements? A. Yes, sir; but not by rail. Very little by water. I ship some by rail. My principal shipping is by the river.

Q. Supposing that agricultural implements (say wire), or any article that can be shipped by water, can be shipped for ten dollars a ton and landed in San Francisco, and thereafter be shipped to the interior points in the State, while it would cost thirty or forty dollars a ton to ship them by rail, would that be discriminating against the interior towns? A. That would depend upon the freight from San Francisco to the distributing points. It certainly would not be discriminating against Sacramento.

Q. Then you do not mean to be understood that if freight was not distributed at points through the State different from San Francisco (to Stockton, Marysville, Los Angeles, and other distributing points), that that would be discrimination against those interior towns, do you? A. No, sir.

Q. Then you think that that mode of transportation, assuming that there would be that rate of difference, would not be discriminating against the interior points? A. I think that that rate would be the best which would distribute the goods at the points where they were consumed at the least rate to the consumer.

Q. If they could be shipped cheaper round by water to that place, that is the whole question in a nut shell? A. Yes, sir.

Q. Do you not think that the special contract system discriminates against shipping freight by water? A. It does if it prohibits the contractors from shipping.

Q. If a man has a general contract that prevents him from shipping by water, it has a tendency to drive ships from the sea, does it not? A. Yes, sir.

Q. Do you know anything about any rebates that have been practiced by the railroad companies in this State, from conversations with the merchants who were reliable, as to whether or not they paid a certain amount in advance of the rate, and then kept it for a certain length of time, and then paid it back? A. I have heard of such things.

Q. Do you believe, as a business man, that that can be justified by any business principle, assuming that freight was $10 a ton, and they charged you $25, and in six months thereafter they gave you back $15, claiming that the actual freight is $15? A. There might be some discrimination where a man shipped a large quantity, and for instance a whole train of cars; they could afford to do it cheaper per car than if shipped by a single carload.

Q. I don't think you understand me? A. I think I do.

Q. If you do I am perfectly satisfied. Supposing I am a shipper, and you come to me to ship some freight, and ask how much a ton it will cost to ship freight to San Francisco, and I answer that it would cost $10 per ton, and you shipped, and I charged you (I will say for purposes of illustration) $30 for three tons, and that when you came to pay that freight they charged you $100; that after six months had passed they come to you and notified you that you could have $70 rebate. Do you think that a principle upon which such a thing could exist would be justified upon any business principle? A. Not that I know of.

Q. Is that what you understand to be rebates? A. No, sir.

Q. What is your understanding of it? A. What I understand by rebate, is, where an individual was shipping at the regular rates and paying at the regular full rate, and that at some subsequent time he gets a rebate from the regular rate.

Q. Then they give him that back as a mere gratuity? A. That is the way that I understand it.

Q. Upon what business principle is that justified? A. No principle of business.

Q. The actual freight is the amount actually and legitimately charged? A. Yes, sir.

Q. That giving back is an excess of the charge, is it not? A. Yes, sir.

Q. Did you ever know of a railroad company to be actuated by motives of generosity in making a man a present of that kind? A. I never had any experience of that kind.

Q. You do not know of any legislation that has ever demanded any such thing? A. No, sir.

SENATOR TAYLOR—Did you ever know of any case such as the Senator speaks of, where a railroad company agreed to carry freight for ten dollars a ton, or any other amount in excess of the regular rate, and then returned it after keeping it three months? A. No, sir.

Q. Did you ever hear of any such thing from any reliable source? A. No, sir. I understood rebate to be from the regular rate.

SENATOR SULLIVAN—I ask you whether you understand rebate to be, where an agreement was made by special contract to ship goods say from St. Louis, and the amount of the expense bill was say $400. That is, paid by the consignee to the agent in Sacramento. He can; not get the goods until that is paid. Then, after about six months, the railroad returns to him, say, $200. That is what you understand by rebate? A. Yes, sir.

Q. The expense bill calls for $400. A. That is the regular rate?

Q. Yes, sir. And then, after a period of six months, the railroad company, holding his money in the meantime, gives him $200 back. A. That is what I understand by rebate.

SENATOR CROSS—Do you know whether any rebates have been practiced in the State of late years? A. Not since the special contract system has gone into effect, there are no rebates. That is my understanding.

STATEMENT OF J. P. WEBSTER.

MR. CHAIRMAN AND GENTLEMEN: I do not know that I have anything to offer of sufficient importance to occupy your time. It is very well known that there is a good deal of feeling in this State, and in the country, and I understand your purpose here, in extra session, is to do justice between the parties and the people. And this certainly would be judicious. It certainly is very much against the State, and against the railroad companies, and other corporations, that this state of feeling should exist, and if the railroad men have an idea of advancing the material interests of the corporations, or of themselves, I should say you are here to-day to reasonably satisfy the demands against the railroad. Our people, as you are probably aware, are a generous people, and an intelligent people; there are none more so in the world. There are none who would require, or be disposed to do injustice to any man. Certainly there is a feeling, and some reason for it, existing against the railroad companies, and especially against their discriminations and failure to pay their taxes, and that has been growing two or three years; and although the railroad companies may prevent operations here, I think that it would be injurious to the interests of the railroad companies in this case, because, even though this Legislature will be forced in this controversy to yield the point, it can never be settled until a fair disposition of the question be had. I understand very well, that in a great many instances, capital has demanded, and is making efforts continually now, to secure itself against the public, and I think the history of the past demonstrates my putting it in that light. The best interests certainly of all the parties concerned is reasonable legislation; that its reasonable demands be satisfied, and the people brought into harmony with the railroad companies and with the railroad industries in the State. Relative to this Barry bill, I have examined it somewhat, of course, not particularly, but to some extent. In some of its details it may be defective, but I think the principle involved is correct.

SENATOR SULLIVAN—Have you read this Barry bill? Answer— Yes, sir.

Q. You understand the aim and purport of the bill, I believe, to prevent discriminations and abuses by railroad corporations? A. Yes, sir.

Q. The principal point in this bill, as I understand it, is to prevent discrimination. Now, in regard to the question of special contracts, have you any knowledge of what these special contracts are, between the Central Pacific Railroad and consignees and consignors of freight? A. I believe I have seen some of those publications in the newspapers which I have read on the subject.

Q. What is your business? A. Horticulture, and agriculture to some extent, and running a paper.

Q. How many years have you lived in the State of California? A. Thirty years.

Q. During that time have you been identified with agricultural matters in this State? A. I have, to some extent. In regard to the question of freights and fares; I have not very extensive acquaintance. Living so near San Francisco our freights have been nominal.

Q. Where? A. Just across the bay.

Q. Have you any knowledge of this present contract system that has been so frequently spoken of? A. As I stated before, from what has been published on the subject.

Q. Do you know of any person who has been injured by the action of the special contract system? A. I have heard of a gentleman of San Francisco who has been very largely engaged in shipping. Something like a year ago he stated that he had stood out against the special contract system for two or three years, and that he was unable to do it longer; that he had been previously shipping heavier goods around Cape Horn, and to get those goods across the continent he had to pay heavier rates. They raised the rates on the outside shippers to such an extent that he was compelled to accept the contract in order to save his business from ruin.

Q. You have studied over this matter a great deal—thought over it, and heard the opinions of varied people in California? A. Yes, sir.

Q. Now, I ask you, from the knowledge thus acquired, what is your opinion in regard to the effect of this special contract system, as practiced by the Central Pacific Railroad corporation, on the shipping interests of the State of California? A. Ruinous.

Q. How, and in what manner is it ruinous? A. In this way: Of course you understand that certain principles as stated here to-day, that the contracts made to which one entering into agrees to ship all freights in that way, and that he is prohibited from selling any goods or dealing with any merchant who does not ship in that way. The tendency has been in this case I spoke of, to bring heavy manufacturing and agricultural implements around the Horn, and in a great measure the shippers of such goods have sent them by special contract, and if the transportation of all goods for the State comes in this way, of course there could be no inducement for vessels to come to this coast. That, as I understand it, is one of the chief objections to the special contract system.

Q. In other words, you say that it virtually cuts off our vessels from competition? A. So far as the signing of those contracts is concerned it has a tendency to break up competition.

Q. I ask you now if the entire State of California, including the various towns of Sacramento, Los Angeles, Marysville, or any other shipping terminal point, even Stockton, Modesto, Visalia, or any of these towns, are not interested in the operation of this special contract system? A. I take it, sir, that they are all equally interested.

Q. For what reason? A. Because it would enable any shipper of agricultural implements to ship around Cape Horn. The merchants here are dealing very heavily, formerly in Stockton and those other places, and now, under the special contract system, as I understand it, they have no discretion in the matter at all. They are compelled to ship all their goods across the continent by the railroads. It is policy that there should be competition, and when there is between several carriers they will regulate the rate.

Q. Do you know if there is any chance, considering this policy practiced by the Central Pacific Railroad, for any individual, or private corporations, to build or own any line parallel with theirs? A. There is only one chance that I see, and that is, to have more capital, and more brains, and more energy, than the company now in operation.

Q. What effect, if any, would the special contract system—the system of discrimination—have, in regard to any new line of railroad started by independent capital? A. Well, as was illustrated in the Northern Pacific Railroad, or as was in the paper, the manager of that road agreed first, not to enter into the special contract system, but they were subsequently forced into it, which would indicate they found it more to their advantage than to run independently.

Q. You would imply that no railroad line built by a corporation, or an individual, could compete with the railroad company, provided this special contract system is enforced? A. It appears to me not. It was reported in San Francisco at the time the agent was there, that the merchants of San Francisco were timid, and so fearful that the Northern Pacific Railroad Company would not be able to carry out its contract, that there were very few, or none at all, that would guarantee their contract to the Northern Pacific Railroad Company.

SENATOR McCLURE—Do you state that of your own knowledge?

5 ᵇ

A. I got it from the merchants. It was reported so in the papers, and also by a very large shipper of such goods.

Q. Do you know anything about the special contract system of your own knowledge? A. Nothing—only what I say has been printed.

Q. What you read and heard? A. Yes, sir.

Q. All that you have stated is based on what you have read and heard? A. Yes, sir.

Q. It is not predicated upon any facts of your own knowledge? A. Not absolutely.

Q. Did you ever run or operate a railroad? A. A horse railroad.

Q. A steam railroad, for the purpose of carrying freight and passengers? A. No, sir.

Q. You don't pretend to know anything about the railroad business? A. No, sir.

Q. As a representative man of the agricultural interests of this State, do you not think and believe that the interests of the farmers and of the railroad corporations should be in harmony for the best interests of all the people of the Pacific Coast? A. There is no doubt of that.

Q. Do you not believe that any law intended to cripple the railroad company would be detrimental to the interests of them as well as the farmer? A. That might be qualified. It would depend upon what your definition of that term is.

Q. You understand: my question is, to cripple; I mean any unjust method? A. Oh! any unjust method; certainly.

Q. After examining the bill, do you think if the bill is permitted to pass, that it is a just and fair bill for the corporations, the shippers, and the consumers, without amendment? A. If that is, to go in that shape or not at all, I should say that it was beneficial to go; but it might be amended in some particulars, possibly.

Q. Don't you think it could be improved by amendment? A. Well, I don't know; I am not well enough posted to determine that point.

SENATOR SPENCER—What part of the country do you live in? A. Alameda County.

Q. I understood you that you have lived in that county about thirty years? A. Yes, sir.

Q. Have you mingled with the community and business men, generally, there? A. Yes, sir; quite extensively, I think.

Q. During the time of your residence there, have you had opportunities of hearing the opinions of the people generally? A. Yes, sir; in a general way.

Q. State whether or not you have had occasion to travel around in this State, and in different portions of it? A. Yes, sir.

Q. What portions of this State have you been through? A. I have been through the northern portions, and northerly to the end of the road, and also to Los Angeles, and the Town of San Diego, and traveled extensively shorter distances around the country.

Q. Do you say that you are connected with a newspaper? A. Yes, sir.

Q. What paper is that? A. California Patron; the official organ of the State Agricultural Society.

Q. Are you a member of the State Grange? A. Yes, sir; Secretary of the California State Grange.

Q. At meetings of the Grange have you ever heard the subject of freights and fares discussed generally? A. Yes, sir.

Q. Have you given that subject any special attention, with reference to going into the minutest details of it? A. Possibly not the minutest details; no, sir.

Q. You have not tried to get up a schedule of fares and freights? A. No, sir; I have not gone to that.

Q. Classified into ten thousand classes? A. No, sir.

Q. Do you know from these different localities, from the people of this State, whether any general complaint as to the mode and manner in which freights are transported by the transportation companies of this State exist, including the Southern Pacific Railroad and the Central Pacific Railroad? A. I know, possibly, more about fares than freights. I have more direct dealings with fares than freights, and of course, in a general way, I have heard complaints. Whether I could state specifically any particular case that would bear directly upon this proposition——

Q. Would you be kind enough to state to the committee in what respect discriminations have been practiced with reference to localities or persons? A. With reference to persons, very considerable.

Q. You think that has been practiced with reference to persons very considerably? A. Yes, sir, it has; a great many cases might be cited, possibly.

Q. Senator Kellogg asked you if any cinch measure would be a beneficial measure. You have been in California twenty years? A. Yes, sir.

Q. Did you ever know a railroad company to be cinched at any time, in the common acceptation of the term? A. No, sir; I think the cinch has always been on the other side.

Q. If they are cinched too tight they buck it off, don't they? A. They never got the girth tight enough to cinch them.

Q. You do not understand that the farmers, or the producers, or the merchants desire any cinch measures, or any unjust measures? A. No, sir.

Q. I understood you to say, as a business man, and a producer, that if this measure, as it is now, should pass, in your opinion it would be better than no measure at all? A. Altogether, sir; while it might be, in some of the details, amended to make it more harmonious.

Q. In speaking of the different sections of this bill, you were not speaking with reference to its legal aspects, were you? A. I could not speak of its legal effect.

Q. You are not qualified to say whether they are constitutional or unconstitutional? A. I am not qualified to do that.

Q. Nor whether it contravenes the fourteenth amendment? A. I never have.

Q. Have you sent any freight under special contract yourself? Can you tell me what is the general opinion among the men with whom you have associated, with the commercial community, and business community, including the farmers and producers, as to the policy of entering into contracts called special contracts, and whether or not you believe that every man should have the right, whether he has a contract or not, to ship the same classes of freights the same distance without discrimination? A. I certainly think so.

Q. Do you know anything about what is called rebate money? A. Very little; I have heard of some very apparent cases, but, of course, it would hardly have a bearing upon this.

Q. Do you know of any discrimination against places practiced by the railroad company? A. In fares; yes, sir.

Q. State them. A. There is one illustration, possibly as good as any would be; that is the fares from San Francisco to Stockton, which is three dollars, and from Stockton to Sacramento it is two dollars, while a through ticket from San Francisco to Sacramento is only three dollars and thirty cents, making a difference between Sacramento and Stockton of thirty cents, when the distance is fifty miles.

Q. Supposing that you bought a ticket from San Francisco to Stockton, and then the next morning go on through from Stockton to Sacramento, what is the difference in fare? A. I bought a ticket from Sacramento to San Francisco, about a year ago, for four dollars, and went down to Elk Grove, twenty miles below here. There I requested the conductor to give me a stop-over ticket; he said that I was too late, that he had not the time, that he had to go through the cars and take up the collections. I was compelled to get off there; but previous to that the conductor had come along and taken up my ticket and had given me a blank check, nothing on it except some distances. I got off at Elk Grove. The next day I got on the train at the same hour and presented my blank check; he stated that it was not good for anything; that I had missed the train for which I had taken a ticket, and therefore had lost about three dollars and seventy-five cents; and I paid that much more and went along, making seven dollars and seventy-five cents from Sacramento to San Francisco.

Q. Do you know of any discriminations against places on account of any positions which they had taken on the railroad questions? A. I don't know positively. There has been threats of that kind, but I don't know of their having been carried into operation.

Q. How about Lathrop and Stockton; what is the name of that road? A. I think it is operated by the Southern Pacific Company.

Q. Do you know anything about discrimination being practiced upon that road? A. I never had any experience, and of course could not speak positively. Of course it would not be proper for me to relate anything which I may have heard.

Q. Do I understand you to state that the effect of these special contracts is to discriminate against shipping by water? A. It is certainly so.

Q. Do you not think that any discrimination of any kind that would operate against the shipping interests of San Francisco would not only thereby increase the price of goods in this State, but would be a discrimination against the interior towns? A. I take it that anything that was discrimination against San Francisco would have its effect upon all parts of the State.

Q. If that was a commercial center, and goods could be shipped there by water for twenty dollars a ton, whereas it cost forty dollars a ton to deliver them by rail in the interior towns of Stockton, Los Angeles, Marysville, and Sacramento, they could make that much difference by having them shipped by water, could they not? A. If that is a correct assumption.

Q. Do you know whether, when goods have been consigned to any place in this State (say Lodi), that they have carried the car past the place, and on to Stockton, or to Oakland, and then shipped it back again, and charged freight for the additional shipment back? A. They have a through rate, and the railroad company claim that in order to get a through rate they have to carry the goods clear through, and that is cheaper for the shipper.

Q. Do you know whether there is an additional charge for carrying that back over the same route? A. I never had any positive experience in that myself.

Senator McClure—I understand you that they transport freight for one person for less than they do for another; that they make a discrimination between persons? That is one of the complaints? A. I believe it is.

Q. Do you understand that all freight of every kind or class ought to be carried at the same rate? A. No, sir.

Q. There is no such complaint as that? You could not carry silks for the same price that you could carry iron? The general complaint is they discriminate between persons—is that the idea? A. It is only between persons, as I take it, and not as to classification of freight?

Q. I understood you that they did discriminate between individuals as to particular classes of freight, and even in the same class between two individuals. Of course that is wrong and ought to be remedied, but do you understand that there is a general desire that the railroad should be compelled to fix a uniform rate of freight with reference to every class of freight and put it all into one class? A. Not into one class, no. To reduce the classification.

Senator Taylor—As the aim of this committee is to get at the views of the people generally and to arrive at a proper conclusion, I will ask you, as you have said that you were a member of the State Grange and had relations with the farmers throughout the State, north and south, and therefore were in a position to give us the general impression of the agricultural people of the State, as to whether or not there exists now any discrimination in the freight by railroad or not? A. I think that that impression is very general.

Q. That those discriminations exist? A. Yes, sir.

Q. You have stated that, in your opinion, the Barry bill, as far as it goes, would be better than nothing at all? A. Yes, sir.

Q. But that it might have certain amendments? A. Yes, sir.

Q. Do you mean by that that some of the sections are too severe? A. That depends upon the legal construction (reading section four). That is a legal question that I do not understand.

Q. Do you think it proper that in a case of this character, even where there is discriminations, whether by railroad companies or by persons, the remedy should be of such a character as to make the punishment of them severe? A. It ought to be severe, but the question of whether it ought to be by a forfeiture of their charter, is one that ought to be made so plain that there could be no quibbling about it, whatever it is. And, whether receiving a charter in another State should forfeit their charter in this, is a question I am hardly able to cope with.

SENATOR SULLIVAN—Would this bill be good for anything if there was not a penalty fixed? A. I think not.

Q. It is absolutely necessary that there should be some penalty for the violation of any section which it contains? A. I think so.

Q. In answer to a question you referred to some track that had been destroyed? A. That was abandoned track. That point was raised here this morning. Of course they may be conditions, and it depends a good deal upon the charter and what that requires, and if there is anything in the charter of the railroad company, or their obligation to the State, that should cause them to maintain the road, if they have that understanding when they take their charter, then it should be forfeited if they abandon, in my opinion.

Q. If that section was amended so as to meet this objection of yours, do you think that would be satisfactory? A. I think so.

Q. Is it not the fact that any classification causes discrimination? A. Yes, sir.

Q. It has been in evidence here, and has been admitted, that the railroad company charge more for carrying ore worth thirty dollars a ton than for ore worth ten dollars a ton. What is your opinion about that kind of classification? A. I do not think it is just.

Q. In other words, you do not think that, under any classification of freights, the railroad company has any right to enter into the profits of the purchaser or consumer? A. Not into the profits, no, sir; but they have possibly a right to enter into the value of the products. For instance, in the transportation of bullion, or anything of that kind, there is some risk. The freight should be raised of course on articles of value sufficient to cover the cost of insurance and the extra expense of handling such goods.

Q. Do you think they should charge more for conveying tea than for wheat, for instance? A. Yes, sir; because there has to be more care in the handling, and the risk is greater. There should be enough additional to cover the additional cost of handling and the cost of insurance.

Q. Well, take two cars of wheat and two cars of barley, and one brings fifty per cent less than the other in the market, and they are classified as A and B. Do you think that the railroad company should charge any more for class A than for class B? A. No, sir; not one cent.

SENATOR JOHNSON—You have been asked the opinion of the Grange. Are you prepared to speak, in answer to that question, as to the opinion of the Grange, at any of their meetings, upon the subject of discrimination? A. Yes, sir. At the last meeting of the State

Grange, in October, there was a series of resolutions adopted by the Grange (I think without any dissenting voice, as far as I remember), in favor of fixing rates of freights and fares, and in calling the extra session for that purpose. I think the resolutions can be produced, if necessary. Mr. Coulter has a copy of them.

SENATOR SPENCER—That does not say upon the subject of discrimination? A. It refers to the Constitution of the State, etc.

Q. I will ask you, then, under the wording of that Constitution, section twenty-one, of article twelve, of it, is included? A. I have not examined them.

Q. Do you recollect this provision in the Constitution of the State: "No discrimination," etc.? (reading section twenty-one, of article twelve). I will ask you whether or not in your opinion a law that will operate alike upon all persons is the proper law to be passed by special legislation? A. I think it should be the province of every legislative body to take it in its broadest sense. It is not for any class.

Q. Can you see any objection to page one of the Barry bill, where the idea intended to be conveyed is this: "that all persons shall be served alike without discrimination?" A. I do not see how there could be any.

Q. Following the provisions of the Constitution, which are mandatory and prohibitory, would not it be the duty of the Legislature, in your opinion, to carry out the provisions of article twelve if there is no other provision in respect to discrimination? A. I think so.

Q. You stated that all persons should be treated alike in respect to the accommodations as regards the moving of freight. Now, will not the same general rule hold in regard to the dispatch and forwarding of freight? A. The only point there is that certain classes of freight are perishable, and there may be such a mass of freight to move that a limited number of cars could not transport it, and thus the perishable freight might become valueless.

Q. Suppose that the provision of the Barry bill was this: "a preference may be given to perishable articles and to fast freight;" would that cover your idea? A. I think that that would be a great amendment.

Q. In your judgment do the words "perishable articles," include live stock? A. That is a legal question, but it occurs to me to say that I do not think it would be a great stretch of opinion to say that it would.

Q. That would be your opinion? A. Yes, sir; because after the shipper has his stock in the cars, it is of the utmost importance that they should be moved.

Q. I understand your position to be that all persons should be served alike with respect to dispatch, and speed, and accommodations, unless it was impracticable? A. There is no question about that, but who is to judge of the impracticability? There is the point right there that it would be possible to cover.

Q. Do you not think that the penalty ought to be sufficiently severe to enforce this bill, if the bill is right? A. Certainly.

Q. Is there any objection to holding a corporation liable for its acts any more than a natural person? A. I do not understand that an artificial person should be allowed any more privileges than a natural person.

Q. If a natural person is an agent, and he commits acts without the scope of his authority, your opinion is that the natural person ought to be punished? A. He is, if I understand it right, now.

Q. Is it not your opinion that the same rule ought to be applied to corporations, if the agent acts within the authority of the corporation? A. It occurs so to me.

SENATOR TAYLOR—Are you sufficiently acquainted with the difference between perishable articles and fast freight and express matter, to tell what it is? A. Possibly not. It is quite intricate, and requires a good deal of study.

Q. Give us an illustration of what you would term perishable articles? A. I think it would be better to leave it to some railroad man to determine.

Q. What would you say about household goods? What class would that be in fast freight, express matter, or perishable matter? A. Sometimes it depends a good deal upon the disposition of the owner. If he wants to pay for fast freight he puts it in as fast freight. Some men would put in almost anything as fast freight, and pay additional charges.

Q. Supposing that it was not desirable to pay additional charges as fast freight, then how would you fix it? A. Well, if it was perishable it would certainly be the disposition of the owner to have it forwarded immediately.

Q. You would not regard household goods as perishable? A. It depends upon what they were, in a measure. If it was furniture that was in a car out of the weather, I would not conceive that it was perishable; but if it was on the platform, in the event of a storm, it certainly would be very badly damaged.

Q. That is the place where it becomes necessary to determine the class, as to whether it is perishable? A. Those are questions which I am not competent at the present time to determine.

Q. How would you class a law library, or the library of a physician? A. It would be better for the public if it were all classed as slow freight, and kept slow all the time.

Q. How about agricultural machinery, such as reapers, and mowers, and headers, etc.? A. I could not classify them as perishable.

Q. How as to being fast and slow? A. If the harvest was ripening I would want them fast.

Q. Supposing that you were to deliver to the company ten thousand tons of wheat, or a million feet of lumber, for transportation; do you say that it should all be transported in the order in which it is received, and that all freights which were not perishable, such as agricultural implements, should wait in the order of its reception till all this other freight was transported? A. No, sir; a man making a contract understands what he is doing.

Q. He may be standing upon his rights in transportation? A. He takes it at his own risk.

Q. I am speaking about the liability of the company under this bill; whether it would be the duty of the company to transport all this freight of wheat or lumber, if it were received first, and make the law library and the agricultural implements and household goods await their order? A. That is a question of law that I am not able to answer.

Q. If this bill should have such an effect as that, would you say that it should pass without amendment? A. Say that it should be left to some power or authority to regulate those matters, I would make it the province of the Railroad Commission to determine those matters.

Q. Then, you do not think that there should be an inflexible rule requiring that freight should be forwarded in the order in which it is received, with the single exception of perishable articles and fast freight? A. I think it ought to be left to the Commissioners to determine what is perishable and what is not. If it is not perishable, it occurs to me that freight should be forwarded in the order in which it is received.

SENATOR WHITNEY—You understand that railroad business should be conducted on the same principles as other business, I suppose, and that the same general rules should be applied as are applied to the conducting of other kinds of business? A. That is the interest of the public.

Q. And it is upon that ground you stated that you thought there should be discrimination of classes, and you recognize the fact that there should be a classification of freight which would enable the railroad company to charge more for certain classes than they did for others; for instance, more for silk than for iron? A. Yes, sir.

Q. How would it be in regard to wheat? Should a person who ships more be allowed an advantage in price because he ships more? A. As I understand it, the charter and the right of way were given for the benefit of the public, and, in my estimation, there ought to be no difference in any amount of cars over one; of course, if you break bulk in less than a carload, there ought to be a difference.

Q. So that if one man ships a hundred carloads of grain, and another man ships ten, he should have just the same advantage as the man who ships a hundred, as far as price is concerned? A. Yes, sir.

Q. There should be no discrimination in regard to the amount? A. No, sir.

Q. Do you not recognize the fact that a railroad company can transport a large amount of freight much more economically than they can a small amount? A. Yes, sir; but there is this point: if there are ten of us, and we each have a carload of wheat to ship, the railroad company can transport that just as cheaply belonging to all as to one.

Q. If in the one instance you had a hundred carloads to transport, and in the other you had ten, you could transport the hundred for less than the ten, could you not? A. Yes, sir; and that is just where the law of the State comes in to say, "we are willing to allow you a fair rate of freight, but you shall not discriminate against shippers where each has less than a carload."

Q. Suppose that the railroad company could, by adopting a classification, increase the amount of freight transported from one to two hundred thousand tons, would not that enable them to make a less charge for each ton? A. Possibly it would, but it is discriminating against the poorer shipper.

Q. It would be discriminating against the railroad company if they could not get as much freight also? A. Yes, sir.

Q. Now, looking at it from a railroad standpoint, can they not afford to transport for me, per ton, one hundred tons of freight cheaper than they can one ton, or one hundred carloads cheaper than they can one carload? A. If they were only going to get one ton by not contracting, and could get a hundred from another man, then I think they could; but there is this point about it: the presumption is always that the railroad is not generous enough to move any freight that it does not get paid for.

Q. If I agreed to give them all of my freight, could they not afford to do it cheaper than if I gave them only one ton, and gave somebody else the other ninety-nine tons? A. I think that broken carloads should be recognized in competition.

Q. If I had a hundred carloads, could not the railroad company afford to transport them cheaper for me than if I had only one? A. I think they could, by making a reduction, and by a general reduction, and a fair average of freights, they could get the whole business anyway.

Q. If they could not get the whole business, except by making that reduction, do you think that they ought to be allowed to make that reduction? A. I think, as I said before, that that is where the regulations of the State should come in to discriminate between heavy and light shippers, provided it is not less than a carload.

Q. Do I understand you that a railroad company can afford to transport a hundred carloads cheaper than they can one? A. If they have to run an engine with one car, they certainly could.

Q. Suppose that they could not do it with one engine, but had to take several? A. If, by one-car lots they were able to make up their train, I don't see where the advantage would come in, excepting to the railroad company.

Q. Do you think it would make a difference with the railroad whether they shipped five hundred or five thousand carloads? A. Yes, sir.

Q. Then any arrangement by which they could get the transportation of five thousand carloads would be better for them than one which only gave them five hundred? A. At the same rates, certainly.

Q. Then they ought to be allowed to make that much, had they not? A. I think there comes in the discrimination again. As I said before, the State should regulate that matter.

Q. You think, then, that they should be compelled to ship one hundred carloads at the same price per carload that they do five thousand? A. I think so.

Q. Notwithstanding it would cost them more? A. Yes, sir.

Senator Kellogg—In regard to the discrimination in your own case, did you ask the conductor for a stop-over ticket before you got to Elk Grove? A. If I had asked in time I presume I might have got it.

Q. Do you think it would have been right for the conductor to have delayed the business of the road, and the other passengers upon it, for the purpose of issuing you a stop-over ticket, when you could have had it by asking for it in time? A. The wrong was for them to take away my ticket and give me a blank check. It should be so arranged that I could get off anywhere on the road and get on again.

SENATOR VROOMAN—Two merchants have each a hundred thousand dollars worth of goods, one sells all his goods to three men, and the other to twenty thousand men; do you not think that the merchant who sells all his goods to the three men can afford to sell them for less than the man can who sells to twenty thousand? A. I can see that there would be a difference.

Q. Would not that same principle run through the railroad business? If they have a hundred thousand tons of freight to transport, and only had to deal with one consignor, would it not be better for them than to have to deal with twenty thousand consignors; could they not transport a hundred thousand tons of freight cheaper for one man than they could for twenty thousand? A. I think, to come right down to dollars and cents, they could; but, as I have said, that is where the province of the State comes in to make it equal between all the shippers with regard to quantity.

Q. In other words, you think that the strong arm of the State should be interposed in this case to prevent the same rules being applied to the railroad company in doing its business as is applied to the merchant in conducting his business? A. There is a difference in the two lines of business; the merchant conducts his business absolutely; the railroad owes a service to the State, and consequently the State has a right to control it to prevent discrimination, as between the large and small shippers.

Q. You think that the power of the State should interpose its strong arm to interfere with the natural laws of trade which govern other kinds of business? A. Yes, sir; because it is a different class of business.

SENATOR JOHNSON—Do you think that any railroad company should be allowed to make any contract with the owners of any vessels, etc. (reading the section of the Constitution)? A. No, sir.

Q. Why not? A. Because it is against the Constitution.

Q. Is it against any principle? A. I think it is against principle. If you have any regulations at all you should certainly have the right to prevent combinations.

Q. Do you mean that it shuts out competition? A. It certainly shuts out competition where several carriers agree to pay the same rate.

Q. Do you think that those special contracts defeat competition? A. Yes, sir.

Q. What distinction do you draw between them; or is there any to be drawn? A. I did not say any should be drawn.

SENATOR WHITNEY—It has been objected that by the special contract system ships are kept out of competition, and that if it were not for that system one half of the freight that now comes to this coast would come by ships and the other half across the continent. By that arrangement the railroad companies would only carry half the freight which they now carry. The price across the continent then would necessarily be increased, because the transportation would be increased. Would you think that would be an advantage to the people of the State? A. In the long run, yes, sir.

Q. So, if by virtue of the special contract the State gets lower rates of freight, you think it would be better off than if it paid more to the railroad company? A. Yes, sir.

Q. You think, then, in other words, that it would be better for the State to pay open rates than to pay special contract rates? A. Yes, sir.

SENATOR TAYLOR—Do you think that there should be no discrimination whatever made by the railroad company between places upon the same class of freight; say now, for instance, in the single article of wheat; should they not be allowed, under any circumstances, to make a discrimination in the amount charged as freight upon wheat between places? A. It occurs to me not; that has been one of the great faults found, where there is no competition by any other line—say from Stockton to Sacramento—the rates have been very reasonable in all classes of freight, except where there is no competition whatever, and no other transportation line; there they have made their rates very heavy, which, it occurs to me, is an injustice.

Q. How would it be with reference to their being allowed to discriminate, and make the freight less per ton per mile from a point distant from the seaboard, than it was from one nearer, in proportion to the distance carried? A. It gives the State and the shipper the benefit of having it uniform, without regard to competitive points.

Q. You do not contend and would not maintain that there must be a uniform rate per ton per mile? A. It depends upon the distance; for instance, it might be and ought to be less per ton per mile from Sacramento than from Stockton; because, as you understand very well, the chief expense is in loading and unloading. The better way to arrange that, it occurs to me, would be to allow a terminal charge, and then allow a uniform rate per ton per mile.

Q. Supposing that there was a uniform rate per ton per mile, and that the company should charge that rate, and not be allowed to discriminate between a competitive point near the seaboard and one that was farther away, would that be right? A. I do not understand you.

Q. If wheat could be shipped at two cents per ton per mile and a party was within ten miles of the shipping point—that would cost him twenty cents to ship his wheat. Now, supposing there was another point four hundred miles away and not a competitive point; the maximum rate being two cents per ton per mile, the wheat raiser there would be compelled to pay $8 per ton to get his wheat to the seaboard, or to the same point. Now, ought not the railroad company be permitted to discriminate in favor of the shipper who was four hundred miles away? A. I do not say it. There should be a difference in the cost of loading allowed at the terminal points, whatever was just, and then he should be charged a certain uniform rate per ton per mile.

Q. Assuming, for the purpose of getting at the point, that it cost just as much to load and unload at one point as at the other, and leaving that out entirely, then ought not the company to be allowed to discriminate in favor of the man who is four hundred miles away? A. No, sir; it is the misfortune of the farmer who has got so far back into the country.

Q. There was something said here about God having discriminated in favor of San Francisco. If that is the case, ought not we, on the same principle, to be allowed to discriminate in favor of our own place, or in favor of some other place? A. I believe that the Lord prepared the place, and that the people found it when they went there. I don't know that he had anything to do with it except preparing it for them.

Q. For the purpose of illustration, we will take the Valley of the Sacramento, or of the San Joaquin, which are much nearer the seaboard than Siskiyou, where the road is now being constructed. In that valley the farmers raise a large quantity of wheat, and they desire to market their grain and to ship it to the seaboard. Suppose that the maximum price were two cents per ton per mile, and that the distance was four hundred miles; that grain would cost eight dollars per ton, say to Port Costa, whereas at the present time the farmers through these valleys get it shipped for thirty and forty cents per ton. Now, would you say that no consideration whatever should be had in favor of that locality? A. It must be a very poor farmer that will undertake to raise wheat for the San Francisco market so far away from the market. If he was a prudent farmer he would turn his attention to something else, to stock raising, for instance, which would justify him in paying the rates.

Q. So you would not allow any discrimination in their favor, but would regard them as poor farmers? A. As unfortunate in getting into a bad place.

Q. Do you not know that it is a fact that wheat is shipped a distance of three hundred miles to the seaboard? A. Yes, sir.

Q. And shipped all that distance by reason of the discrimination of the railroad company in favor of that locality? A. Yes, sir; I know that it has been the case.

Q. Would you have all of that industry stopped to prevent the railroad company from discriminating in favor of that locality, and cause the people to turn their attention to something else? Would that be right? A. It occurs to me that if I had a contract to fix I would put it just as low between the railroad company and the farmer at that distance as would justify the railroad company in carrying it, and if they could not carry it to the seaboard at that rate I would say for them to turn their attention to something else. The State cannot afford to accommodate every farmer because he happens to get away back in the backwoods. The whole system should not be overturned simply for the benefit of a few farmers in the interior.

Q. Is it not the policy of the State to attempt to settle up the country, and to encourage immigration to its uttermost parts? A. Yes, sir.

Q. How would that policy coincide with the manner in which you have spoken of farmers in the backwoods? A. There are various inducements besides farming.

Q. Suppose that the lands of Siskiyou County are especially adapted to raising grain, and much better for that than for raising live stock? A. If they are adapted for raising grain they are for raising live stock also.

Q. Well, do you think there should be no discrimination allowed to the company in the transportation of live stock? A. Such produce will bear a very heavy rate of transportation.

Q. Well, as between the farmer who lives in that remote section, and one who lives in Sacramento Valley, must they all be treated alike? A. I take it so; yes, sir.

Q. Suppose that the business which is done by the company outside of the transportation of wheat and stock, is such that they were compelled to charge the maximum rates? A. I think that if they were allowed to discriminate between two places, and to take wheat and stock and other products at such rates as the producers there could afford to pay, and transport it to the seaboard, that they could lessen the whole rate of freight through that section. I think that they never take any freight, from any section, that does not pay for taking it out; that they have their rates, and always will, so as to make a profit on every ton of produce moved.

Q. Then you do not believe in the idea, that the more business the less the rate? A. Well, the principle generally holds good; but as I said before, the interests which the State have in railroads are such that it is the province of the State to regulate those matters.

SENATOR SPENCER—What one man calls discrimination is not discrimination in another man's mind. In other words, that word discrimination, as used in fares and freights, is subject to a good many interpretations? A. Yes, sir.

Q. You mean simply to be understood as saying, that where freight is shipped from the same point they should charge the same rate of transportation? A. Yes, sir; in anything above a carload.

SENATOR CROSS (Senator Johnson presiding)—I understand that you, especially in the relations which you hold to the State Grange, and to the journal which you edit, have an opportunity to become reasonably familiar with the agricultural and horticultural interests of the State. Do you believe that there is any demand in the State for any legislation which would punish any person for acts which they neither control nor are in any degree responsible for? A. No, sir.

Q. Do you believe there is any demand in the State that a law should be passed by which the mere bondholders of railroad companies should be punished for the acts of the company? A. Well, of course the charter is granted on certain conditions and restrictions. Every stockholder and every bondholder knows the conditions when he takes the stock or bonds, and consequently that would qualify it to some extent; but as I said before, that while I agree in the main features of the bill, and possibly the penalties attached may be too severe, yet they ought to be sufficiently severe to compel a compliance with the law.

Q. From your associations with the people of the State and with the State Grange, do you believe that there is any demand that penalties should be inflicted upon any person who is not responsible, either directly or indirectly, for the act for which the penalty is inflicted? A. Well, I dare say that it would occur incidentally and unavoidably; but as I said before, in cases of bondholders, they take their bonds under certain restrictions, knowing that the Legislature has the power to forfeit the franchises whenever it permits discrimination or violates the law.

Q. I am asking you whether you think the people of the State demand that a property worth, for instance, four millions, ought to be forfeited because one carload of freight was forwarded out of its order? A. Certainly that would be an extreme case. It ought to be in such shape that where there was a disposition to obey the law, or by any mistake or otherwise, freight was forwarded out of its order, they should not suffer the penalty without there was a general disposition to disobey the law.

Q. Do you think that, from your knowledge, and the associations you have had with the people of the State, that they demand that a minority of the stockholders of a corporation ought to be punished for the act for which the majority was responsible and which was against the wish of the minority? A. That is just how the minority generally suffers in all corporations.

Q. Do you think that the people of the State demand legislation inflicting penalties to that extent? A. In this case it would be unavoidable, in order to compel a compliance with the law.

Q. Do you not think that the people of the State and the State Grange would be satisfied with penalties being inflicted upon those who committed the act of discrimination? A. If the penalties can be so shaped as to be sufficient to compel a compliance with the law it don't make much difference to the people of the State what means are used. I think, so far as the bondholders are concerned, if they could be protected in consonance with the interests of the State it would be done.

Q. Do you think that the State Grange demands that if there are, for instance, twenty stations upon the road, and all the freight is offered at one of those stations at a time when freight is also offered at another station, which should be forwarded first? A. As I understand the bill, it simply requires that all freight shall be forwarded in the order in which it is received at each station.

Q. Do you think that the State Grange, or those whom you heard express an opinion, would be satisfied if the bill provided that the freight received at each station should be forwarded in the order in which it was received at that station? A. It occurs to me that that is the spirit of the bill as it stands.

Q. I am not allowed to ask you as to the effect of the bill. I am simply asking you as to the opinions of the people upon these questions as far as you have been able to ascertain them? A. There might be cases where it would work injustice.

Q. Supposing that a thousand carloads of wheat were tendered at one time at Chico and that at the same time a hundred tons were tendered at Stockton, do you think that it is required by the people of whom you speak that that whole thousand tons at Chico should be moved before any was moved at Stockton? A. It occurs to me that that would be discriminating against the town.

Q. Suppose that a quantity of live stock and a quantity of wheat were tendered at the same time, and that the quantity of wheat was sufficient to exhaust all the cars at any station for ten days (which would be possible by some of the large shippers, I believe), do you think it would be wise legislation to fix a rule so that all the wheat should be forwarded before the stock? A. No, sir.

Q. In the meantime the stock might eat up the profits of the shippers, while the wheat might not suffer any disadvantage at all? A. Yes, sir.

Q. Do you know of there having been any complaint that freight was not forwarded in the order in which it was received, to the injury of any person? A. I have no case in my mind at present.

Q. Have you any reliable information that such a case has transpired within the State? A. I do not recollect any. I have heard incidentally of cases, but none sufficiently important to present here.

Q. Not of sufficient importance to present with reference to the enacting of a law? A. No, sir.

Q. Have you known of any complaint against any railroad company because they would not make known, upon demand, the rates which they charged for carrying freights within the State? A. Not positively.

Q. Have you any reliable information of anything of the kind? A. I do not know that I have.

Q. Do you know of any case in which the removal of any structure has worked any hardship to any person? A. What do you mean?

Q. Any structure; I suppose that would include any building, warehouse, railroad depot, or anything of the kind? A. Not to my knowledge. Only from what I have heard.

Q. Have you heard of any removals which worked no hardship? A. I do not think of any at present.

Q. Do you know of any changes in the line of tracks, or roads, in this State which worked no hardship to any person? A. I think not.

Q. Do you know of any place in the Sierra Nevada Mountains where the track has been removed for the purposes of shortening the line, or improving the grade, and then relaid in a different place from where it was originally? A. Possibly some small distances, but nothing material.

Q. If such changes should be made for the purpose of improving the grade, or anything of the kind, do you think there is any demand on the part of the people of the State, or of the State Grange, that for so doing the railroad shall forfeit its charter? A. I think not, unless it was done intentionally for an injury.

Q. If it were done merely for the purposes of transportation, you think no penalty should attach? A. Not without they are under obligation to the town, or something of the kind.

Q. Do you know of any case where any person, or the State, has suffered in any way from any railroad company within the State having a charter from any other State, or from any other government besides the State of California? A. There was a question before the Legislature last session upon that point, in which it was claimed that if it operated under a Federal charter, the road was released from its obligation to this State.

Q. Have you known of any hardship being worked within the State to the people of the State, or of any person within the State suffering any disadvantage from a railroad being operated within the State which held a charter from other States? A. I think there is a case decided which would bear upon that question.

Q. I will ask you if the complaints which you hear are not with relation to rates of charges, and with relation to non-payment of taxes? A. Yes, sir.

Q. They complain of onerous charges? A. Yes, sir; and of discriminations.

Q. The discriminations which you speak of grow out of what are called special contracts? A. I understand there are discriminations between different places and persons in different parts of the State.

Q. If the matter of discrimination between places and persons, and the matter of charges, and the matter of taxes, were reasonably adjusted, do you think that the demands of the people with regard to railroads would be satisfied? A. Do you include in that the special contract system?

Q. If it amounts to discrimination, yes, sir. A. Well, sir, it would make a very different kind of feeling from what now exists.

Q. Are not those the real complaints of the people of the State? A. I understand so.

Q. Do you know that the people of the State demand that the railroad charters be forfeited, and that the railroads go back to be the property of the people of the State? A. No, sir; I think not. Not with any equitable disposition on the part of the companies to do the service of the State.

Statement of Mr. Overheiser.

Senator Spencer—Where do you live? Answer—At Stockton.

Q. How long have you lived there? A. Since the Summer of forty-nine. I am a farmer, and a member of the State Grange.

Q. What position do you hold in that body? A. Unfortunately, I have been the State Lecturer.

Q. How long have you belonged to the State Grange? A. Since its organization in California, for ten years.

Q. I presume that from the position you occupy in the State

Grange, you are conversant with the general impressions, and of opinions that are entertained upon the question of freights and fares in this State? A. I have heard the expressions of many.

Q. Were these matters ever discussed in the Grange? A. Not to any great extent—somewhat; but you have got about all the information I could possibly give you through Mr. Webster. He has given it as near as I possibly can. I hardly think it necessary to go over that again.

Q. Have you any reluctance to testifying here? A. Not at all.

Q. Do you know anything of what is called the special contract system? A. I know something about it.

Q. Will you be kind enough to state without these formal interrogatories, what you know with reference to any discrimination practiced? A. I will state right here that I have never seen a contract, or examined one, but I am connected with a house that has a contract, and it is through the manager of the house, and its director, that my information comes. Our first contract was broken off by the railroad, because of failure to live up to it.

Q. Be kind enough to state what you mean by "failure to live up to it." A. The contract, as I always understood it and as I understand it to-day, is this: That a party making the contract with the railroad obligates itself to buy of no person except those who have a contract; that is, of no importer. They are forbidden to buy of any importer that sends goods round Cape Horn or by water. The contract that I speak of was broken off by the railroad for this reason: a firm in San Francisco got out of a certain article. Their goods around the Horn not arriving in time, they applied to this firm for goods and the goods were sold to them—goods which had been brought across the continent. They were shipped from the depot in Stockton and went down on the high water and were sold to this firm, and in a very short time after they were notified that their contract was void.

Q. The firm in Stockton had one of these special contracts? A. Yes, sir.

Q. The firm in San Francisco dealt in the same class of goods that the firm in Stockton was dealing in, and the firm in San Francisco, having refused to join in these special contracts, wrote up to the firm in Stockton for a lot of goods? A. Yes, sir.

Q. The firm in Stockton which had the special contract complied with the request, and sent them a carload of goods? A. Sold them a carload of goods.

Q. Have you any objection to stating the character of the goods? A. A carload of nails.

Q. About how much did the firm down there buy? A. Ten or twelve tons.

Q. And after they had shipped these goods to San Francisco, they received notice from the railroad company that their contract was forfeited? A. Yes, sir.

Q. Do you know whether that was put into effect, or whether it was a mere notice? A. It was put into effect, as I understood. The house changed managers, and the other manager went to San Francisco and renewed the contract.

Q. State whether the merchant in San Francisco, who had no contract, to whom you sold these subsequently, got a special contract? A. The merchant I have reference to at that time had no contract, but since that time he has been coerced (I call it) into the contract system.

Q. Coerced into it? A. Pretty near.

Q. Did you say coerced? A. That is the way I understood it. He refused to take a contract a long time.

Q. Did you use the word that I spoke of, or did I suggest it? A. I think I did; I felt as if it was coercion.

Q. So both of the firms have contracts now? A. Yes, sir.

Q. Do you know of any discrimination practiced by the railroad company in this State against places, or do you know of any instances of any threats being made or carried out by the railroad companies? A. I know of threats.

Q. Will you state the extent of your knowledge as to whether any discrimination is practiced in that county against places in times past by the railroad companies? A. As regards fares, I have some knowledge, if it includes that.

Q. State the discrimination in reference to fares, and illustrate it as near as you can? A. I have had favors as far as fares are concerned, but I learned, by traveling over the road from Stockton to San Francisco (for a dollar and a half by second-class fare), that parties can go from Lathrop to San Francisco for that money. Now a ticket to Suisun, which is nearly half way, is a dollar and a half. I don't know whether that is discrimination or not.

Q. You are on the same car? A. Yes, sir; on the same trip.

Q. The same conductor, and he has the same coat on? A. Yes, sir. In going from San Francisco to Stockton, a first class ticket is three dollars; in going from San Francisco some six years ago, I used to travel the road very frequently, the fare was four dollars, and from Stockton to San Francisco at that time, it was two dollars.

Q. I did not wish you to go back to that time? A. I only wished to cover the ground because there has been a change. To come down to the present time: a friend of mine lived in San Francisco, he bought a ticket to come and the price of a ticket was three dollars and thirty cents; he stopped over until Sunday at Stockton and then came up on his ticket. From San Francisco to Stockton is three dollars if you stop at Stockton, and a ticket from Stockton to Sacramento is one dollar and ninety cents. I wish to make a correction of one of Mr. Webster's declarations, because he was under a false impression. The fare now from Stockton to Sacramento is one dollar and ninety cents; from San Francisco to Sacramento is three dollars and thirty cents, by way of Stockton.

Q. And from San Francisco to Stockton on the same train, it is three dollars? A. Yes, sir.

Q. Then, if you want to go from Stockton to Sacramento, you pay one dollar and ninety cents more? A. Yes, sir.

Q. And you can buy a through or stop-over ticket from San Francisco to Sacramento for how much? A. Three dollars and thirty cents.

Q. Then if going the whole distance, by simply getting a stop-over ticket, you make how much? A. Figure it up.

Q. Is that the extent of your knowledge as to discrimination in fares? A. I don't know that I think of any other at the present time.

Q. State where the principal depot or station is with reference to Stockton? A. When this firm that I have reference to commenced business some six or eight years ago, Stockton was evidently left out in the cold, there was no place there. You could not ship freight from the East and land it there. We had to go to San Francisco for goods, or to Sacramento. Since that time—I don't know exactly the time—Stockton has been made a shipping point, and now we can stop our cars at Stockton.

Q. What is the principal station some six or eight miles from Stockton? A. Lathrop.

Q. How came that to be made there, do you know? A. Senator Baldwin is here and I would like to have him state it, but I will state it as near as I can. When the railroad was about getting their right of way to build their road they came to Stockton and they wanted to go through the center of the city. The Common Council objected. They could not make any arrangements with the railroad magnates and they left in disgust, and said, as I understood it, "that they would cause the grass to grow in the streets of Stockton before they got through with it." And, gentlemen, we have had a good tug at it, although there is not much grass there now.

Q. They didn't get the right of way and for that reason they put the depot down at Lathrop? A. They did not get the right of way through our city, but went outside there and then built the road, and then Stockton, for some reason or other, reached out and took them in and embraced them.

Q. At the time they built the road there, was there any special reason assigned for making Lathrop a station? A. The reason assigned was to make a pasture of the City of Stockton.

Q. Will you state how it is there now with reference to transportation by water. Can you give us the facts by giving us the history? A. If the Senators will indulge me. I came to Stockton a long time ago, before there was any town there and before the railroad was an incorporation, and we had a company there after that called the California Steam Navigation Company. They run from Stockton to San Francisco. After the railroad was built the railroad company bought out this California Steam Navigation Company and put on their own boats. A man by the name of P. C. Walker put on an opposition boat and run it for some little time and it was bought off by the railroad and he was employed by the railroad company in their shops. After some little time had expired he was out of employment and he took it into his head that he would put on another opposition boat, and he went around among the citizens of Stockton to get them to sign a contract that they would patronize his boat at a certain price which he said he could carry freight at, which was very much lower than they had ever paid before. They signed the contract and he put on his boat and commenced freighting, and the people were very anxious that he should carry passengers, and he afterwards changed his boat so as to accommodate passengers and carried passengers. During that time, to my certain knowledge, this corporation carried passengers for nothing to try to break that boat up, but the citizens of Stockton stayed right with their agreement, and the result was that in about three or four months the railroad drew off their boats and they have never been there to my knowledge since. The water is all that saved Stockton.

Q. If it had not been for the water communication to San Francisco, Stockton would have been in a bad fix, wouldn't it? A. There wouldn't have been any.

Q. What were the rates from San Francisco to Stockton before the railroad was built? A. I can hardly tell. First the fares were sixteen and twenty dollars, and then it ran down, and I have not kept the run of it.

Q. What were the rates for passengers from San Francisco before the railroad was built, or there was any railroad communication direct to San Francisco? A. I do not recollect exactly.

Q. What do you know, generally, with reference to discrimination against localities? A. If I understand the point, any place not a shipping point from the East have to pay extra to those points. For instance, if a merchant at Lodi wanted to ship a carload of wire from the East, they have got to ship it to Stockton or Sacramento. I believe there is no way station where they will switch off eastern freight cars till they get them there, and then they have to pay back freight back to Lodi.

Q. There is additional freight charged for pulling that back? A. The local freight is always charged.

Q. They charge the local freight, notwithstanding it is shipped past Lodi from a point East? A. They say there must be a general terminal point, and it goes to Stockton—the freight paid takes it there—and then they carry it back to Lodi. Several years ago they used to carry it to San Francisco, but since Stockton has got to be a terminal point, they bring it there.

Q. And then they charge the local freight. Do you know any other circumstances of discrimination against persons. What is your knowledge of such? A. I know of none excepting the contracts.

Q. Is that the subject of complaint among the citizens of Stockton that you are acquainted with? A. No, sir.

Q. Are you sufficiently acquainted with the commercial community of Stockton to know whether they have any reluctance in making complaint about this before any Court of justice, or in going before the Railroad Commissioners, or an investigating committee? A. All I know about it is the impressions I have drawn from what I have heard.

Q. To what effect? A. I would be very reluctant to come before this body and state what firm I belong to, or represent, for fear that the railroad might chastise me for it, or my firm.

Q. Is that opinion generally shared among the merchants? A. As I understand it, that is the general opinion.

Q. What do you mean by the word "chastise"? A. They might take our contracts away from us.

Q. They thus work forfeitures for a simple violation of their contracts, do they? A. I cannot say that they do, but we are afraid they will.

Q. Are you acquainted with the mercantile business houses in San Francisco? A. I think so, somewhat.

Q. Do you know some of the wholesale merchants down there? A. I know them, but personally I have no dealings with them. The house I am connected with has a manager.

Q. Have you examined the provisions of this Barry bill in relation to its rules of shipping? A. I looked over it to-day closely, for the first time.

Q. Do you see anything in this bill that would militate against the commercial interests of this State? A. I don't know that I do.

Q. I will ask you whether, if you were in the transportation business, and you would bring goods to the depot to-day, and another man should bring goods there to-morrow, and he was compelled to wait until you shipped your goods, you would consider that an inequitable rule? A. If I were to take an article to the depot to-day, and you took yours there to-morrow, and yours was shipped first, I should consider that I was badly treated.

Q. You believe that goods ought to be shipped in the order in which it is brought, so far as it can be conveniently done? A. I do.

Q. Do you believe that there should be any exception with respect to perishable articles? A. I do.

Q. Do you believe that the same general rule should be observed with regard to perishable articles. That they should be forwarded in the order in which they are received or tendered for shipment? A. I do.

Q. You think, then, that each man should have equal facilities for transporting his goods? A. I do.

Q. Do you think that live stock should have a preference over wheat in shipment? A. That depends upon circumstances.

Q. Do you not think that the same rule should apply to stock as to other goods. That the man who brings his stock first should have it shipped first? A. If I understand the shipping of stock, it is simply this: in order to secure a certain kind of a car, you must give your order ahead two or three days. It is but just to notify the railroad company that you want to ship a carload of stock.

Q. Isn't that the general rule among stock dealers? A. Yes, sir.

SENATOR WHITNEY—Ought not this bill to be prepared so that the railroad company should receive notice of intended shipments? A. So far as stock is concerned, I think it had.

Q. You think an amendment to that effect would be a good amendment? A. It occurs frequently that the railroad folks have not a large number of cars at a shipping point, and that it would be very unjust to them to require them to ship a carload of stock without notice.

Q. You do not believe that they should be required to forfeit their charter if they fail to do it? A. I think not. The people are reasonable, as a general thing.

Q. Do you think that the people of Stockton would be satisfied to give up the privilege of shipping by special contract and go back to the open rates? A. I think they would.

Q. You think that they do not consider this any privilege that they have of being made a shipping point? A. By being made a shipping point—don't misunderstand me—we want to be a shipping point. We would not be willing to give up being a shipping point, but we are willing to concede that to every depot on the road.

Q. Are you willing that Lodi should be made a shipping point as well as Stockton? A. We are willing that all should be.

Q. There is nothing there now that compels the people to take these special contracts. They can take the open rates if they prefer them? A. Yes, sir; but I never heard of a merchant that was compelled to take that special contract that did it freely.

Q. What is the objection? A. The objection is that the railroad company requires them to do certain things. They prohibit them from trading with certain men on this coast that bring their goods around Cape Horn, and they claim the right by the contract to go into the office and examine the books to know that you are living up to your contract.

Q. Nevertheless, they make the special contract? A. They are obliged to take the special contract to protect themselves.

Q. Because it is an advantage to them to do so? A. Well, if A takes a contract and B don't, B has got no chance at all.

Q. So that the special contract is really an advantage? A. No, sir. It shows compulsion, no advantage about it.

Q. It is an advantage to A, but a disadvantage to B? A. I will illustrate by a man in the City of Stockton, who has been here many a time. He is a harness maker, and he told me here at the convention that he could not go to San Francisco and buy from a firm there that did not ship by railroad; that he was prohibited from doing that.

Q Do you know the reason why the railroad company makes these special contracts? A. The reason is to control freights.

Q. Why? A. To get business.

Q. In other words, they can make more money out of it? A. As a matter of course.

Q. Do they make more money out of it? A. They can prohibit the produce from going by water and bring it across the continent.

Q. In that way they handle a larger amount of freight, do they not? A. There is no question about that, if they can prohibit the shipping of it.

Q. And if they handle a larger amount of freight they can afford to do it at less rates, looking at it from a railroad standpoint? A. We are like a man driving swine, we do not like to be coerced, if we do we turn right square round.

Q. I am looking at it from both sides. A. So am I; I am a railroad man in one sense of the word. We couldn't get along without them.

Q. You recognize the fact that the more they ship the cheaper they can afford to carry it? A. I recognize the fact that they are in competition with vessels that carry goods around Cape Horn, although they cannot ship them across the continent as cheap. If we can ship goods cheaper around Cape Horn, then let them go around there, and if it is cheaper across the continent then let them go that way. Give them the privilege of doing as they please about it.

Q. They can do that now? A. No, sir; I understand that they can't. If A has a contract and B has none, A can undersell B, because he can get his goods quicker across the continent, and in this case, it seems to me that the party in San Francisco is an illustration. One of the largest houses in San Francisco got out of a certain line of goods—out of nails. The ship was coming, but did not get in in time, or as soon as expected; the same case I referred to. Another party that had a contract was out of goods; he went to another house and ordered a full carload of goods—ten tons, or whatever it may be. The goods were shipped to him and hauled to the landing in San Francisco. Now, the railroad company sought to prohibit that, and make that man go without his goods till he could get his goods around Cape Horn. Do you see the point?

Q. Is it not a fact, that as far as the railroad is concerned, they could give you a smaller rate if you gave them the shipment of all your goods? A. Will the Senator allow me to answer the question by asking one?

Q. Answer the question in your own way. A. The question was asked to Mr. Webster, who was just here, whether the man who shipped the largest amounts ought not to have the best rates? Now, I will take a man and put him on a farm of one hundred and sixty acres of land, and he raises a carload of wheat there. I will take another man there that raises on five thousand acres of land as much more in proportion. Now, according to the argument of the gentleman, the man that raises on the five thousand acres should have his wheat carried to market cheaper than the man that raises wheat on the one hundred and sixty acres. I want to know if you think that is correct?

SENATOR WHITNEY—I do. A. You do?

SENATOR WHITNEY—Yes, sir. A. Well, I call that discrimination, and making the rich richer and the poor poorer.

Q. That seems to me the common rule of business. A. Here is ten thousand acres held by one man, and he is a farmer. If the same land were cut up into farms of one hundred and sixty acres the wheat would go over the road at the same rate, and the company would haul just as much wheat, wouldn't it?

Q. Yes, sir. A. Then every man would have his freight alike, wouldn't he?

Q. If I am to answer your question, I will say that they do not make any such distinction as that. In fact, I understand that they haul at just the same rate that they do for five thousand. A. I understand they do. A friend of mine in Merced County told me that it cost him to ship a carload of seed wheat from San Francisco to Merced three times as much as it did to ship it from Merced to San Francisco. Now, what do you call that?

Q. Isn't that one of the abuses that the Railroad Commissioners have lately corrected? A. I hardly know what the Commission has done.

Q. Do you understand that that has been corrected? A. No; I do not understand it.

Q. Is it not your idea that a merchant should live up to a special contract, if he makes it? A. Not if he is compelled to make it.

SENATOR SULLIVAN—When did this occur that you spoke of, of sending the seed wheat from Merced to San Francisco? A. Within eighteen months.

SENATOR CROSS—The ingoing freight was higher than the outgoing freight? A. Yes, sir.

SENATOR WHITNEY—That is no longer a cause of complaint? A. I am sure I do not know. I do not know what has been done lately. These complaints I have heard in traveling over the country.

SENATOR CROSS—Do these special contracts relate to freights within the State or to freights across the State line? A. I think to freights from the East.

Q. It relates only to inter-State commerce? A. Yes, sir.

Q. Do you know of any special contracts with relation to carrying freights wholly within the State? A. No, sir.

STATEMENT OF N. D. RIDEOUT.

SENATOR CROSS—You are interested in a railroad near Marysville? Answer—Yes, sir.

Q. Running where? A. From Marysville to Oroville.

Q. How long is that road? A. Twenty-six and a half miles. I suppose the idea is to have testimony in regard to this Barry bill, in case it becomes a law, and the effect it will have upon transportation, upon freight, and what effect it will have upon shippers, the benefits that will result to the people, and vice versa. First, as to section one: "All persons and companies engaged in operating any such road, or in transporting freight or passengers over the same, or which shall hereafter operate or engage as aforesaid, shall forward, move, and carry impartially for all persons offering freight to be transported or moved, without discrimination, preference, or favor, to one over another." I suppose there is no question but what that means that the railroad company is to charge the same price per ton for all kinds of freight; I believe that is the construction put on the bill. I simply wish to state that it is impossible to run a railroad and charge the same rate per ton for all kinds of freight. It is against the interest of the people, and against the interest of the shippers that ship freight, and also against the interest of those who have freight to be transported. I will, in a few words, give my reasons why I think it is against the interest of shippers to pay the same rate per ton. For instance, on this little

Oroville road we carried, during the last year—and we are developing quite a trade in lumber, and also in wood—we carry a large amount of wood, and carry it very cheap. We carry wood from Oroville to Marysville for six dollars a car, and we get about seven dollars for lumber. The merchandise and up freight pays—two cars at about twenty-five dollars and one at fifteen. For a car of merchandise we receive about twenty-five dollars a car, and for bran and millstuffs fifteen, so that the two cars up freight are about fifteen dollars. That is the daily average, and we take down each day a car of grain at ten dollars a car, and a car of lumber at seven dollars, and wood at six dollars; making an average (figuring up) of one dollar and forty cents per ton for freight carried over the road. Now, it would not pay to operate the road at less than one dollar and thirty cents or one dollar and forty cents per ton, but on that average up and down we make a very fair profit. If we were compelled to charge the same for up as for down freight, we would have to charge upon lumber, instead of seven, fourteen; for wood, instead of six, fourteen; and on our up freight the same. So that you can very readily see how it would affect us. It would be a prohibition as far as lumber is concerned, and also wood; therefore we would carry no lumber and no wood. If we had two carloads of wood at twenty-five dollars a car, and one at fifteen, it would make an average of three cars at forty dollars, and we would have to raise that to a larger amount to enable us to run the road. Now, during the last year there has been a V flume built forty miles up on the ridge between the North Fork of the Yuba and the South Fork of Feather Rivers, and it is bringing lumber to our road, and wood, and it is the expectation that they will carry this through. They have spent one million two hundred and fifty thousand dollars in getting it in, and have built a large number of sheds for the wood business. There has been a great amount of wood cut, and a great many men engaged in cutting this wood. Now, those wood men would be discharged, and the men would go to some other place; and we think that would be detrimental to our part of the State and retard its enterprises. Our lumber business is increasing quite largely, and there is now a mill being put up on the Peavine Ridge, and they are hauling wood in wagons to Oroville. We are going to carry that freight at about seven dollars a car, and if we are compelled to charge fourteen, of course, the mill will shut down and go off somewhere else, and the people go away; which is again a great hardship to the people of that section. It is a detriment to the shippers, and they don't require it and don't demand it. If it is put in force it will be necessary to charge more for up merchandise, and that will be particularly hard on the merchants of Oroville. If we have to charge them forty dollars instead of twenty or twenty-five, of course, they would go to some other town to trade—to Chico, or some other town where they could get it cheaper. We say that this section of that bill should be amended; that after the words, "one over another," there should be inserted, "offered of the same kind or class," so that the railroad would charge the same price for the same kinds of freight. That, of course, would prevent any discrimination as against persons. I do not think that any railroad should discriminate against persons, and as far as our railroad is concerned, they are punished if they do.

SENATOR DEL VALLE—Suppose that the meaning of that section is just as you want it construed—a portion of the section at least—that one person should not be charged more than another as to difference of the price of goods, and that goods of the same character should not be charged differently to different persons; would that be satisfactory to you? A. Yes, sir; but if that is meant it is better to say so.

Q. Suppose that you illustrate the sentence as you desire, would that be satisfactory to you? A. No, sir.

Q. From that you would imply that it should only mean that there should not be any discrimination against persons? A. Against persons.

Q. How does that discrimination exist now, as you understand it; is it the special contract system? A. Discrimination against persons? I don't know of any.

Q. Do you construe the special contract of the Central Pacific Railroad to be discrimination? A. I have never seen any special contracts.

Q. Do you know of the existence of such? A. Only from what I have heard; I have heard that there are some; that is all I know.

Q. You are not informed of the facts? A. I have only heard generally that there is such, and that every man can sign them if he wants to. I never saw one of them.

Q. Does that railroad belong to a corporation, or to you alone? A. It belongs to another man and myself.

Q. It is a company? A. Yes, sir.

Q. Have you read the remainder of that section? A. Yes, sir.

Q. What is your statement in reference to that portion of the bill which requires the company to carry freight in a certain manner? A. It says "all freight shall be dispatched and forwarded in the order in which it is received or tendered for transportation." That would prevent the railroad company from doing any business.

Q. Explain that? A. I think they would do some business, but it would not be a satisfactory business. It is not what the people want. Of course the clause as it is, without amendment, would be construed that any man that had any amount of freight (for instance, wood or lumber), and notified the agent that he wanted the freight shipped, would prevent all other kind of freight except perishable articles from being shipped till this wood was all taken away? Now I will take a simple instance in regard to our road: These men are hauling lumber there to the depot and piling it up; now a man comes to us and says, "I have got two hundred thousand feet of lumber piled up here beside your track; I have an order from San Francisco, and I want to ship it; order the cars and ship it as soon as possible." If there is two hundred thousand feet it will take thirty cars to carry it. The agent says to the man, "Very well, I will get the cars here as soon as possible." The probability is that, without taking any other freight on our road, we could carry that in five or six days—as soon as we got the thirty cars. In the meantime if a man should come in with cattle from Big Meadows, or Oregon, as they do every little while, and take perhaps four or five cars, and say, "We want to send these cattle to San Francisco as soon as possible; we want to deliver them there at a certain time, and we want to ship them; it will only take four or five cars." The agent says, "Very well, as soon as this lumber is off I will take your cattle, but I can't do it before." The consequence is that the man has to keep his cattle there until the lumber is all taken away.

Q. Do you not think that live stock ought to be made one of the exceptions to the bill as to the transportation? A. Well, I think that there ought to be the same amendment put right in there that they ought to be of the same class or kind. When I have got twenty men, all having lumber, the first coming with his lumber ought to have it shipped first, but not over any other kind of freight.

Q. Suppose that I came with a lot of wheat and you came with a lot of drygoods, do you think that a preference ought to be exercised there? A. I think there should be a preference exercised.

Q. Why so? A. Because I think if a person has a carload of drygoods that he wants shipped to San Francisco or Marysville that he should not wait until a hundred cars of wheat were shipped, or wait three or four days, or a week. I think the railroad ought to be allowed to discriminate. They could take some of the wheat and take the drygoods, and not block up their road with one class of freight to the exclusion of all other.

Q. Supposing that it was of the same character as barley? A. That is about the same thing, of course.

Q. Suppose that you bring a carload of wheat and I bring a carload of barley to the railroad, and that I bring mine first, and they say, "All right, I will take your carload," and day after to-morrow the car comes and they take yours in preference to mine. Under your statement that should not be prohibited. Do you think that discrimination should be permitted? A. You mean as between barley and wheat?

Q. Yes, sir? A. Well, they are about the same. I don't know, if you allow the company to classify freight, as I think you must, whether there should be anything to compel them to put it in the same class.

Q. They don't do it now? A. I think it is about the same. The freight is about the same on wheat that it is on barley—I mean on the Central Pacific.

SENATOR CROSS—Is barley of the same weight, or about the same, as wheat? A. Yes, sir.

Q. Weighs about fifty or sixty pounds? A. Barley is a little the lightest. I think that they charge about the same on barley that they do on wheat.

Q. Suppose that a man brings a carload of wheat to Fresno, to be shipped to San Francisco, and another comes with a carload of wine, and the one with the wine comes first, but the wheat is shipped first. Do you think that ought to be permitted? A. If there was only one carload, the man that came first should have the right to ship first.

Q. Suppose that there were ten carloads of wine, and five carloads of wheat, does that make any difference? A. Well, for that matter, any company could take it all.

Q. Supposing they can't? A. Well, I think they ought to be allowed to take the most valuable freight first.

Q. You think that discrimination should exist? A. I do; I think that the railroad company ought to be allowed to discriminate so as to accommodate their customers.

Q. Do you think that they should be permitted to discriminate in their freights where the goods are not of the same class? A. Yes, sir; but in goods of the same class there should not be any discrimination.

Q. How many classes have they? A. I do not know. We do not have many on our road.

Q. On those goods as classified they are obliged to charge a different rate for every different class? A. I think they do charge every class a little different; I am not thoroughly posted on that. This road of mine does a limited business.

Q. There is another portion of this section with regard to preference of one over another. A. I am not talking about price, I am talking about dispatch. Supposing you come to the agent of this station, and say, "I have ten thousand tons of wheat here that I want taken away. I have men here ready to load it." Under the provisions of this bill we could take no other business till that is all taken away. Now, you know very well that that would take up the business of the road, and that if a man should come in with a lot of country produce, sheep, hogs, furniture, or anything of the kind, the company could not take it till that ten thousand tons of wheat were taken away; and I say that is not right. I say it is injustice, and that the company ought to be allowed to discriminate in such cases. Of course I concede that often in discriminating, as to classes, you make trouble, but I think it is the best we can do. Under this bill, if a man has ten thousand tons of wheat he might control the road for a week or a month as against the small shipper. Some farmer might come in and want to ship a hundred or two hundred tons down to San Francisco, and providing we could ship it in time he could sell it to advantage; and if the other could monopolize the shipment for a month he controls the wheat market, and the man with a small lot has got to sell to the man who can keep it on hand a month. I say that is very disastrous to the small shippers. I think this bill discriminates between them in favor of the large shippers, and against the small ones; but I do not see how you can change this bill in any way, except to allow discrimination as to classes, and not allow it as to one class. If you allow a man a preference as to class he will then get the advantage of the small shipper. Suppose that we have lumber to ship from Honcut and Oroville, we say to the man at Honcut, "We will give you six cars to-day, and we will take the others on to Oroville."

Q. What amendment would you suggest there? A. The only amendment that you could put in would be an amendment as to freight of the same class or kind: "All freight of the same class or kind shall be shipped in the order in which it is received or tendered for transportation." Of course that would allow the man with the ten thousand tons of wheat to get in ahead of the man with a small number of tons, but still it would allow the man to get in with his furniture, and his sheep or cattle.

Q. You would not have a great number of classes for your road? A. No, sir.

Q. Do you know the classification of the Central Pacific Railroad, or the Southern Pacific Railroad? A. No, sir; we have it in our office; we have a schedule, but I do not remember what it is.

Q. It is quite a volume? A. Yes, sir; quite a volume.

Q. Of different classes? A. Yes, sir.

SENATOR SULLIVAN—I understand then, that you are perfectly satisfied with the bill, especially with section one, if it were changed as you suggested in regard to class and kind? A. Yes, sir; I do not think it would hurt our road.

Q. Have you, on your road, what is known as the special contract system? A. No, sir.

Q. Whereby you discriminate between persons and persons? A. No, sir.

Q. I believe your road is called the California Northern? A. Yes, sir.

Q. What is the length of it? A. Twenty-six and a half miles.

Q. Does it connect with the Central Pacific? A. Yes, sir; at Marysville; and also with the water communication there. We get lots of freight from the Central Pacific.

Q. If the words "of the same class or kind" were inserted in there, would it not do away with the very object for which this bill was passed? A. I think not.

Q. In other words, would it not allow the very same discrimination that has been practiced by the railroad companies? A. I should say not. I don't see how you can.

Q. Assuming that there are two kinds of wheat or of barley, and that one brings in the market fifty per cent more than the other, you would have them in two classes. Wouldn't that allow the common carrier to discriminate between the two classes, so as to charge the producer more? A. Of course I take it that "class or kind" there, would mean wheat, and that wheat would be but one class.

Q. Your idea would be to put wheat in one class and barley in another? A. Yes, sir.

Q. Upon your own road have you discriminated, and charged according to what the commodity would bring in the market? A. No, sir.

Q. It is shown in the Railroad Commissioners' report, and has been stated here, that the railroad companies make a distinction in regard to charges on ore according to the value of it in the market. I will ask whether, if such a change is made in that bill, they would be allowed to make that distinction between ores—say in Class A and those in Class B—and to charge more for ores that will bring fifty dollars in the market than for those that will bring ten dollars? A. Perhaps they had. I heard Mr. Yerrington's testimony in regard to that, and according to his ideas, if they are correct statements, I think he should charge more for ore worth forty than for ore worth ten dollars; otherwise they could not carry ore worth but ten.

Q. In your experience, have you ever known a railroad to transport merchandise or ore that did not pay anything. A. I never have on our route. I don't know anything about others.

Q. Do you not actually refuse freight that will not pay you to ship? A. I will answer that by saying, that this wood that we are carrying at six dollars a car, pays us to ship at cost on our road. If the cars were not going up with merchandise they could not carry wood. In other words, if we had to take that and nothing else, we would refuse to take it.

Q. You are of the opinion that the charges of common carriers are arranged according to what the goods or merchandise will bring in the market? A. Not altogether; that depends upon circumstances.

Q. Take the cost of chairs, for instance. The chair upon which you are sitting will cost about two dollars, or two and a half. Take walnut chairs of the same kind; they would bring two dollars and seventy-five cents in the market; they take up the same amount of space in the car; they are not any more trouble, nevertheless, the rate upon the walnut chair is more, because it brings twenty-five cents more in the market. Do you think that is right? A. No; I think they should be charged alike, unless there is some difference in the insurance.

Q. Have you ever known, in your experience, of the Central Pacific Railroad making such distinctions? A. No, sir.

Q. You would be surprised, would you not, to learn that such discrimination was practiced? A. No, I don't know as I would, if it was shown; that discrimination that you speak of is a small one.

Q. In examining you I only desire to show how far this classification could be carried out; then I ask you if that would not defeat the very purposes of this Barry bill? A. My opinion is this: That it would be better to have them discriminate than to block up the whole commerce and trade by leaving it as it is. You can't get everything equal; you can't prevent men from carrying goods from the East and discriminating in any particular amount, but in the meanwhile, the whole State is being blocked up, and the railroad companies are prevented from carrying on the business of the State; I don't think it is right in principle to discriminate, but it may have to be done.

Q. In your intercourse with the people of the section through which your railroad runs, of course you have occasion to make contracts, and to arrange about transportation and freights? A. Yes, sir; in a small way.

Q. Have you ever said to them that this thing ought to be divided equally between the carrier and the producer; that is, that they ought to go in as partners in the sale of merchandise, or wheat, or whatever it may be? A. No, sir.

Q. You do not know that such a thing has been done upon your road? A. No, sir; I don't think it has.

Q. Then, with these amendments that you spoke of, you think

that the bill is a good bill? A. I am only speaking about the one clause. I think, if that amendment was put in there, allowing them to charge different prices for different amounts of freight, and allow them to discriminate and reduce one class and take another, it would be satisfactory to our road. We would have some trouble, as I said before, about taking heavy lots of lumber, but that would be better than excluding all other kinds of freight. I don't see but that is the best amendment that you could put in there.

Q. You are aware that this goes further than making discriminations, and that it strikes at the question of freight? A. Yes, sir.

Q. It says that it "Shall forward, move, and carry, impartially, for all persons offering freight to be transported or moved, without discrimination or favor to one over another." Don't you think the amendments you propose would be a discrimination between person and person? A. No, sir; I think under that I would be compelled to charge the same price for all kinds of freight.

Q. If that section does not mean what you think it does would you be satisfied with it? A. If it does not mean that, and there is any question about it, why not state it so as to make it plain?

Q. Assuming that the words "Class or kind" would allow discrimination again, then would you not be sorry that the bill was so amended? A. Well, you can't make the thing any worse than it is now, and you might make it better. You desire to punish people for making discrimination against persons; it ought to be to punish them for discrimination against crime.

Senator Taylor—"Without favor to one over another, in price, dispatch, speed, or accommodation of any kind." As the bill reads do you think that it would prevent discrimination by the railroad company by reason of distance? A. I was taking that in connection with section two. You will notice line seven. Take that in connection with section one and you would have to charge the same rate per car for all distances.

Q. I understand you to say that you have two stations upon your road—one called Honcut and the other Oroville? A. Yes, sir.

Q. And that your general rate is seven dollars a car for lumber? A. We are carrying some lumber for that.

Q. If you charge the shipper seven dollars a car for lumber at Honcut, and it is only half the distance that it is to Oroville, in order to comply with this bill, and not discriminate in price, would you not be compelled to charge fourteen dollars from Oroville per car? A. That is the way I look at the bill.

Q. Is that the way you do now? A. No; we charge six dollars to Honcut and seven to Oroville. That is about our rates.

Q. If the rates were uniform between the two places, per mile, per ton, you would have to charge twice as much from Oroville as from Honcut? A. Certainly; that is a matter of figures.

Q. The shipper at Red Bluff would have to pay, if there was no discrimination in price, per mile, per ton, much more for his freight than the man would who lived in San Joaquin Valley? A. There is not much difference in distance in the two places.

Q. The distance from Red Bluff is nearly three hundred miles?
A. About two hundred and twenty-five miles.

Q. Then, under this bill, at the same rate, per ton, per mile, whatever the distance might be? A. That is the way it seems to me. I may not be right in regard to that, but I should say that, taking the bill altogether, without amendment, it would be that you would have to charge the same rate, per mile, per ton. Of course, then your men in the valley would have to pay a pretty high price for wheat, per ton.

Q. Do you have any idea that that would prevent the raising of grain in some places? A. If they were too far off it would.

Q. How is it in regard to that at the present time? A. The farther they get away the less rate they pay per mile per ton. It would not bear shipment if they paid the same rate. In other words—at the end of the road they would not get as much per ton for it as they do now.

Q. How would it be with regard to cattle? A. I could not say positively in regard to that. The principal places where cattle are shipped in Sacramento Valley is in Cottonwood and at Chico; some from Marysville.

Q. Is it not a fact that during the time when the harvest is ripe and wheat is being shipped cattle are procured in California for the San Francisco market? A. To a limited extent. Most all of the cattle come from the outside.

Q. Is it not a fact that nearly all the cattle come from Oregon and Nevada and other places without the State of California in the Winter, and when there is no wheat being shipped? A. Yes, sir, I think there are more cattle shipped then than during the Summer.

Q. Then, under this bill, if the company were required to transport freight in the order in which it is received, would there be any great hardship or inconvenience raised if they were compelled to take the cars which they were using for one purpose and use them for the other? A. I have already stated that.

Q. And you have stated that, in your opinion, it would completely bar out the smaller shippers by the large ones? A. Yes, sir; it looks so to me.

SENATOR KELLOGG—What, in your opinion, is the effect of a sliding scale of prices? If a mandatory rule was established upon long hauls, what would be the effect upon the industries of the interior of the State—would it be beneficial or otherwise? A. It would be otherwise. I think the rates, as now established, discriminating, and charging less rate per mile for long distances, better for the State than to make that rule.

Q. Would it not almost cripple the interior—say three or four hundred miles from the seaboard—to undertake to establish a positive rate per ton per mile upon wheat and farm products? A. I think so. I think that Senator Taylor's constituency up in the mountain valleys would have to go into another business.

SENATOR VROOMAN—There is an exception made here as to perishable articles and fast freight. Isn't it a fact, that cattle are generally shipped as fast freight? A. Not in my experience. The cattle trains go down the road along past Marysville on the same trains as wheat.

7ᵇ

Q. That is in small lots, but where there is a large quantity there is a lot of special cars, is there not? A. I don't know. I never knew any cattle in Sacramento Valley to be shipped on any other trains than the freight trains; it may be different in other parts of the State.

Q. Has your experience been with many carloads, or only with a few? A. Sometimes ten to fifteen. I have seen as many as twenty-five or thirty going along the road; and sometimes a lot of special freight trains going and coming on the same time as the other freight trains. As I understand the time table the freight trains are all limited to so many miles per hour.

Q. Don't you consider them as belonging to that class of freight? A. I never considered it so; I never heard it mentioned.

Q. What is fast freight? A. Sometimes they put a freight car on the passenger train going to Ogden or Omaha. I have seen them going by here. That is fast freight.

Q. All freight would not come under that head? A. I should say not. I don't know of any fast freight trains that have been run in this State as freight trains. I think they all run on the same time, and that any fast freight that has been carried has been attached to a passenger train. That is my opinion; the same as any fast matter.

Q. They speak in ordinary phraseology of fast and slow freight. Does it mean, in the ordinary acceptation of the term, the cars attached to a passenger train? A. I don't know about that. I think in the East they have a fast train at a different rate of speed. It may be so; I don't know.

SENATOR CROSS—How would the law work if a large amount of down freight were tendered before any up freight, or a large amount of up freight before any down freight, and you were compelled to take all of the down freight before any of the up freight was transported, or vice versa? A. Of course that wouldn't work. Are you alluding to this bill now?

Q. I think I am. Supposing that a thousand carloads of wheat were tendered to you on Monday, and that on Tuesday, Wednesday, and Thursday other freights were tendered from San Francisco, Oakland, and other points; what would be the effect if all that down freight had to be hauled before any up freight subsequently tendered could be hauled? A. Of course that would have a bad effect.

Q. Would it tend to increase the price which would have to be charged for freight in order to enable the transportation company to realize a profit? A. I don't see how that would cut much figure; it would injure the shippers more than the railroad company.

Q. How would it injure the shippers? A. If the freight came from San Francisco it certainly would; we would have to haul the cars up without it that had been previously sent down.

Q. How would a law work which provided that if a thousand tons of freight were tendered at Red Bluff at nine o'clock, and five tons at Marysville at eleven o'clock, you would be required that the whole of the thousand tons tendered at Red Bluff should be carried before any of this at Marysville? A. If that was the law I would think it was bad. It would be simply an inconvenience to the man at Marysville.

Q. What effect would it have upon the intermediate points? A. It seems to me that the question answers itself. I don't see any need of answering a question like that.

Q. You think that the law which made a provision like that would be upon its face absurd? A. I certainly think so; 1 don't see that this bill does that.

Q. What it says is a question of law. I ask you if that is so, what would be the effect? A. It would be very bad, of course; anybody can answer that.

Q. If a rate were adopted, and it was uniform as to all kinds of freight, would there be any kinds of freight which you now carry which you would not then be able to carry? A. Yes, sir.

Q. Would it increase or diminish the prices which would have to be charged for all classes of freight? A. It would be an inconvenience, of course.

Q. Supposing that a uniform rate were required upon all kinds or classes of freight, including furniture, would that increase or diminish the rates which would have to be charged for transportation of crops from the country to the seaboard? A. It would increase the down freight; bound to. Of course, the wheat in the Sacramento Valley is taken to San Francisco at a very reasonable rate; from Marysville, two dollars and forty cents; from the other side, two dollars and fifty cents.

Q. Some questions were asked you concerning special contracts. Have you ever read, or have you any knowledge, of any special contract which related to other than inter-State commerce? A. No, sir.

SENATOR VROOMAN—"All persons and companies shall, at all times, keep posted in a conspicuous place, etc., a printed table or schedule of all rates of freight and charges in force for transportation between all points and stations to or from which they carry," etc. What is your idea in regard to that provision? A. I should say, that 1 do not think it necessary to keep at every station a schedule of the rates of freight between all the different stations in the State. In other words, I do not think that they ought to be compelled at Honcut and Oroville and Marysville, to keep the rate of freight between Los Angeles and other different points. 1 don't see any need of it; it would be of no benefit to the shipper. I should say that there ought to be an amendment put in there; something to this effect, "To the particular stations to which they carry;" that ought to be put in there: "At the office or station."

SENATOR SULLIVAN—Do I understand you to say that you think they should only have a schedule at the point or station where the goods are shipped to? A. From that station to all other points to which they ship them.

Q. Then you would amend it in that respect? A. I would say that at the stations from which freight is to be shipped, they should keep a schedule of the rate from that station to all the stations for freight upon the road. "Such rates shall be equally available," etc. I don't know about that. I don't know whether that would compel us to charge the same rates per mile or not. The amendment in section first would perhaps cover that. You might amend it if you kept the first section. "Different rates may be charged for fast freight," etc.; I think that is all right.

Q. What do you understand by the word "rebates," on line ten? A. That is to charge a man a certain price and then pay him some back afterwards. We do not do that.

Q. You have an open rate for all? A. Yes, sir. I understand that "rebate" is this: A man often goes to the railroad company with some proposition for us. We say: "We will ship your goods provided you ship a thousand tons; go on and ship and we will make you the regular charge. If you ship the full amount, we will pay you something back."

Q. There is no such customer upon your road? A. No, sir.

SENATOR KELLOGG—Are you well enough acquainted with the system of rebates to explain to this committee just what it is as practiced on the eastern and western roads and the roads in California, so far as freights and fares are concerned? A. I don't know that I am.

SENATOR CROSS—Suppose that in shipping freight there should be an overcharge made, and that it was afterwards discovered, and the money be paid back, would that be a "rebate?" A. No, I think that would be an error, or overcharge.

Q. Wouldn't that be "rebate?" A. No; I think not. You are a lawyer; you can tell better than I can.

Q. I didn't know but the word might have a technical meaning in the railroad business. A. Sometimes; for instance, a theater company comes along and says: "We have got twenty-five. We can't afford to pay you the regular rate." I say, "All right; if there is twenty-five, we will take them at a certain price. If there is less than twenty-five, you can pay the regular rate."

Q. How would it be in regard to commutation tickets. I suppose that would not apply to that class of freights? A. I suppose not. It might be in a technical sense. Well, that is section two. There you provide for some discrimination, and I don't see why you should object to it in section one. I think it should be the same all the way through. I think the company should be allowed to discriminate some, and that they should be allowed to discriminate some under section one. Now, we will go on to section three (reading it). I wish to say, in regard to that section, that I cannot see what benefit it could be to the shipper, or to the people, or to the seller, if the railroad company are responsible. If their road got out of repair in any way, and they had a difficulty in consequence of their carelessness, they are responsible for it. I can see, on the other hand, where it might be very annoying, especially on this road of mine. Three years ago, we had our road under water for four miles, and there was some trestlework washed away, and we had it replaced again. We might not have done it as it was before, but that would give the power to any man that did not like us, whom we had refused to carry over the road for nothing, to say, "Why, this structure is not built as it was before; it is not safe." He might not be able to maintain a complaint, but he could put us to a great deal of trouble. It might not be as good, but that would be very annoying. We have now our track running to Oroville, and a depot at D Street, in Marysville. The depot used to be there. We have an old depot there. It is more convenient for passengers, coming by rail, for us to go to the city for them, so we have a depot in another part of the city, and take the passengers there. This old depot is now out of repair, and to be compelled to repair it, beyond what is necessary for keeping our engines over there, would be needless; but I think that under the construction of this statute, we would have to keep that in good repair. We intended to take up the track, and run it in another way, so as to connect with the Central Pacific at A Street. We have a track running there for a mile, which ought to be taken up, but we can't take it up if that section becomes law. It would make us trouble. The people do not demand it. It don't pay the company, and we should not be compelled to keep it there. Now, at the Honcut, we have put in some side tracks, running out to different places to take a little freight, or wood, or lumber. We might want to change them, and, as I understand that section three, it prevents it.

Q. What amendment would you suggest? A. I would suggest leaving it out entirely.

Q. You would not put it in at all? A. No; I don't see any need of it, or what good it does.

SENATOR SPENCER—Suppose there were an amendment put in there to meet that objection, to the effect that it should not apply to side tracks or temporary structures? A. If you can put any amendment in there that will not compel the railroad company to keep the track in good repair when there is no necessity for it, it ought to be done, but I have not heard any complaint of any company in this State not keeping their track in repair or not keeping it safe. The very first thing I did when I found the road in bad condition three years ago was to spend a large amount of money to make it safe. There is no railroad company that would keep a road in bad repair. Self-interest would compel them to keep it up and in good repair. It will only make an annoyance and cause trouble.

Q. You have heard of the wharf at Santa Monica? A. I have heard it mentioned. I have never been there.

Q. Suppose a case of that kind, where a fine structure is allowed to go to decay through the collusion of the railroad company. Don't you think there ought to be some law that would prevent a wharf being ruined and merchants being thereby injured and trade depressed? A. Are they operating a road there and running freight?

Q. The company is operating a road from Los Angeles to Santa Monica. A. Mr. Stubbs knows more about that than I do. Do they use this wharf for transporting freight?

SENATOR DEL VALLE—They don't transport freight at all. A. If the railroad company are running freight to any particular wharf they ought to keep it safe, and especially as there is a danger to life, for which they are liable.

Q. Do you think that they should have the right to allow a structure, such as a wharf, to go to decay, and do a wrong to the citizens of a place, simply because they desired all the freight to go by rail?

Would you not put such a provision into the law of our State as would stop such things from being done? A. If I could do so without doing more injury in some other way. You must take these things all together. If you could not put this section three in as it is without doing greater injustice to others, I say let the wharf stay as it is.

Q. I am asking you if that might not be amended so as to meet this objection? A. It might be.

Q. Suppose that there was a provision put in there that it should not refer to side tracks, or temporary structures, or anything that occurred from the act of God? A. A fire is not the act of God sometimes, and you could not replace it again as it was.

Q. Well, we will say any certain contingency? A. If you can arrange it so as to avoid this difficulty it should be done, but I am of the opinion that, as the section stands now, it ought to be taken out.

Q. Suppose that a railroad company had a cause of complaint against a community, and would remove their tracks in order to injure the people of the town. Don't you think there ought to be something in the law of the land to prevent them from doing so? A. I think so, if there is business enough in the town to pay them for running a railroad there, and if it don't pay them they ought to be allowed to take it up.

Q. I am not alluding to that at all; I am alluding to their trying to injure the people of a town? A. I don't think they should do that.

Q. Don't you think there ought to be something to prevent it being done? A. Yes, sir; and I think you could do that without putting that section in. You can pass a law to prevent them from doing that. I don't think the railroad company ought to be allowed to discriminate against persons.

Senator Kellogg—Would you have any objection to section three with the last paragraph left out, say all after the word "adopted," on line four, if it is the intention of the companies to keep their roads in good repair? A. They must do so, or they can't operate them. I think that would be safe enough. Perhaps it would not be just the thing for my road, but it might be for other roads. Mine cost a great deal of money to build. It was built in an early day, and if I was compelled to put it as it was originally, I could not do it.

Q. This does not refer to that section. You must keep it all right to the freighting points? A. I suppose that would be safe enough.

Q. The last clause is what you make objection to? A. Yes, sir; I see no necessity for it.

Q. Now, as to section four? A. I don't know as I have anything to say about that. That does not interest me. I suppose that any road that has a charter in the United States can come in any way. I have nothing to say about that. It may retard the building of roads, and might retard the development of the State, and injure the people.

SENATOR SULLIVAN—You have not studied that proposition at all? A. I have been studying only these propositions that affect me.

Q. You do not know anything about foreign corporations at all? A. No; I do not know much about them. I am not a lawyer.. I cannot say that I can see any benefit in section four.

SENATOR CROSS—Do you know what section five relates to? A. It relates to the Political Code.

Q. It is that a railroad corporation cannot be organized to exist for more than fifty years. Now, one corporation might organize in 1850, and another in 1860, and a third in 1870. There is a section of the Code which would allow these three corporations to consolidate. That is, a provision of the Code, which, when amended, would read so that whenever the first charter expired then the rights of all would expire. A. I do not see why you could not allow them all, when joined together, to run as long as the youngest. I don't see that that cuts any figure.

Q. It don't affect you? A. No; it might if I wanted to consolidate. There might something or another happen that another road might come in from the East that would want to connect with us, but if these things were put in the way it would be that much against. If that is done I do not see how the Union Pacific could ever compete with the Central Pacific in California.

Q. You think if this section four is adopted that the Union Pacific could never build a competing line in California? A. They could build under a new incorporation. They could not connect together.

Q. They could by getting a charter in California? A. Yes, they could by forming two corporations, and have one in California, running to the State line, but that would be inconvenient, and it wouldn't be the Union Pacific. (Reading section seven.) Now, I think, of course, that an officer or agent of any company ought to be punished for disobeying the law, and I think that section ought to be amended in some way so that if you pass a law it will punish the parties violating the law, by some heavy fine or something of the kind, without forfeiting the charter. In the first place, to forfeit the charter and to take a man's property as against a mortgagee, who is an innocent party.

Q. The author of the bill says that you can. He claims that that is the effect of the bill. A. You might pass a law punishing a man for doing a certain thing, but you cannot confiscate his ranch as against a mortgage. If I put a mortgage of two hundred thousand dollars on a railroad and borrow the money from you, and a certain agent of mine violates the law and the road is confiscated, can the State take the property, as against the man taking the mortgage, and hold it?

Q. You have made a radical error in that, and that is that the road never belonged to you, but it belonged to the people. The mortgage belonged to the wrong man? A. Of course I admit that if you pass a law you want a penalty. There ought to be a penalty to enforce the law. All laws ought to be enforced, but if this penalty is put on, it retards the development of the country. It prevents the building of new railroads. I will give you the extent of my experience, and it is this: We have been making a survey this last Summer up the Feather River, intending to extend our road up the North Fork of the Feather River to Big Meadows, about one hundred miles. We have surveyed the route, and the engineer has been making up his reports and maps, and about two weeks ago he had it finished. The gentleman who is interested along with me is quite wealthy, and he proposed to put up the money for this road and to extend it if possible, and we were to have a meeting in San Francisco and decide whether the road should be built, and take the engineer's figures and see if it would pay, but the gentleman says now: "It is no use to have a consultation if this Barry bill is to pass with that section in it." He will put no money into the road, nor he can't get anybody else to put any in. He could not incorporate or bond the road for the cost of building it. Whether the gentlemen interested with him took the bonds or not, he would not take them with this clause in the bill. I say, therefore, that that provision will prevent any capitalist from taking any bond of any railroad in California for the building of a local road. While it may not be constitutional and could not perhaps be enforced, yet, at the same time, people do not want to take any chances about those things. I think that this clause, with the forfeiture attached, would injure railroad building in this State. If this bill does not forfeit the charter, then of course it has no effect, but if it does, people would not put money into them (reading section six). As I understand it, that takes in all the real property except buildings. Perhaps it does not take in the rolling stock.

Q. Would the road simply be the right of way? A. No, sir.

Q. The rails and sleepers? A. I should say the rails and sleepers and the appurtenances.

Q. What do you think the term "appurtenances" means? A. I think it means the ties and rails, and everything required to run the road.

Senator Sullivan—You are familiar, no doubt, with the turnpikes of the various counties of California? A. I used to be in early days, but not lately.

Q. I ask you as a matter of fact, if, when the grant of a turnpike has expired, it does not become a public highway? A. Unless the parties owning the turnpike procured the right of way from the landholders for certain purposes, it goes back to the original landholders. So in regard to a railroad; I suppose it goes back in the same way.

Q. I only ask you for the fact. Do not these turnpikes become public highways, and belong to the people of the State? A. I suppose that is correct; if it is not, it ought to be.

Q. What difference is there between a turnpike and a railroad? A. A turnpike does not require any rails, and that is an expensive matter, besides being more expensive to construct.

Q. Would it affect your opinion any if you knew that other States have a similar provision and their railroads were carried on and made a success? A. I don't see how it could be done with such a law as this in force.

Q. I understand that in several of the States like this—or of the same character—I understand there is such a law in Missouri, and that no injury has been done to the interests of the State there? A. If there is a law like this in Missouri, that allows the State to take the property of a corporation, except the rolling stock, I would not like to loan money and take a mortgage on the road.

Q. What would you suggest in the way of a penalty? What would be a fair thing between the railroad and the people? A. That is a matter that is difficult to answer. It seems to me that the people make laws here and they can find some way to fix a penalty and have it enforced. If imprisonment were too severe, you might fine them so much, quite a large amount perhaps. Possibly the railroad might have to pay it.

Q. Do you think the penalty would be too severe upon a corporation that will persistently violate the law, if it forfeits its charter? I am not speaking of little matters that may be an oversight—not that an agent might do this or that—but suppose that a corporation, in its corporate capacity, by the voice of its Directors, persistently violate the law, do you think that would be too severe a penalty? A. I would, for the reason that it would injure innocent parties. I think you could punish the company in some other way; I don't think you should confiscate the road. I think you could punish the party who commits the violation without confiscating the money that I may have in a mortgage. That section six might be boiled down a little bit, but that is my objection to the penalty.

SENATOR CROSS—If you simply forfeit the charter under that section, do you understand that you forfeit the right of way and the roadbed? A. If you forfeit the right of way and the roadbed, that would be all that belonged to the people of the State.

SENATOR SULLIVAN—Of course, the privileges granted to this company are granted by the people of the State for the benefit of the public, and when the corporation violates the law, the public are interested in the matter, and can forfeit the charter and the roadbed and right of way? A. I suppose that would be an injury to the public.

Q. I suppose that would, incidentally, be an injury? A. When you come to study this bill, you will see that it is a very binding bill.

Q. It is intended to be binding? A. As I said, I do not object to punishment, but I think those two sections could be amended so that you could punish the managers of the road enough to prevent them doing these things without confiscating the property. You might amend it so as to punish them in some other way, without taking the property away from the parties who hold a mortgage on it. If there was no mortgage upon the road, then I don't know but I should pay the penalty, because a man ought to be very careful about disobeying the law. I think it will operate against the mortgagees of roads. I think the Central Pacific Railroad Company ought to be punished if they disobey the law, but in some other way. I would not retard the interests of the State or of the mortgagees of the road.

SENATOR SULLIVAN—With these amendments which you have suggested, do you not consider this a good bill between the railroad companies and the people of the State? A. Allowing me to qualify those parts of the bill, yes, sir; if you will amend section one and section two and take out section three.

Q. You did not strike all of that out? A. Well, leave out part of it; and really section one and section two is about all there is of the bill. Section one is in regard to discrimination between persons, as I understand it. That section ought to be amended.

Q. You do not believe in forfeiture? A. No, sir. I have explained why.

Q. You are in favor of a penalty sufficient to enforce the violation of the law? A. Of course. All laws ought to be enforced.

Q. That bill would not be worth the paper upon which it is printed without the penalty? A. Unless you enforce the law it would not be worth anything.

Q. Would you put the Directors in the State Prison? A. I think that would be better than to take the property from the stockholders. I don't see why you cannot punish the manager of a railroad company as well as you can the manager of a hotel. You put a penalty upon the manager of a hotel if he does not keep a certain door swinging in a certain way; and you impose certain laws upon different people. I don't see why you can't put a different punishment on railroad people without confiscating the property.

SENATOR McCLURE—I want to ask you if the words "other structures," in the first sentence of that section, does not cover the very cause that you spoke of? A. I supposed at first that if I didn't keep those structures in repair, it would be forfeited, but perhaps not. I am opposed to the whole section, but it would be better than it is now by taking out that clause, "for the purposes for which it is used." There ought to be no objection to that.

Q. You do not wish it to be understood that you are in favor of the bill at all under any circumstances? A. I don't know whether I ought to be compelled to answer such a question as that.

THE CHAIRMAN—You are not compelled to answer any questions. A. I will simply say this, in a general way: I am pretty well acquainted in California, and have business connections with five or six different kinds of business, and ship grain, etc., and I don't know of any demand on the part of the people for this bill. I don't know a man in Sacramento that says he wants this bill passed. Also, in Marysville, I don't know of a man in the city of five or six thousand inhabitants who wants it done. I have not heard anybody say they wanted it passed. I heard people say they didn't want it passed. There may be people who want it passed, but I don't know of any.

SENATOR DEL VALLE—According to your proposition, those amendments leave the matter exactly as it is now? A. I don't know as it would; but if the bill is to be passed, I would like to see these amendments in, because it would not be so bad.

Q. Wouldn't it leave it almost as it is now? A. The part of it discriminating against persons? I have no objections to passing a law preventing discriminations against persons.

Q. You suggested that they should be allowed to discriminate in classes? A. Yes, sir.

Q. Do you not know that there are hundreds of classes in the classification by the railroad company? A. I know there are a great many; I don't know just how many.

Q. Couldn't they to-day discriminate in favor of grain as against iron, for instance, and to-morrow discriminate in favor of iron as against grain? A. Yes; but you should put in an amendment, that they should not discriminate against classes. That would not allow them to take freight of one class as against another.

Q. To-day, for instance, they could discriminate in favor of wheat and against barley or iron, and to-morrow they could reverse it? A. With that amendment in, you could prevent it.

Q. Therefore the conditions would be just the same as they are now? A. It would not be proper for them to do it, but at the same time I think you could allow some discrimination to the managers of the road.

Q. Your understanding is, that with your amendment in, it would be just the same as it is now? A. No; I understand now that they can charge one man more than another if they want to.

Q. I mean so far as dispatching freight is concerned? A. It would be as it is now in regard to classes; it would not be in regard to prices. They could take a man's ten thousand tons in preference to the other. As it stands now, they could take half of your wheat and half of mine, but with this law they would have to take all of yours and none of mine.

Q. If all the freight was of the same class, they could not discriminate between you and me? A. No, sir.

Q. But on freight of different kinds, you say they ought to be allowed to? A. Yes, sir.

Q. Then, suppose they discriminate to-day in favor of Class A, and to-morrow in favor of Class B? A. You don't mean in prices?

Q. No; in forwarding. Could they not do so under your amendment? A. I think they could, but at the same time I don't think that any railroad company would be foolish enough to conduct their business in that way, and against their own interest, and against the interest of the people. I don't think they would do it.

Q. Supposing that you had a difficulty with the railroad company, or even with the agent, and they say, "Here, you just delay this freight as much as you can; throw any obstacle you can in his way; don't you think that such things would be done; would not an amendment in a case of that kind be a necessity? A. In cases of that kind, I think it would.

Senator Kellogg—An amendment, to the effect that they would be required to give five or ten days notice of any change, would save all that trouble? A. I don't know whether it would or not; it might.

Senator McClure—I understood you to say that if such a case did occur, that it might be left somewhat to the managers of the road? A. Yes, sir; you can't pass a law that would cover every particular case; you would have to allow a little power to the managers of the road, or you cannot make it successful. If you protect the interests of the people, and of the shippers, and the railroad company, in doing so you may have to put some clause in the bill allowing the agents of the company to discriminate occasionally. I don't see how you can do it without.

Q. You don't consider that that is the best way of doing? A. Yes, sir, I do.

Q. You have, for instance, printed Classes A, B, C, D; you change them every few days; or, do you think there should be no rule at all? A. I think they ought to have the privilege of changing the classes, or else they couldn't manage the road.

Q. Therefore, you mean that it should be left just the same as it is now to carry on the business with discrimination as to persons only? A. Yes, sir.

Q. You are simply opposed to any portion of the bill; isn't that the exact fact? A. Well, that is pretty near it; but I think those amendments would affect these matters.

Q. Don't those amendments contemplate the striking out of one of those clauses? A. That may be so; I say if that bill cannot be amended as I have suggested, it ought not to be passed.

Q. You believe that freight should be dispatched without reference to who is the owner of it? A. Yes, sir.

Q. But as to classes, you think there ought to be allowed some discrimination; for instance, to forward furniture before ten thousand tons of wheat? A. Exactly.

Q. Your road is one of the oldest in the State? A. Yes, sir.

Senator Cross—Do you know anything about any discrimination that is usually made with regard to explosives, or powders, or any other substances of that character, which are to be carried; do you know whether or not they forward those cars containing explosives along with the other cars, or whether they have special days for forwarding that class of freight? A. I think they have certain days to forward them.

Q. And they carry them in such a way as not to endanger the safety of other goods? A. I understand so.

Q. Do you think that such a discrimination as that is necessary for the protection of property? A. I think it is for the protection of the railroad people. They are responsible; if the cars are blown up, the property upon the same cars would have to be paid for.

Q. They have some rule about sending acids and that class of freight? A. I think so.

Q. Do you think that the company should be allowed to discriminate as to when they should forward those articles? A. Yes, sir.

Q. You think that they should be allowed to classify them so that they may carry them with safety to the property of other people? A. I think they ought to be allowed to discriminate as to all classes of goods, and to take one class in preference to another.

Senator Vrooman—Are you a large shipper? A. Yes, sir; I am interested——

Q. I mean over these roads? A. Yes, sir.

Q. How long have you been in the shipping business? A. Twenty years.

Q. Has there ever any case come within your observation of personal discrimination, either as to price or dispatch, under the same circumstances? A. No, sir.

Q. Have you ever applied to the Central Pacific Railroad Company to get special rates? A. Yes, sir; I have sometimes.

Q. Wanting them to discriminate in your favor? A. I asked them to take some lumber over once or twice.

Q. Did they give them to you? A. No, sir; they told me if they gave it to me they would have to give it to all at the same price.

Q. In fixing the price of goods do you take into account the value of the goods to be transported to a certain extent? A. Yes, sir; we take into consideration the value of our lumber to the merchants and more to some of them.

Q. You have a flouring mill? A. Yes, sir.

Q. And you make different grades of flour? A. Yes, sir.

Q. Do you charge more for one grade than for another? A. Yes, sir.

Q. Do you make shorts? A. Yes, sir.

Q. Do you charge more for shorts than for bran? A. Yes, sir.

Q. Does it cost you any more to make it? A. No; we make it at the same time that we make the flour.

Q. Do you conduct your railroad upon the same principle that you do your other business? A. I do if the State allows me to.

Q. I will call your attention to section two, commencing at line eight, of this bill (reading it). If a theater man came to you and wanted twenty-five, or thirty, or forty tickets for his company, could you give him a rebate under this law? A. I should suppose that we would have to charge the same.

Q. You could not call them commutation tickets for a single trip? A. No, sir.

Q. Do you think it is in the interest of the patrons of railroads that you should be permitted to discriminate and make a rebate in cases of that kind, where a large number of persons are upon an excursion, or wanted to go at one time. Don't you think that they ought to be allowed to make a rebate in those cases? A. We do it sometimes on a special train; I don't know as it is a rebate; we take them out Sundays and charge four bits apiece, while the regular trains are a dollar and a half.

Q. Do you think that you would be allowed to do that if this bill became a law? A. That is a legal question; I should be afraid to do it.

Q. Supposing that your road from Marysville to Oroville should cease to pay operating expenses, and become useless, do you think there should be a law passed that would prevent you from removing it without sustaining the loss of your charter? A. No, sir; I do not.

Q. Would you, as a prudent business man, attempt to remove it under section three, if a portion of your road ceased to pay? A. Of course I would have no right to remove it, if the State could take the rails and sell them.

Q. Did you construct this road yourself? A. No, sir.

Q. Do you know how it was constructed? A. The California

Northern Railroad Company bonded it and sold the bonds and built the road.

Q. Do you know who paid for the ties and the rails that were put down? A. The company paid for them, and obtained the money from the sale of bonds, from private persons.

Q. Do you know who macadamizes the roads in your county? A. The county roads are macadamized by the county.

Q. By taxation of the people? A. Yes, sir.

Q. Do you think there is any similarity between the county roads, which are paid for by taxation of the people, and the ties and rails of your road, which were paid for by the company? A. No, sir.

Q. Do you think any law is just, that forfeits to the people of the State the ties and rails that were paid for by private persons, because a forfeiture is worked upon a road paid for by the public? A. No, sir; I don't think it would be just.

Senator Sullivan—Who pays for the macadamizing of any turnpike road that you know of in this State? A. Do you mean a private road, owned by a corporation?

Q. Yes, sir? A. The people that own the roads.

Q. They collect toll, do they not? A. Yes, sir; where they own the road.

Q. Supposing that they did something to forfeit their roads; do you not think, then, that the people of the State would have the right to take the road as a public highway? A. They should either forfeit it or be punished in some other way.

Q. Do you not think that any railroad company who holds property in the same manner should have their charter forfeited if they violated the law? A. I stated before that I did not, for the reason that I thought they should be punished in some other way.

Testimony of A. E. Davis, of San Francisco.

Senator McClure—I wish you to take this bill and make any suggestion; first, as to the railroad you are interested in? Answer—The South Pacific Coast Railroad.

Q. What relations do you bear to that road? A. President and part owner.

Q. How long has that road been in operation? A. The Southern Pacific Coast Railroad was commenced at the terminus on the first day of April, eight years ago.

Q. Between what points are the termini? A. San Francisco and Alameda Point by ferry, and thence by rail through Alameda and Santa Clara, and across the Santa Cruz Mountains to the Town of Santa Cruz, in Santa Cruz County.

Q. The road is projected beyond that? A. We have many projections beyond that; but no work so far, except in the way of surveys. Nothing of any particular importance except a branch. We are constructing, or rather have made a survey, for a branch from the old town of Felton to Pescadero by the San Lorenzo River, and through the redwood country. We have also a survey completed from our terminal point at Alameda now, where we have a new route to Stockton. The survey is completed, and the profiles are in the office, but the work of action has been suspended.

Q. You are a part owner? A. Yes, sir.

Q. Has this railroad been constructed by subsidies or by private capital? A. By private capital entirely.

Q. You have never received any subsidy from the General or State Government? A. In no shape whatever. No State, county, town, or individual.

Q. Of course, if you have any objection to answer these questions you have only to say so. About how much money have you invested up to this time in those roads? A. If the Assessor wasn't about I would be more willing to tell you. I admit, however, that I have paid more than it is worth.

Q. There has been a large sum of money expended? A. Yes, sir; over four millions.

Q. Now will you please take Assembly Bill No. 10 and make any suggestion to this committee, commencing with section one, as to the provisions of the bill, with reference to the operations of your railroad? A. I scarcely flatter myself that I can give this committee any information. I am willing, however, to endeavor to try, if I am allowed to state in my own way. I am no lawyer or legislator. If there is anything about me it is a practical way of putting it. If I was asked what I thought of this bill, I should say, if I was asked how I would amend this bill, I should say by striking out the enacting clause. If I was asked, "What for?" I should simply answer: "Because, in my judgment, the character of such legislation is meddlesome and pernicious." "Why?" "Because it is calculated to do a great deal of harm without doing any commensurate good that I can see." So much for that. Now, commencing at the first section, I read: "All railroads built or owned by corporations, or organized under the laws of the State, are public highways, over which all persons are entitled to transportation for persons and property on equal and impartial terms." I should add to that, if I was asked to amend the bill, "according to the services rendered." That might help that to some extent. (Reading.) "All persons and companies engaged in operating any such road, or in transporting freight or passengers over the same, or which shall hereafter operate or engage, as aforesaid, shall forward, move, and carry, impartially, for all persons offering freight to be transported or moved, without discrimination." Now, there is the plum of the whole business. I should say that that cannot be done. I undertake to say so, and I undertake to say, and I would not state an unfair proposition, either in my own favor or ortherwise. That is the pith of the whole business, "without discrimination." Now, gentlemen, that word "discrimination;" it makes a great deal of difference whom that word is applied to, doesn't it? If you discriminate in favor of a shipper it is all right. If you discriminate in favor of yourself it is all wrong, isn't it? Isn't the true proposition whether I shall discriminate either against you or in your favor, as you please? Now, I say that in running this road of ours, constructed as I stated, and operated entirely in the interest of the people, and to the best of our ability to do so, we discriminate every day; badly, too. But I do it in favor of my patrons. I don't hesitate to say so. I may be in fault, for what I know, but I am not aware that I am. I will illustrate, and give you examples, if you desire to hear them, of how it occurs.

SENATOR CROSS—We want to get facts, if there is any good reason for them, and if there is not we want to know it. A. My patrons say that there is, and I venture to say that on my road, six miles long, every patron I had would have as good a reason. Our road, of course, is short, and it is chiefly for its travel we depend for Summer patronage for any returns that amount to anything considerable. Our business travel amounts to very little. We discriminate, if you please, in favor of all sorts of societies. We do that in order to meet them at a price they can pay; that is to say, we increase our resources as much as possible, but we discriminate in freights too every day. I will tell you why. I know the propriety of it under very close reasoning might be doubted, but that is all right. The upper end of our railroad runs through a redwood country. One of our chief resources for business is in the shape of lumber and wood. Now it runs to the Town of San José, which is a large consumer of redwood lumber, several million feet of lumber every year—eight or ten probably—and before the construction of this road the common freight over the mountains was seven or eight dollars per thousand. As a result of the building of this road, it was to reduce that freight to four dollars, which I believe, as far as I have heard, is entirely satisfactory to the consumers, and I know it is to the shippers; I am certain of that. And like all other things of that character it stimulated the building of a great many sawmills, and it increased the price of timber lands from five to forty dollars an acre; and increased in the production of lumber; they found they were producing more lumber than they could sell, and the lumber people came to me and said, "We desire you to give us relief, if you can." I said, "What relief do you require?" "Open up further markets for us." "How?" "Send our lumber into Alameda County." They never had that market before.

SENATOR CROSS—How much further would that be? A. About forty miles by rail; but they say, "You must carry it very cheap." "Why?" "Because they have got redwood lumber in Mendocino County, and there were water, and ships, and boats between Mendocino County and the Bay of San Francisco." I said, "I will see how I can serve you, and I will serve you if I can." I concluded I would make myself believe that if I could haul sixteen millions of lumber through the expensive part of the road, through the tunnels, and to San José, at four dollars, it would be better than to haul eight millions, so I agreed with my shippers that I would carry the lumber the other forty miles for a half a dollar a thousand, because they say, "If you charge us eight dollars, we can't sell any lumber. The Mendocino fellows sell it all." Now, I say, if that is not discrimination between places, I do not know what it is. Is it right? Am I doing wrong, and should it all cease? I was, certainly, if I know or under-

stand the reading of that bill. I apprehend, if the delegation here
from those counties could hear their constituents, they would not
wish to stop it. I think they would not, but, to my mind, that
is the result of the word "discrimination," in section one, line
nine, in this bill. That would be the practical result of it. Now
I can say no more upon that, that is the fact. I can't say anything
more on that section. That is all there is about it, and that is the
word "discrimination" here. It happens here to be in favor of the
people. I hope I shall not lose anything by it. I don't know that I
have. I am very certain that I don't make anything by it. I know
I help them all I possibly can myself, and give them the best end of
it. I would like to make one other application here that applies to
the discrimination that is practiced. I was about to make a contract with a lot of gentlemen who contemplate constructing a sugar
manufactory at Alvarado, in the County of Alameda, twenty-five
miles from San Francisco. A delegation of gentlemen waited on me,
including the proprietors of the beet sugar manufactory. We have
only one in the State that I know of, and that is this one of ours, that
is successful. We have found it extremely difficult to get into the
manufacturing of beet sugar. They wanted to connect their business
with the cane sugar. They sent an agent to the Sandwich Islands to
contract with several planters there who are producing large amounts
of cane sugar. They were looking anxiously for a favorite location
for their manufactory. They came to me and said, "Mr. Davis, what
can you do for us?" "Well, I don't know; I am willing to do anything I can." I have expended a great deal of money in railroading here, and I have never been able to make anything out of
it yet. Although our gross receipts last year were nine thousand
dollars a mile it did not meet our expenses. Our payroll was
twenty-three thousand dollars a month. If my lines were longer
I should expect to receive more. Of course, my terminal facilities
would be just as good for one thousand or two thousand miles as it
is for one hundred miles. Now, I said, "What do you want me to
do?" "We want you to enable us to compete with Claus Spreckles."
I said, "That is a pretty tough job to do, but I will do the best I can
for you. State your proposition." "We want you—we have offered
us five acres of land, located at Alvarado, and we want you to stand
in and help us; we think it would be to your interest—we know it
would. We want you to carry our crude sugar from your wharf
at San Francisco, and ferry it across to your new mole on the
Alameda side of San Francisco Bay, and carry it to Alvarado,
at fifty cents a ton. We want you to bring back our refined
sugar and deliver it on your terminal wharf at San Francisco at
fifty cents per ton. We want you to handle all our coal from your
new wharf at fifty cents a ton, and no wharfage, either." "Well," I
says, "That is a pretty tight proposition; I hardly see what there is
in that for me; I don't see how I can make any money out of that."
They said, "Yes, you can, you don't understand this thing." "Well,
please to show me, if I don't." They said, "You know, if we open a
refinery up there, there will be at least one hundred people go there
to operate it, and they will start coal yards, grocery stores, etc., and

8 b

they will make a flourishing town, and you will benefit the people, and you will get the benefit of all the freights upon which you can charge freight, and make money." "Well," I said, "It does look plausible, and I will consider it." I went off and thought about the matter. I told them if they would call around in a day or two, I would consider it and let them know. I studied over the matter and went back, and said, "Gentlemen, I would like to make it for you, but it is pretty hard work for me to make land as valuable in Alvarado as it is in San Francisco, but I would like to accomplish it, if it was possible; I will do it for you for sixty-five cents." They said, "No, we can't do it; you must do it for fifty cents a ton; you will make it back in the increase of your business that you will do." I didn't have the Barry bill in my mind just then, and I finally said, "In order to accomplish it I will tell you what I will do: I will carry it for sixty-five cents, bearing in mind all the time that I would charge the other fellows something—the coal yard man, and the groceryman. I made them that proposition which they are now considering, to give them a five years' contract to do that, but in the meantime somebody sent me down the Barry bill, and I began to study the Barry bill. I says, "Here, why that goes to the coal yard, and the groceryman, and all. Every fellow will want his stuff carried at the same rate. How am I going to do that? And I can't do it, because I cannot discriminate between persons and places." Now, if that is the fact and the conditions, I am opposed to the Barry bill and anything that is in it. If you can tell me any good way that I can carry out that enterprise without running against that law, I would like to know it; I can't see how it can be done. I can't see what good the bill does anybody. I might do these people some good. The factory might do the people some good; it might increase the volume of my business, so that I would be able to get a portion of my money back that I have put into railroads. And am I to be deprived of that? I come here to this Legislature—I think this is the most remarkable instance on record—asking this Legislature to please let me alone because I was fool enough to put my money into a railroad. That is the practical sum of it; it is nothing more or less. If you will pardon the expression of my mind, it seems to me that all I have learned in eight years is this: That I have got into the wrong business; that an honest man can't live in it; that a railroad is not worth anything unless you can steal it. I can't do that, but the fellow that can is the fellow to run it. That is a pretty hard experience, isn't it? And that is so much for discrimination. I think that is plenty to say of it. I don't know what more I could say if I talked a week. If there is any crime on the part of the railroad people of this State, please not visit their sins on me. I don't know that there is. I think there is more talk about it than there is reality in it, although I think, if I might venture an opinion, if I had had the system of railroads of the Central Pacific Railroad and the Southern Pacific Railroad, I would guarantee that I would not have had much money. But that is a question between the people and them as to who is to get it all. I don't want it all. It is too much trouble to me, I want somebody else to have some of it. The fact is that there are just the same difficulties in every branch of life. I saw my friend Webster here with his bank; he loans money for less than Michael Reese; I only say that as an illustration; it is the difference between men; everybody and every interest ought to be put on a plain, fair footing; and these are simply my practical suggestions. If there was some man in this State who could get hold of the right end of this puzzle and eliminate it to the satisfaction of everybody, he would be called a very big man. There are difficulties here to my mind almost impossible to overcome. I cannot believe, to start out with, after buying as I did a right of way through three counties, and I never invoked the right of eminent domain only in three instances—one in each county—in most instances I took a deed in fee; I had to pay for the land in all cases by private agreement, or by arbitration. I didn't have any suits where it was possible to avoid them; and it seems to me that while all the world is building new roads under the law as it now stands, the new Constitution, and the correlative legislation under it, and that which is proposed to be made, that it is almost impossible to build a railroad in this State. But I bought this land, and I paid for it clean. Some of it I bought directly in the name of the South Pacific Coast Railroad Company; or rather, I might state, that we have three or four corporations; I got it originally for the South Pacific Coast Railroad Company, starting from Dumbarton Point on the Bay of San Francisco, and running through Santa Cruz, and through the upper end of Alameda County, but I found that it was impossible to do anything with that, that I would never do anything at all with it till I put in new money and built new lines, and made new incorporations under the control of the same stockholders and the same President, excepting that we made a nominal change in the Trustees, but none of the Trustees are owners except one and myself. It was easier to make new incorporations than to amend the old ones. We thought we would call it the South Pacific Coast Railroad Company, as I said, starting from Dumbarton Point and running to the junction of the Santa Cruz and Fulton Railroad, and which we afterwards bought. That is about seven miles in length; it terminates at the junction, a little below Big Trees—the Felton Big Trees. We maintain that corporation still, and maintain and operate the road, and call it the South Pacific Coast Railroad Company. Then we have what we call the Bay Coast Railway, and a third line running from Newark, in Alameda County, down Alameda Point down to the middle bridge, at Oakland, that is the end of that. After building that we found that we had not enough to do yet, to do anything, so we thought we would run into Oakland, and we got in there; but I don't want to try it over again. We quit in Oakland at Fourteenth and Webster Streets. Now, we need another corporation, which we have just made, that we call the Felton and Pescadero; that is the one that I spoke of. We have the surveys made, and are now trying to procure the right of way, and would probably have begun the construction of it the coming Spring. Then, we have another incorporation—the last—which is the largest one of all; that is the San Francisco and Colorado River. That is the one we have got in our minds. That is several hundred miles long; that is, the papers are, but that is like a good many others—a good deal of paper about it. We have built our new mole and new depot under the incorporation. The line was not covered by any previous surveys. We hope, if railroad matters turn more favorably, that we will be able some time to build that road. I don't know whether we will be able or not, but I am sure I cannot if this legislation is carried on. I mean to say if the promoters and sponsors of this legislation, believing, as I believe they do believe, that it is right. I think they are prejudiced, to say the least. I don't think there is one of them that is prejudiced against or would do me any harm as far as I am concerned, in any way; I don't think they would. But I will say: Suppose that I (being the one honest man in the railroad business)—that I should come here and say: "Gentlemen, I will stand in with you; we will adopt the Barry bill; I have lost more than I can afford; now we will steal more than my profits could aggregate in a hundred years. I will show you how to do it under this Barry bill; it is very easy. I don't think you ought to give me or any other man the power to do it. But say everything is lovely, the legislation all suits me, and I will stand in with all you people, I am not going to contend with you about property or property rights; that is all nonsense; I don't care anything about it. I build my railroads, say some three hundred miles. I have a fair standing and credit. As I said, we have never had a mortgage upon our roads; it was built and paid for with good sound gold coin; I think the stockholders could very easily manage that part of it, if we desired. We say we will organize now with this three hundred miles of road. I go out in San Francisco, or go down to San José; I have my Senator in San José, reputed to be a man of wealth. I say to him: "I have some railroad bonds to sell; you know me; you know what I have done; you know that further roads will be a benefit to you, because you have a large property here, and I ask you to take about twenty thousand dollars' worth of these railroad bonds; they are all right." He finally starts out and looks it over, and he says: "I think I will take them." I go on to various capitalists, and I finally raise enough by this sensible way of doing business, to build a road with somebody else's money, and after I had built the road I would say, under the Barry bill and kindred legislation like this, I would say: "Never mind your bonds; I will kick up some deviltry now and you will sell the bonds for half what they are worth, because I will frighten you." I say that it is quite in my power to do it, or of any other man. I am learning something new about the railroad business every day; I am very sure I shall learn more about it. Now, I don't believe myself that the provisions of the bill could ever be carried out, because I don't believe, from what I have observed, that if we found our property taken to pay the taxes, and the next fellow took it, and because he didn't pay the taxes it would be sold again, I don't know where we would catch it, it would be running round so. It would depress the value of the bonds so that any designing man could buy them up at his own price. I don't know what good that would do anybody. It might be denied that it could be done, but I believe it can. I am not a lawyer, but I believe if that bill is carried, just as these men here propose to pass it, that it could be done. Now, there is only one other thing to say: You say that it is necessary to declare in all solemnity, to the assembled wisdom of this State, that no railroad shall come into this State without incorporating in the State. Now, if there is anything in that, I declare I don't see it. I say that the power of the State has jurisdiction over the State in a paternal and parental way. The laws ought to be made and maintained and obeyed; and though they ought to be and will be obeyed, yet I say there is no wealth for the people of this State, excepting in the encouraging of roads. The people of this State cannot afford to cast out all its securities—they want more roads. If there was anybody in this State that could devise means by which we could get more roads, and make those that are here do right constitutionally, I have no objections. I know very well that, so far as I am concerned, or anybody associated with me, we do not wish any more. We will not sink new money, or put it into undesirable securities; it is unreasonable to suppose that any sensible man would do so. That is all I have to say.

Q. What is the name of your road? A. The San Francisco and Colorado River.

Q. Projected from what point? A. The survey commenced at our terminal point in San Francisco Bay, a little south of the estuary of San Antonio, and adjoining the front wall, and follows up that and over to the Marin coast, and crosses and takes up the valley there.

Q. If this bill becomes law, will that road be built? A. Not by me; I will not try it. I can't do it myself, and I can't get the money to do it with if I desired ever so much; and I would not advise a friend of mine to put it into it. This may be considered a remarkable statement for a man who is a railroad man to tell. Most people are bolstering up their things, but I declare that that is the naked truth.

SENATOR KELLOGG—You bought the land and right of way in fee. Do you own that? A. I don't know that I made that entirely clear. We have what we call a sister corporation with our railroad corporation; that is not exactly au fait in that line; it buys and pays for all it gets; it don't build any railroad; we call it the Pacific Land Investment Company. In various places we have had to buy considerable tracts of land in order to get the land we traversed. If we couldn't get the piece of land that we wanted alone, we bought the entire tract. It is owned by the same parties, and controlled entirely in the same way as the railroad. Now, I was wondering what would be the result of confiscating that land. Some say that it would go to the State. It is my opinion that it would go back to its original owners, if it did. The portion of this land which is deeded in fee to the railroad company we would take anyhow. I was trying to figure out how much I could save of it if this did pass. All that portion which is deeded to the Pacific Land Investment Company and the title derived through them would come back to the corporation.

SENATOR CROSS—You think it would revert to them? A. That is

my opinion. But I do not think that they mean it—I believe in the American people. I don't believe that anybody desires it. They say it, but they don't mean it.

SENATOR KELLOGG—What do they say so for? A. I don't want to say; I might be accused of being prejudiced; but I know that I don't want any more.

SENATOR VROOMAN—Are you a candidate for Congress? A. No, sir; I beg leave to decline. I couldn't be got up.

Q. How much of this Colorado River and San Francisco road has been constructed? A. From the end of the new mole to Alameda Point—about two miles and three quarters—to the trestle and bridge.

Q. Is that where the new depot is, on the Alameda side? A. Yes, sir.

Q. From what States did the constructing parties get their charter? A. From the State of California.

Q. Would that road, when constructed, extend outside of the State? A. Of course it would extend to the Colorado River—but I shall not do it myself, and I would not recommend a friend of mine to put his money in railroads in the present condition of the State.

Q. I understood you to state that you had suspended work on this railroad. Is that true? A. No; we have suspended action. We went far enough to carry out the organization. We suspended financial action because it looked to me like we would be able to get no securities. We are entirely willing to do it, but we want to be safe about it.

Q. When did you suspend action? A. About the beginning, or just after the adoption of the new Constitution. Of course, we have spent some money since, because we were obliged to. We desire to save our investments. Our road is doing a considerable business. Last year we earned nine thousand dollars a mile gross on our road, and it paid a profit because the line is short and the service first class, and the patrons all satisfied; but the proprietors are not.

Q. How long have you been operating the Alameda County road? A. Five or six years.

Q. Have you had a good deal to do? A. All the business of that county.

Q. State whether or not there is any demand on the part of the people of that county for such legislation as is contained in the Barry bill? A. Not to my knowledge. I am free to say that there is no patron of our road that has ever intimated to me anything of the sort.

Q. Have you heard any complaints from any persons that were considered reliable concerning the present transportation facilities furnished to the people of that county? A. Yes, sir; of course.

Q. Any complaints? A. Yes, sir.

Q. Were they well founded? A. No, of course not. Some people would complain if they were going to be hanged, but I have heard of nothing that is worth noticing at all.

Q. What are the conditions with respect to manufacturing in Oakland as compared with what they were five or six years ago? A. A benefit to the people wherever there is any reasonable competition;

an unmitigated benefit everywhere as to their being transported and to the value of their property. I mean to say, so far as would be consistent with the terrible times we have had for the last three or four years—at the time of the great depression, when property went down fifty per cent in San Francisco; but it did not affect the property value in Oakland; it held its own. And I am continually requested by the property owners to push the road out—that is the way to help us. I say, "Yes, I would like to help you; I would like to help myself a little, too."

Q. Isn't it true that there has been, during the last three or four years, large manufacturing industries started there in consequence of the competition of the railroads? A. Certainly.

SENATOR SPENCER—Your idea of "discrimination" is illustrated by saying that you wanted to start a manufactory? A. A sugar refinery.

Q. And your idea was that under this bill you would have to transport all persons and freight to that point at the same price? A. I so understand the bill.

Q. And that is one of your objections on the basis of discrimination? A. That is one of my objections.

Q. Do you agree with section twenty-one of article twelve of the Constitution? A. That is a legal question, and I can't answer anything about such things.

Q. Wouldn't that provision comprehend your idea of discrimination? A. No; that Constitution was passed after I commenced this iniquity. I commenced to do this before you commenced to interfere with my operations.

Q. You would never have built a railroad, then, subsequent to the adoption of the new Constitution? A. Not an inch.

Q. Do you understand that previous to the adoption of the new Constitution there was not any discrimination between persons as to the same character of freight? Do you claim that freight was ever charged to one more than to another? A. I want to answer that in this way: There are a great many things said in that new Constitution, and some of them have been entirely explained away by the Supreme Court, and I hope they will explain that away.

Q. You do not believe in the principle enunciated by the Granger cases? A. No.

Q. You do not believe that it is right? A. No.

Q. You differ with the Supreme Court of the United States? A. I do, so far as I understand it. I don't like to put my opinion up against theirs, but for myself I am going to disagree.

Q. I understand you to say, that in shipping freight to your terminal points, you should be allowed to discriminate between two persons? A. I do in some cases.

Q. That is for the purposes of the success of the railroad people in developing the country? A. No. There is another way of putting it. Human nature is very much the same all over the world. If I kept a grocery store, and two men came in who were both anxious to be served at the moment, I don't think I should wait on the man who bought the fewest goods first, would you?

Q. I am not answering. I don't understand that to be a parallel. You understand that transportation companies have a lien on goods for the freight? A. I understand that.

Q. Therefore your illustration is not a parallel? A. I think that the groceryman has a lien, too.

Q. He has a lien as long as he holds on to it? A. I believe in people paying their debts; I would not favor any law that would allow men to avoid them.

Q. Do you believe in a railroad company paying all the damages done when they injure a party? A. Practice is a little better than theory. I always proceed to investigate into the matter. I have paid damages.

Q. I am not speaking about you. I think there has been no complaint about you. But do you think that, if a farmer at Santa Cruz should bring an action against the Central Pacific Railroad, it is right that it should be transferred to San Francisco, instead of being tried in the Court nearest to him? A. It is a pretty hard case for him. I don't know about the abstract justice of it.

Q. Don't you think that the corporations of the State doing business in the State should be subservient to the State and to State sovereignty, and be governed by their laws? A. Yes, sir; I think so.

Q. If a foreign corporation is doing business here is there any question that they should be subject to the State laws? A. That is a legal question; I don't think so.

Q. If this provision of the bill would prevent the trouble in that direction you would not so seriously object to it? A. There is no way by which I can see any good in the bill or any part of it.

Q. Did you not start in a little prejudiced against it? A. May be so. I think I am a little; I think I am a good deal. The fact is, if all men conducting railroads conducted the business honestly, the same as they do other business, there would be no need of laws.

Q. Do you think that there ought to be any more privileges granted to corporations than there are to natural persons? A. They ought to be all on the same footing. Then, there is another thing—let me follow it out logically: Is there any reason why a corporation should not have equal rights with others?

Q. No, sir. A. Then that is all there is of it.

Q. Do they not want their privileges and immunities greater? A. They may on account of their extensive business and the necessary capital and resource to carry on the business; and they may be in many instances tyrannical and overbearing.

Q. Do you say that you have heard no complaints in this State against the Central Pacific Railroad Company on account of discrimination? A. I said no such thing; but I mean to say that all the stories that are told are not true; there are many of them true. I don't think that they are treating the Legislature or the people of this State right; I think that they are being wrongly guided. From my standpoint I can't say that anything we have ever done, or any view that we have ever taken, goes to the real merits of the question. I don't know exactly what is needed, but certainly nothing is to be gained by tearing down; what we want to do, is to build up.

Q. Do you believe that, under any circumstances, there should be any forfeiture of the charter of a railroad company? A. No; I don't think a man's property ought to be taken away from him at any time without consideration; I consider that a very great crime. I think to take a man's property is a pretty tough business, and it is not often done; with that there is apt to be kicking and some little explanation; if it is carried on to any great extent it will cause some kicking.

Q. Then you assume that every railroad holds property in the State the same as a natural person holds private property? A. I never said any such thing.

Q. What property do you have reference to in this case? A. If some gentleman should step into my office and quietly set down and say, "Davis, you don't own this railroad;" I would look at him first to see whether he was insane or not. I don't own this railroad; then what have I been setting here signing checks for all this time; am I crazy, or you? I begin to argue with myself which it is.

Q. You believe that if a man has property in this State, that it should come under the jurisdiction of the State Government? A. That is what I believe.

Q. Do you recognize the difference between the roads built by subsidies, and those built by private capital? A. I do, decidedly.

Q. To what extent would you discriminate between them? A. That I didn't get any of it.

Q. I suppose, in looking over this subject, and trying to ascertain how it was that you didn't get any of it, it must be attributed to your natural modesty? A. No, I didn't begin early enough; I don't profess to be so excessively modest as all that.

Q. Now, outside of the funny side of this I will ask—— A. Well, that is right; this is a grave subject; I tell you, it is; it is a big subject, and it is not to be laughed about.

Q. Well, you put us in a good humor, and we had better discuss in that manner than in a bad humor. Do you claim that you have a right to discriminate where a road is not subsidized, the same as where one is subsidized? A. None that I could define. I have business experience and judgment, and my notion, founded upon that is, if I have given anybody anything, it is mean to take it back; that is what I think; I say they never should have done it; I say that it is pleading the baby act; it is not manly or just; I say that; I say that if the General Government gave the Central Pacific Railroad Company large sums of money, from this State and from the counties, and if there was no condition to it—if they received large sums of money as a donation, and I understand it was put in that form—I say that if they did, I don't know any better owner for it than the people who received it.

Q. But you think that if they did give it to them that they should act squarely and honestly by the people? A. Now you reach the point that is not law; it is only the result of men's actions—I think they are very ungrateful.

Q. If the moneys and lands were given to them upon conditions you think that the conditions should be complied with? A. I certainly do.

Q. In running your railroad you have no serious complaints as to your manner of conducting it? A. No.

Q. Do you think that under this bill there would be any liability to injure you if there has been no complaint against you? A. Well, I declare there is only one answer. I don't desire to be so well off as this bill would seem to make me.

Q. Supposing that there were other men building roads in other portions of the State that did not act as well as you; we could not make a special law for them. Would not this be better than no law for them? A. I am not mean enough to punish one man for another man's crime.

Q. You are old enough and wise enough to know that these laws have to be general in their character? A. Certainly they do.

Q. And you know that a general law works hardships sometimes in particular cases? A. Why, certainly; there can be no perfect justice—not on this side of the river, anyhow.

Q. Do you believe that if I brought my freight to you for shipment before another man brought his, that his should be shipped first regardless of my wishes? A. If you can devise any law to prevent anything of the kind without taking my railroad, I have no objection. I say that it is wrong, and I think it ought to be remedied, but the remedy is so serious that I confess that I cannot see the necessity for it, or for any such legislation.

Q. Do you think that there would be any trouble in living up to the reasonable requirements of a law of that kind? A. In my opinion there is not a man in the State that would be satisfied if the principles enunciated in this bill would be carried out, if he has any business with the railroads. I say this in connection with this bill— that it is needless and mischievous, and does not in my opinion give any redress commensurate with the damages that it is liable to do.

Q. Supposing that I take three hundred tons of wheat to your station and have it there for a week, asking that it be shipped, and that at the end of that time another man comes there with a like amount, and his is shipped first; do you think that would be right? A. If I deliberately hold that wheat, I should say that it was a very dishonest act.

Q. Supposing that that is practiced generally, do you think it is right? A. If it is practiced generally, it is not right, but I don't believe it is.

Q. Do you not think that the penalty ought to be severe if it is practiced generally? A. Yes, sir.

Q. If it can be practiced, can it not be practiced to the ruination of a man's property? A. Certainly it can, but the penalty ought not to go to the extent of confiscating the property.

Q. Don't you think, if the railroads would be more accommodating, that there would be less trouble? A. Certainly; you can't drive the people.

Q. You do not pretend that, if this bill is passed, you will not have a right to contest any of these matters, and have your day in Court? A. I don't want to go into Court upon any such pretext.

Q. The railroad men don't like to go into Court, anyhow, do they?
A. If you make a general application I will make you an answer. If you include me——

Q. You seem to think that this bill is made for your road; this is made for all roads. A. Yes, but I am in the bundle.

Q. I understand that your conduct is so admirable in the conducting of your road that your patrons have no cause for complaint?
A. I do not desire to say anything about that; I would rather somebody else would say that. I wish that that reputation would do me some good.

Q. In regard to the lumber business in Mendocino County, you claim that discrimination is necessary there in that instance? A. In Santa Cruz County; yes, sir, there would be a discrimination against Mendocino County by taking that lumber. Isn't that a discrimination between persons and places?

Q. Is that the way you construe this bill? A. That is the way I understand it.

Q. Your opinion of this bill depends a good deal upon the construction you put upon it? A. Of course, I am only giving my understanding of it.

Q. One of your reasons is that under this bill if you wanted to be dishonest you could incorporate, and then run the stock down almost to nothing, and that you could do this by committing some act of forfeiture, and force them to sell at a very small price. Would not a man be guilty of conspiracy in doing that? A. I think very likely.

Q. You can't legislate to make men honest? A. I have never known of such a case.

Q. Such a thing is an exception to the general rule? A. I know that men frequently take the chances of going to jail, and a good many of them slip through.

Q. We can't help that? A. I can't either.

Senator Sullivan—Does not this road to Alameda and San José run between the Bay of San Francisco and the Central Pacific nearly all the way? A. It does. It runs between the Western Pacific and the branch. The Western Pacific goes up by Niles.

Q. So that you have competition by the Central Pacific Railroad and the bay? A. For that distance we have.

Q. Then, on the Santa Cruz side you have the other? A. Yes, sir.

Q. The fact that you have competition makes you exceedingly pleasant and agreeable with your patrons? A. I imagine that has considerable effect upon me.

Q. It goes a long way towards making your road popular? A. Yes, sir.

Senator Murphy—Is there any special contract system upon your road? A. Not that I know of.

Q. Do you oblige any shipper for whom you carry goods to carry all his freight by rail? A. No, sir.

Q. Do you make him agree not to buy from or sell to any merchant who does not ship by rail? A. No, sir.

Q. Do you have the right in any manner to examine the books of the shipper to see whether they are doing so? A. No, sir.

Q. Do you not know, as a railroad man, that there are such practices in the State of California? A. Not of my own knowledge. I have heard that it is so.

Q. Have you heard of any complaints upon that ground? A. I have heard them loud enough to threaten the road; I have heard a great many.

Q. Are you of the opinion that such contracts are against public policy? A. I don't know of any contracts.

Q. Do you know of the existence of such contracts in any way? A. I never saw one; I have heard people speak about them.

Q. Assuming that such contracts exist, do you not think that such contracts are detrimental to the people of the State of California, and to the shipping interests of the Pacific Coast? A. It is a serious question. If they do have such contracts with the people, and enforce them, they must have some good reason for it. Whether it is merely mercenary or not I am not prepared to say. If it is, it is all entirely wrong; if I knew of the reasons why they do make them, I would be willing to venture my opinion upon it. If there are good and justifiable reasons, I don't know of any.

Q. Assuming that those contracts exist, and that their effect is to drive away the shipping interests from the various portions of the State of California, do you not think they are against public policy? A. If it is wholly for mercenary purposes, it is wrong and against public policy, and ought to be suppressed; but they may have good reasons that I don't know anything about.

Q. Do you know of a certain suit brought by the firm of Richards & Harrison against the Central Pacific Railroad? A. I have heard something about it.

Q. Are you familiar with that suit in any way? A. I have not heard enough about it to give you an intelligent opinion about it.

Q. If these special contracts exist, do you not think that the law should correct them? A. If these contracts exist, and they are used for a mercenary purpose; that is, if they set themselves up as a power above the law to make and unmake individuals, I say it is all wrong, and if it is true, they ought not to be allowed to do it.

Senator Sullivan—Why should they desire to inspect the books of the shipper? A. That is beyond my knowledge.

Q. Why should they forbid one man to buy goods from another, simply because they came around Cape Horn? A. If it be true, I don't know why; I don't know of any right that they have over those people; I don't know that such a thing is so. It they did it with me I know what I would say.

Q. What would you say? A. I would tell them to go to the devil.

Q. Supposing you couldn't tell them to go to the devil? A. But I could.

Q. What would you do if there was no competition? A. If it was so that I could not cure it I would just endure it; I wouldn't stop to growl about it. In the course of my life I have found that it is not a good thing to buck my head against a stone wall.

Q. Would not you want the Legislature of the State of California to relieve you from that? A. Not if it hurt somebody else a great deal more. I believe in just laws. I said that I did not think there could be any perfect justice on this side of the river. It is impossible for laws to be made to cover everything.

Q. Then, you do not know of the existence of special contracts? A. No. If they do exist for mercenary purposes, or for tyrannical purposes, they ought to be severely punished.

Q. Do you think that forfeiture of the charter would be too severe? A. Yes, sir, I do; I am not so handy with that sort of an ax.

Q. Do you think that a penalty inflicted by the officers of the company would be correct? A. Yes, sir; but I would not take the property. .

Q. Would you consent to the company being fined a certain sum of money? A. Yes, I think that would prevent it.

SENATOR CROSS—What would probably be the effect of the passage of this law upon the volume of railroad business? A. I have stated that I thought it would be meddlesome and pernicious, and be of no possible use to anybody, but on the contrary, it may do a great deal of harm.

Q. Do you think it would increase the volume of business? A. I could not say so and have my answers consistent.

Q. Could you state approximately the number of persons employed in this State by railroad companies? A. Ten or twelve thousand.

SENATOR VROOMAN—Do you know of any person who has been ruined, or has suffered the ruination of his property, by the railroad business? A. No, sir.

Q. Have you, in your business in this State, had occasion to transport freight over roads other than your own? A. I have.

Q. Have you ever known a case where freight has not been transported in the order in which it has been received, as nearly as it could be done? A. No; I don't know of any such instance.

Q. How long have you been transporting freight over railroads? A. Since the commencement of our road. All of our rolling stock, and engines, and locomotives came over the Central Pacific Railroad.

Q. And during all that time you never saw the necessity of a law compelling the railroad company to forward freight in the order in which it is received? A. Not at all.

SENATOR CROSS—By whom is the forwarding of freight attended to upon your road? A. By a general freight and passenger agent.

Q. In the different localities, at the different stations, who has charge? A. The agent, subject to orders. On the Central Pacific Railroad I think that they have a station agent, who has charge of those matters.

Q. At each station there is a local agent? A. Yes, sir; except at the flag stations.

Q. Those local agents have the power to forward freight in the order in which it is received, or in a different order? A. Certainly, if they chose. If they choose to behave wrong, it is in their power, because the general freight agent might not be able to go there to see him more than once a month or longer.

SENATOR SPENCER—Do you require freight in advance? A. I

believe that there is some such instances, but I don't know that they enforce any such rule, unless it is shipped to a station where there is no agent to collect.

Q. Do you have a system of "rebates?" A. Of course we make rebates.

Q. Let me hear you define "rebate?" A. All that I understand it to mean is that a company are to pay back a certain amount of the regular charge. You understand that people in the railroad business will make mistakes the same as anybody else—and they may make an overcharge—or they may classify goods in the wrong class. If there is anything overcharged that is a rebate, and it is repaid.

Q. Suppose that a person were shipping goods over your road, and that you charged him twenty dollars, while the regular charge was ten—and then return him the ten dollars at a subsequent time? A. I would not knowingly overcharge him.

Q. Do you know of such a system being practiced in this State by the railroad company? A. No, sir. If it is so, it is wrong, and ought not to be allowed.

Q. You believe that everybody should be allowed to ship their goods at open rates? A. Certainly; every man ought to be charged alike for like services, and I don't think that any railroad company would do any other business.

Q. Supposing that a contract is made by the Central Pacific Railroad, or by any other company, to the effect that they shall ship all their goods by rail and none by water, and that they shall not deal with any person who does ship by water, or by any other mode of transportation; that if he did he would have his contract broken; do you think that would be right? A. I hardly know how to answer that question.

Q. Supposing that such a contract did exist; would it not have a tendency to lessen the shipping by water? A. Evidently.

SENATOR VROOMAN—If any such contract exists by which men shipping freight from New York to San Francisco, by rail, can send it cheaper than by water, does that lessen the shipment by water? A. Certainly it does, but not to the disadvantage of the shipper.

Q. Not to the disadvantage of the people of the State? A. No, sir.

Q. Is it possible to reduce the classification under the railroad system down to thirty or forty classes, or down to five or ten classes? A. I am not expert enough to answer the question as it ought to be. It is an intricate subject. There is enough to be said upon it to fill a book, that I am aware of. I know that the classifications are as various as the motives of men and the mutations of commerce. There is everything to be had in this world, and in this country, and they all come under some sort of classification, and some fixed rule. The true policy would be to make a just rule and apply it to all. There is no absolute wrong; on the contrary, there is an absolute necessity for classification. Supposing that you send furniture worth five hundred dollars to my people. Under the law of common carriers, we must deliver that as good as received. We should get more pay for carrying that. We have to use extra care in handling it.

We have to pack it so that it will not bruise. If we break a looking glass we are obliged to pay for it. So we would have to charge more for carrying a piano. That is classification. Classification, as a rule, is a factor in the business. If you bring me an animal worth fifty dollars, and I charge you five dollars for carrying it a certain distance, and you bring me one worth a thousand, and if I say, "This should be worth no more for carrying than the one that is worth fifty," you would say, "Why, this is my choice animal; I expect you to charge a certain amount more than you do for the other;" and so the rule of classification will run away into the intricate mutations of commerce.

Q. Then you would take into consideration the value of the article? A. Yes, sir; and there is another reason, and that is the character of the goods to be transported. Suppose that you carry explosives, powder or niter, or any other dangerous article which you have to handle with extra care and precaution, and where the risk is great, in consequence of the nature of the goods, to other merchandise, that is another branch of classification.

Q. Is it necessary to have such a classification that every article will have its separate classification, or is it possible to group them together in a few classifications. How many have you on your road? A. I do not know.

Q. Of course it would cost about the same, as far as freight is concerned, to carry a thoroughbred horse as it would to carry a mustang? A. Exactly.

Q. Do you consider the charge of one in excess of the other in the nature of insurance? A. Yes, sir. That is insurance, and there is no mode of getting at it without insurance, as I understand it, without classifying them.

SENATOR DEL VALLE—Do you know that they tried to enforce the rule that you could not recover more than one hundred dollars for the value of an animal that was hurt? A. I heard of it.

Q. If the question of insurance were eliminated from this, you could carry a thoroughbred as cheap as you could a mustang? A. I think so. If both are of the same weight I don't know that it could make any possible difference.

***

STATEMENT OF MR. DONAHUE.

SENATOR SULLIVAN—You have examined the Barry bill? Answer—Yes, sir.

Q. With what road are you connected? A. The San Francisco and North Pacific Coast Railroad.

Q. Through what counties does it run? A. Marin and Sonoma.

Q. What is its length? A. The length, including the side lines, is about one hundred miles.

Q. Was that road built by private capital, or by the assistance of subsidies? A. The road was built by my father out of his own personal means.

Q. How much was invested in that road? A. I cannot tell exactly how much, because the earnings of the road were put back into it; but the investments. including the earnings and expenses of the contemplated branch which we are now building, is about four millions.

Q. Isn't it a fact that you did receive a subsidy from Sonoma County? A. I don't know that only from hearsay. The matter was brought out at a hearing before the Railroad Commissioners, and I understood that a subsidy of two hundred and sixty thousand dollars had been granted; if so, it was at the time that the Central Pacific Railroad Company owned it.

Q. Who built the road? A. My father. When the subsidy was first granted it was granted to some other parties, and they built a road from Donahue's line, about thirty-four miles from San Francisco, almost to Santa Rosa. Then some other parties started an opposition route, and they were forced to sell out, and they sold to the Central Pacific Railroad Company, and they completed the road to Cloverdale, and when the Central Pacific Railroad Company, in 1876, were undergoing some difficulties with the Government, my father had their notes and bonds for a large sum of money, and he gave them their notes back and took the road. And since that time he built a branch twenty-two miles long to Petaluma, which laid idle four or five years, and another branch sixteen miles. We never got the interest on what it cost us.

Q. What do you transport over your road? A. General merchandise and farm products.

Q. You have steamers connected with the road? A. Yes, two steamers have been plying for the last two or three years and we will have another one in a few weeks.

Q. You have competition by water? A. We have for forty-two miles.

Q. State what you think about the Barry bill; whether you think it will be favorable or unfavorable to you? A. In its present form the effects of the bill will be to cause us to give up the operations of the road. The first section prevents classification, and without classification we would be unable to operate the road, because you can't carry a carload of silk at the same price as you can a carload of brick, and the remuneration ought to be different. They say that there are hundreds of classifications. That is a mistake. We have only four—one, two, three, four.

Q. Upon what does that classification depend? A. It depends upon the liability in case of damage to the goods, and in other cases to the quantity of the goods.

Q. Is not your classification based: First, upon the distance; second, the measurement; third, the bulk; and, fourth, the insurance? A. The three last, yes; but not the first.

Q. Why? A. Because distance does not come into the classification of goods. All goods of a certain class must be carried in the same manner as goods of the same class for all distances, of course upon a graduated scale.

Q. If you ship goods from Cloverdale to San Francisco, you charge more than from Santa Rosa to San Francisco? A. We do, but not per mile. The goods are not so much per ton per mile; and that is the objection in this bill. It says, in the first section, "except as hereinafter provided," and gives, on line seven of section two, the conditions. Now, our objection to that is that we have competition for forty-two miles by water; and secondly, that fixes a minimum rate on the road to that point. Our rates now are under the minimum rate between the two points, and we are not to-day paying expenses there; and if it were applied to the whole road we couldn't run it any longer. I asked the gentleman who introduced the bill if that was not its meaning, and he said it was. Then our present minimum rate per mile would be the maximum rate for the whole road.

Q. What would you suggest as an amendment to section one, to avoid this difficulty that you speak of? A. I would suggest that no discrimination to any person should be made at the same shipping points; that everybody in Santa Rosa and everybody in Healdsburg should have the same open rate, and Petaluma the same. We have no objection to that, because we always give an open rate; but this bill would forbid that, and force us to give a minimum rate. For instance, we made our road for the purpose of enabling shippers to ship wheat, and at one season of the year our cars would lie idle; and it is better to have them doing a little something, and so we have been trying to ship some wood; and we also do something in the way of sending up provisions for men that are chopping wood, and the freights and fares are helping us out in that way. If we were forced to put a minimum rate on our road, we should be compelled to make the same rate on the whole road.

Q. If the words you suggested were inserted, would that meet your objection to section one? A. I would insert "at the same point or under similar circumstances."

Q. What do you mean by that? A. If two or three wagons of freight came up to the station, we would not take one man's, and make the other wait to the last, but take them all as convenience offers, if they are at the same point, and forward them in the order in which they arrived. If they were delivered at a side track out of town, that would not be under similar circumstances, and we would have to make a different rate.

Q. Have you any special contract system upon your road? A. No, sir; we have open rates for every one.

Q. You have heard of the special contract system? A. Yes, sir.

Q. Do you know of any such contract upon your road at all? A. No, sir.

Q. You charge all men alike, whether they are friends or foes? A. Yes, sir. If an agent has a grudge against anybody, and he lets us know that he has not been properly treated, we will discharge the agent.

Q. Do you discriminate in any way against shipping. Do you bind any person by any contract not to ship by water? A. No—not even upon our competitive points where there is water. We are in fact carrying freight so low that we leave a car, and they put the goods in it themselves, and we take it back. I don't know whether they also ship by water. If they do we go to them and offer them inducements to ship with us. Sometimes they ship one time by water, and then come back to us.

Q. Have you any knowledge of the special contracts in force upon the Central Pacific Railroad? A. I never saw one or heard of one being in anybody's possession that I know of.

Q. Is there anything on page two that is not satisfactory to you (reading it), "without preference," etc.? A. There would be a half a dozen teams all coming up at once—one five minutes ahead of the other—and of two or three different kinds of goods; and we take them and put them in the cars, and then take the others next; but this would enable people to make trouble for us.

Q. You would amend that so that it would read, "without unreasonable delay or preference?" A. Yes, sir.

Q. Do you think that would avoid the difficulty in that portion of the section? A. I think it would, except in cases where a man had received a large lot of wheat, five thousand tons, and a small farmer comes in with ten or thirty tons. If the first one demands the cars, the other has got to go to the warehouse, and we will not be able to send it till the man who makes the large shipment gets through with his demand upon the road.

Q. How would you amend that? A. It would be difficult to word an amendment to that.

Q. How would you say? A. I would say, "with reasonable discrimination, or without unreasonable discrimination;" but the word "discrimination" carries so many points that I don't know.

Q. Would not that do away with the very object of this bill? A. No, sir.

Q. Is there anything in section two to which you have any objection? A. The words "or any part thereof" should be stricken out, because if you say that you shall not discriminate in favor of one person over another, that carries that. If you leave that in, it would make a maximum rate out of the present minimum rate, and it refers to that "as provided in section one hereof." The result of that clause would be that in about two years the large railroads would own all the other small ones, because they are the only owners who could operate them.

Q. Is there any other portion of section two that you specially object to besides that? A. I would like to go back to section one and say that this which applies to a "preference to one over another" would prevent all return rates, or picnic parties and commutation tickets, and make us carry our passengers at the minimum passenger rates.

Q. Is there anything in that section of the bill that you wish to make remarks about, or in sections three, four, five, and six? A. Section three, as I understand it, forces us to keep up track that we want to abandon. There is the Northern Pacific Coast Railroad. They have gone to an expense of two hundred thousand dollars to shorten their line and to avoid heavy grades, and by doing so they have been obliged to abandon about two miles of road. It is true that those two miles of road run over a pretty good property and that they are maintaining that road, but there are on it two very expensive high trestles. They want to avoid them for the safety of the people, because we all understand that if an accident occurred on one of those trestles it would cause a loss of life, and loss of value almost enough to forfeit the whole road. We would be obliged to operate that, under this section, the same as heretofore.

Q. Do you object to this: "All railroad corporations shall at all times maintain all their track and other structures in good and sufficient repair?" A. Self-interest makes us do it anyhow.

Q. Is there anything objectionable in that sentence? A. The whole sentence is objectionable.

Q. You heard the statement of Mr. Rideout, of the Marysville road? A. Yes, sir.

Q. Did you notice that he said that sentence was not objectionable, and that the only part he objected to was the latter portion? A. The last part of that says that they shall keep the "track." Now, you might construct a track two miles to get out some wood, and after it was out there might be nothing left there. Now, under this, you would have to maintain that track "for the purposes for which it" was constructed.

Q. Supposing there was an amendment put in there, "necessary for the operation of the road;" would that obviate your objections? A. Certainly, because we do that now.

Q. Do sections four, five, or six specially affect you (reading section four)? A. That don't affect us.

Q. Section five; does that affect you? A. Yes, sir. Our working company consists of three corporations, consolidated, and under that section the youngest or last constructed corporation would lose its charter at the expiration of the first constructed. It is some ten or twelve years ahead of it, and virtually says that the laws of the State cut off that twelve years.

Q. That is your construction of it. Have you been legally advised about it? A. No; I had construed it myself; and then I went to a lawyer and asked him if that wasn't so.

Q. And he agreed with you? A. Yes, sir.

Q. Is there any other section of this bill to which you have objection? A. Sections six and seven are a virtual forfeiture of the road for any small acts of discrimination that may be practiced. Section six makes it the same as a turnpike road. It ought to be omitted. Section seven makes the railroad companies liable for the act of any agent, no matter whether they are cognizant of his acts or not, and whether they authorize the acts or not they forfeit their road. But that can be amended by saying, "That if the Board of Directors of a railroad company ratify the discrimination or unjust act of its agent or agents, then they shall be guilty;" but not forfeiture.

Q. You would, then, object to forfeiture of a road for any purpose? A. Certainly.

Q. What would you suggest—imprisonment of the Directors, by confinement in the county jail for one hundred days, in case they are found guilty of any discrimination? A. I would suggest that they be convicted of a misdemeanor in the Courts, and adjudged the punishment that would be given them by the Court.

Q. You would insist on having some penalty? A. Certainly.

Q. Would this bill, with these amendments which you have suggested, benefit the people of the State of California? A. Leave out sections four, five, and six, and take out the forfeiture clause.

Q. No; we do not want to leave out any section at all? A. No; I don't think so.

Q. You do not think it would be a good bill? A. Not if you leave in sections four, five, and six.

Q. I understood you to say that section four did not affect you? A. It does not affect us, but it does the State.

Q. Section six you decidedly object to, on account of the forfeiture? A. Yes, sir. Our railroad is a private corporation, built by private capital, and the stock is not in the market. It has always been held by my father, and we have just finished nine miles of road, from which we are not going to get any special returns, and it will cost us $800,000. We are forced to do it, in order to save our property. When we are through, it will cost us in round numbers a million of dollars. What benefit do we get from that? None in the world. We have got to spend money to keep an outlet to the Bay of San Francisco, and from competitive roads trying to kill us. We want to take our road up to Eureka, and we have a survey already made, but we cannot do it alone; that is out of the question. If this section passes, we will not be able to get money for our bonds. This is a fine country, and it is settling up fast. There is no better country in the State. If we run our road up there, that whole portion of the State will be populated and be brought into close connection with us. My father has often expressed himself as sorry that he did not sell out when Villard tried to buy him.

Q. How much did Villard offer? A. I do not know.

Q. Have you read the Constitution in reference to the railroad corporations? A. I have read portions of it.

Q. You are satisfied with our Constitution, are you not? A. I will not answer that, because I have not studied it sufficiently to know that I am.

Q. Is it not a very good character of law? A. For the public, yes.

Q. And also for the common carrier. Don't you think so? A. I am not able to answer that.

Q. What does your road pay per mile net results? A. I do not know the figures.

Q. Is it a paying road? A. It would pay some profit, but is not paying a reasonable profit on the investment; we have never declared a dividend. Every dollar that we got we put right back into the road and back into the county. We have not taken a dollar outside; it has been paid to the people in the county where we have employed them.

Q. Have you been operating this road at a loss? A. Some portions of it.

Q. As a whole? A. No.

Q. In other words, you have made money out of it which you have placed in again in building it up? A. Yes, sir; but we have not had a reasonable compensation for the money invested, by any means.

Q. You say that you did not receive a subsidy from Sonoma County? A. Not a dollar.

Q. Do you not know as a fact that Sonoma County has been paying taxes upon those railroad bonds? A. I know it from hearsay; I never saw one of them, or the accounts, or books of record.

SENATOR KELLOGG—I understood you to say that the author of the bill informed you that the object of it was to allow railroads to charge the same price per ton per mile on long and short hauls? A. Yes, sir; I asked him yesterday afternoon in front of the Golden Eagle Hotel.

Q. Would not such a rule prevent the farmers in the interior from competing with those nearer the seaboard? A. Yes, sir; it would be impossible to compete.

SENATOR McCLURE—I ask you to look at the bill, and see whether this would meet your ideas: "All freight of the same class or kind shall be dispatched and forwarded as near as may be in the order in which it is received." Would that cover your objection? A. Supposing that you had freight for a half a dozen cars at each station and you haven't got them there. You may have three cars, and you distribute them as near as you can. Sometimes, then, it would happen that you would have to keep the stuff in the yard two or three weeks, or let it go by. We can't do that. If a man offers us freight we have got to take it. We have got to unload it, and under this law, in that case, we would have to furnish him storage as well as anybody else.

SENATOR SPENCER—Have you not a competing railroad connected with the water traffic? A. Yes, sir.

Q. What is the name of that? A. Our road is a competing road, connected with the water line.

Q. The water line runs up to Petaluma, and from there the road runs up to Duncan's Mills? A. That is the North Pacific Coast Railroad. That will be a competing line in about two weeks. It starts from Saucelito.

Q. It runs from San Rafael now? A. It runs through San Rafael.

Q. It runs from San Quentin? A. From Saucelito to Duncan's Mills—that is, about sixteen miles.

Q. How far is it from Petaluma to San Francisco? A. The way that we have been running, it is forty-two miles.

Q. What do you charge on that road? A. One dollar.

Q. You charge one dollar and a half for forty miles, and one dollar for fifteen? A. That is water competition.

Q. Where the water is in competition, you drop the rate? A. Yes, sir; but we have got competition.

Q. From Petaluma up you have it all your own way? A. No, sir: we have not.

Q. Up to Healdsburg, Cloverdale, and Guerneville? A. I refer you to the testimony before the Railroad Commission on that subject.

Q. That road is about fifteen miles long? A. Yes, sir.

Q. Did not the citizens of the county help to build that road. Did they not subscribe a large amount to build that road? A. Not to my knowledge. They did not subscribe a dollar. They may have given one or two rights of way.

Q. Do you mean additional to the stock?

SENATOR CROSS—Either? A. Not to my knowledge.

Q. Has your road a bonded indebtedness outside of the county? A. No, sir.

Q. Your father and yourself are the exclusive owners of that road? A. Yes, sir.

Q. Do you know the cost of running that road last year? A. No, sir; I do not.

Q. Do you not know as a matter of fact that it is one of the best paying roads in this State? A. No, sir; I do not.

Q. If you do not know the cost of running it, how do you know that it is not one of the best paying roads in the State? A. If I did know, and knew the cost of running the others, I might answer it.

Q. Where you have water competition do you make the same proportional charge? A. I could not tell you, I never figured it out.

Q. You say that you have but four classes on your road? A. There are four classes, I think; articles that are to be shipped in a car in bulk, such as live stock and wheat, and lumber, redwood, and stuff of that kind. Then we have one, two, three, and four—and A, B, C, and D.

Q. Do you know what class of articles go into class one? A. I do not know, because we have just changed class one, and we were figuring on making it class four, to help the people out in understanding the matter.

Q. A man that is not a railroad man cannot understand these matters anyway, can he? A. Not unless it is explained to him.

Q. He has to have a mathematical expert by him all the time, does he not? A. No, sir; all that he needs is to have one or two explanations made to arrive at them. Like a man taking up a railroad time-table, a stranger that don't know anything about it, if you explain it, he understands it. It don't take more than three or four days for an agent to understand our tariff.

Q. You only have about four or five different classes of freight? A. As far as my limited knowledge of the freight department goes, that is all.

Q. Do you discriminate between persons and places on your road? That is, do you permit one person to ship cheaper, on account of the greatness of his trade or transportations? A. No, sir; not to my knowledge.

Q. The branch of the road that was built to Guerneville was built out of the earnings of the road? A. My understanding is that the greatest portion of that was taken out of my father's private business, outside of the railroad.

Q. Isn't it a fact, that the extension was built out of the dividends of the main line? A. Yes, sir; what was made was applied to that, but we have taken also a great deal of money that was made outside from private capital.

Q. Had you not expended that on the building of the extension, you would have had a dividend on the road originally made? A. No, sir.

Q. Why not? A. Because we would have had a parallel road.

Q. You mean that you would have had competition? A. On one portion of the road, we have now. I think that they built it to sell to us, and we had to take it. We never would have constructed it ourselves. We have a narrow-gauge on that twenty-two miles that was built expressly to sell to us. They forced us to buy it. We run a steamer a third of the distance, and we have run as much as $8,000 short. Now we have to run the boat. The whole freights of that part of the line won't pay steamer expenses. They are a loss to us of $100,000.

SENATOR SULLIVAN—Why do you run the steamer? A. Because they built a road parallel to ours, and did it in such a way that it would affect us, and would hurt us, and take half our travel away from our road.

Q. Then you are running this steamer to break up competition? A. Not to break up competition, but to do a double business, and to carry the business up to the Donahue Landing. We deliver the freight there, and it is actually at a loss, but the property is there and we hope some day or another it will pay us.

SENATOR KELLOGG—And to accommodate the people? A. Yes, sir; and we hope, that in the next year or two, the country will develop sufficiently to pay us.

SENATOR SULLIVAN—I understood you to say that it was for the purpose of preventing the competition of a parallel line? A. We have bought it, and we have got to run it now. If we don't, somebody else will. That is one of the difficulties in railroading.

Q. Was your construction of this bill put upon it by your legal advisers? A. No, sir.

SENATOR VROOMAN—What facilities were offered for travel, on the first day of January, 1884, between Donahue's Landing and Petaluma? A. We were offering one fast train and the accommodation. We were running one train through and back. We were doubling the road.

Q. When this through line is completed, will you still continue running that train for passenger travel? A. No; we cannot do it.

Q. You will not be allowed to discontinue it under the last part of section one of this bill? A. No, sir; we are not.

Q. Have you compared the fares and freights over your line with other lines in this State? A. No, sir.

Q. So you do not know whether your fares and freights are lower than others? A. In some instances they are higher and in some they are lower.

Q. In what particular? A. I cannot say, I will have to refer you to the tariff to compare it with other roads; still, I know that to be the case.

Q. How is the general tariff on a commodity fixed? A. I can't say. I have not seen the original in years; it is not as it was originally fixed.

Q. Will it not fix itself after awhile? A. It fixes itself now.

Q. In other words, the freight is coming down every day? A. Yes, sir; in fact we are making a new tariff to-day in which we have reduced it fifteen to twenty per cent, all freighting above Healdsburg. Our agent has been working at it now for three months.

SENATOR WHITNEY—Is it not to the interest of the railroad companies to reduce freights as fast as they can? A. If by reducing they can increase the volume of their business, it is for their interest to do so. They never fail to increase it when they can, and that is a benefit to the producer.

Q. The interest of the railroad company and that of the people would be identical in that respect? A. If they do not work in harmony they will never get along. They are both losers by it; a liberal policy will make more money for the people, and make more money for all. That is what we are aiming at.

SENATOR SPENCER—You say that the interests of the people are the interests of the railroad, and you think they ought to be harmonious. Isn't it a fact that it turned out on the investigation at Santa Rosa, that the merchants shipped their goods by Healdsburg, and by so doing they were delivered both in and at San Francisco, at a comparatively small price, and that the railroads put it up higher and they had to pay it? A. That took place about a year ago, and not as you state it.

Q. Give us the statement of how it was done? A. I don't know the particulars of that, but Wells, Fargo & Co. began to play a little opposition on our road. It was unknown to us, and we found it out and told them, "Here, if you are going to carry perishable articles and express matter on this road, come out and act squarely and don't go behind us."

Q. When did you find it out? A. Through an investigation of a freight train not over a year ago. And to-day I believe Wells, Fargo & Co. carry the butter and eggs and poultry, and I think deliver them in the city, and it is to the advantage of both the shippers and buyers.

Q. Was not that developed at the time the railroad went up to Santa Rosa? A. No, sir; there was some discussion on that, but that was later. I forget what it was.

Q. A merchant was shipping eggs at fifty cents a box by Wells, Fargo & Company, for them to deliver in San Francisco? A. I don't know the figures, but to show you the absurdity of that, the railroad company had never at any time handled a box of eggs, or butter, or anything else, because they wanted them to have it.

Q. Didn't it cost them twice as much afterwards to ship it by Wells, Fargo & Company? A. No, sir; not to my knowledge. What you refer to took place over a year and a half ago.

SENATOR VROOMAN—Is there any stations between Donahue and Petaluma of any kind? A. No, sir; there is a junction, that is all.

Q. After you get your new line done will the people of Petaluma have as good accommodations as by the other way? A. They will from San Francisco, by way of San Rafael, by an hour and forty minutes.

Q. That would be much better for the people of Petaluma than the present route? A. It gives them nearly three hours and a half longer in the city.

Q. If the road from Donahue to Petaluma is discontinued, would any portion of the community suffer in any way, shape, manner, or form. Would it be any detriment to the community if you should take the other line up? A. No, it would not, because there is no travel between Petaluma and Donahue.

Q. If you were compelled to run the road the same as it was on the first day of January, eighteen hundred and eighty-four, you would be subjecting the company to very great expense without a corresponding benefit to the people? A. Certainly.

SENATOR SULLIVAN—Do you understand that "equal and similar facilities" mean what the Senator from Alameda says they do. Don't it mean that you shall run a passenger car of the same quality as you do now, of the same kind and size, and furnished in the same manner? A. It don't go, that particular part of it; but it could be so construed.

Q. It is the most extreme view? A. It is the view I take.

Q. "Equal and similar." You have a certain kind of car in which you send express matter, or furniture, or things of that kind? A. We have box and flat cars.

Q. Does not this mean that you shall not put matter, like furniture or something that would receive injury, on an open car, but that you shall put it in a box car? A. That is the custom of railroads. They make us do that anyhow.

Q. Does it not mean that you shall place articles in cars fitted to carry them? A. If it don't say "heretofore," it means so certainly. For we have always got box cars for certain classes of goods. We can't be compelled to do so hereafter, because we were doing so before.

SENATOR CROSS—You say that there are four classes of freight, and some sub-classes? A. We have got what we call general merchandise stuff, of four classifications, and then there are, I believe, three or four that run a little beyond the classification. We have A, B, C, and D, and one, two, three, and four, and then carload lots. Wheat, for instance, is very low, the farmers can't afford much. We have cars lying idle and can't afford it, so we cut the freight down a half a cent, that puts it into another class, may be, but the classification is made on all kinds of merchandise.

Q. What is the basis of charges on your roads? A. The classification: they have the name of nearly every kind of freight shipped or handled arranged alphabetically. A shipper comes down to the station, a shipping merchant, for instance, and the agent shows him the rates, class two, so much; he has perhaps a bundle of silk, class one, so much. It is to facilitate the charges. Of course, we have to have classification, because if you take an article of freight that there is no danger of breaking, you can handle it in half of the time that you could a sewing machine in putting it into the car.

Q. On the classification you base your rates of charges? A. Yes, sir.

Q. Suppose that you were compelled to charge one uniform price for all classes of freight, what would the result be upon the prices that would have to be charged upon the shipment of the main products of the country? A. We wouldn't ship any, unless we took our minimum as it is at present. It is a loss to us.

Q. Suppose that you were to make an average rate of all, what would be the price necessarily charged in shipping the great products of the country, such as wheat, or live stock? A. It would be an injury; you couldn't ship it at all.

Q. If they were to be shipped, what would be the prices that you would be compelled to charge? A. Close to the water they are at a minimum now. It would make very little difference there.

Q. Suppose that your road, instead of being a hundred miles in length, was some thousands of miles, reaching to all the principal cities, and carrying goods to all parts of the United States, do you think that any other classifications would be necessary than those which you have? A. The further we went the less per mile we would make on bulky articles.

Q. Do you think that any further classification would be necessary under those circumstances than that which you now have? A. I could not answer that, because I have not examined the classification lately. I naturally suppose so.

Q. By whom is the forwarding of freight attended to on the line at the different stations? A. By the agent in charge.

Q. He is the man who sees that freight is put into the cars and sent forward? A. Yes, sir.

Q. And it is in his hands, if it is in anybody's hands, to discriminate? A. Yes, sir; altogether. He could make us have our road forfeited at any time if he wanted to.

Q. Do you think it possible that you could always have at those stations agents upon whom you could rely in such matters? A. No, sir; we could not. Suppose that we authorized an agent to have charge of our station and of all our freight, and that he appoints a sub-agent. Another company could come to our authorized agent and with a little matter of a hundred or two hundred thousand dollars (and he would go to jail six months mighty quick for it), and his act could make us forfeit our road and we would not know anything about it. He could fix up the job at any time that he wanted to.

Q. Then the property, instead of vesting in the owners of the road, vests in the hands of each particular agent? A. Yes, sir; that clause should be: "If the Board of Directors sustain, or ratify, or authorize the station agent." Then the Directors would be responsible for the commission of these acts.

Q. Do you think that a personal penalty inflicted on the representative of the road would be sufficient? A. I think it would be more than sufficient. The penalty should be on the person who authorizes the act. If the representative of the road, then let it be him.

Q. Do you think that would be sufficient to compel a compliance with the law? A. I should think so.

Q. Do you think that the people who conduct the railroad or the company should be held responsible for the acts of the agents? A. That question would require a little explanation.

Q. If the railroad company could always say that it was the employés that disobeyed the law, then the railroad company would always avoid the penalty and the liability? A. Of course. If they could always avoid it, the agent could always keep on doing that. Now, if you would put the penalty very heavy for the first offense, mister agent wouldn't do it any more.

Q. If you put it entirely upon the agent, it would not be proper to say that the company were responsible at all, even if they did cause the agent to do it? A. That would be wrong. We want to see the agent punished.

Q. Wouldn't the company always say that they never authorized the agent to do it? A. Suppose they did say that; then we have got the agent to punish ; he did it, didn't he?

Q. Yes, sir. A. Well, punish him, then.

Q. You would not forfeit your charter for any act of his. Do you know that when an agent does any act out of malice, or out of the scope of his authority, that the company would not be responsible for his act in any sense of the word? A. No doubt, but under this bill he would be.

Q. If he is an engineer, and running on the road, and willfully and maliciously runs over a man, he is responsible? A. Yes, sir; according to law.

Q. Do you think the company would be responsible in that case for his act? A. In Court—I don't think any Court would deliberately hold him responsible.

Q. I have asked all these questions simply for the purpose of showing that they are not proper questions to be put.

Statement of Mr. W. N. Hawley.

Senator McClure—What is your business? Answer—The hardware and mercantile.

Q. Where do you conduct your business? A. On Market Street, San Francisco, under the firm name of Hawley Brothers.

Q. How long have you been engaged as importers of hardware? A. Nearly thirty years.

Q. How do you import your goods? A. At the present time, entirely by rail.

Q. How long have you been importing your goods by rail? A. I think about two years; that is, consecutively. I dropped out two years, and then for four years I carried entirely by rail, making about six years altogether.

Q. To what extent do you import goods—great or small? A. Our freight bills amount to $200,000 a year.

Q. You are acquainted with a great many of the merchants of San Francisco? A. Yes, sir.

Q. You import goods by the Central Pacific Railroad Company? A. Yes, sir.

Q. Are you acquainted with the special contract system? A. Somewhat so.

Q. Do you import your goods under a special contract? A. So I understand.

Q. Will you please state to this committee anything that you know about the special contract system, and as to whether you have any objection to it, and the effect which it has upon the business community of San Francisco? A. At the present time we have only a verbal contract. It is a verbal continuation of the old contract, with some few modifications. We have been running under it and the modifications for about six years. In the first place, Mr. Stubbs made the first special contract with myself for all our agricultural goods about eight years since. We tried it for one year, and after that we, without any notice to the railroad company, abandoned it, and shipped round Cape Horn. After one year shipping round Cape Horn, they made a proposition to us to get our freight back. We told them that we would carefully consider it, and tell them what we would do. When Mr. Stubbs came to us, he asked us, "What can you afford to pay the company to ship all your goods overland?" We named a certain figure, and told him that we had made careful estimates, and told him what we thought we ought to pay. We had put a man on it, and he was three months working it up, and we presented it to him with every article brought to the State for six months, and showed him the average of all that business, and what it cost by water, and the cost of insurance on the goods, and what the cost was of what we had brought by rail for six months.

Q. Who is Mr. Stubbs? A. The General Traffic Manager of the Central Pacific Railroad Company.

Q. At the time you were making these estimates there were but three routes—the overland, by the Panama, and round Cape Horn—and in making your estimates, you took into consideration the matter of bringing freight by either of those routes, and the question of insurance and of delay? A. Yes, sir; and we also estimated by the freight bills for six months overland, and got at the total amount of our freight. We then took a special contract tariff and figured the same classes of goods under the tariff, and showed him that if we continued the business of shipping overland under the special contract for a year we would have a loss of sixty-seven thousand dollars, and we told him very plainly that we would not make a special contract unless he reduced the rates to us.

Q. Were the rates subsequently reduced? A. Not that year; no, sir. He told us that our figures were incorrect; that they were doctored for the purpose of getting lower rates of freight. We submitted the matter, and told him he might go on and prove whether we had made an error. He tried them for about three weeks, and then said he had sent them to the General Freight Agent of the Union Pacific Railroad. We told him at that time that our business being with the agricultural community, we had to have contracts running at certain seasons of the year. We were not like any other party, making a contract every month, nor could we make a contract from January to January. Our contracts commenced in July or August, and they must commence then, or we would make no contract at all, and I told him that on the first day of July we must know what he would charge. He said he would not accept it in the first place. He thought the matter over, and sent the figures on to Mr. Vining, who at that time had the control of the matter. Vining would not accept of it. He told me that he did not have a positive answer, but that he wanted to investigate it. I told him if we didn't have a positive answer on the first of July I would make a contract to ship around the Horn. We did make a positive contract to ship that way. He came to us two or three days after that to negotiate and we told him that we could not negotiate. We had telegraphed to New York and it was closed; that we had entered into a negotiation for the year, but the next year, when the time came round, we would take up negotiations again. The result was, that we entered into a new contract on the first of September to the first of last September, with the privilege, on the first day of July, of shipping around the Horn or to state our case on sixty days' notice.

Q. From year to year, you had your goods overland? A. That was the year which terminated last September. We had our goods overland, and that continued under a verbal contract, and we have been shipping overland.

Q. Was the matter satisfactory to you? A. We would not have entered into a contract unless it was entirely satisfactory.

Q. Was there any compulsion at all? A. Not at all; we told him we would give certain figures, and when we got the figures, that was satisfactory, and when we bound ourselves to agree to it, we would naturally stand by the contract.

Q. If it were for your interest, could you have gone on shipping around the Horn? A. Certainly, our contract gives us the privilege of going around the Horn, and whenever we see fit to do so, we shall certainly go around the Horn with our freight. There is no compulsion of any kind on one side or the other. It is a matter of dollars and cents to us.

Q. I presume you have talked with other merchants, then? A. Yes, sir.

Q. Do you know of any special complaints as to the system from the merchants of San Francisco? A. I do not, sir. There are complaints, but no substantial complaint. There is always some growling done; and the reason is, on the part of a good many of them, that they have had contracts with the Central Pacific Railroad Company, and have violated them and had their contracts withdrawn, and now they are howling against the railroad company and the contract system.

Q. Do you regard these contracts as a detriment to the commercial and business community of San Francisco? A. I do not. I claim that since these special contracts are allowed to be made, it would be a detriment to the interests of San Francisco, and a very great detriment to the interests of the Central Pacific Railroad Company, and would take 'from them, perhaps, twenty million dollars' worth of freight should they be stopped.

Q. Do you think any substantial gain would be secured to the people of the State if they were done away with? A. It is a question of dollars and cents. We want to get our goods here at the lowest possible rates. We can't compete with other merchants unless we do, and when the company come to us and give us contracts, which we think are better, we accept of them; and when we do, we try to live up to them.

SENATOR DEL VALLE—Your business is in the hardware line and agricultural implements? A. Yes, sir.

Q. You have stated what the bulk of your freight cost you at a certain time of the year? A. Not the bulk of our freight. As to that, I may say that the bulk of our freight comes from March until June; that is, our agricultural implements, and we have to have them right at that time. The other classes of goods we can manage to ship round the Horn, just as well as to make a contract every month in the year; but on the agricultural implements, we want to know what we need, and ship them from January to December, around the Horn, and get them here at a prior time. We would be tied up if we started them after January first, and have to get them over the roads.

Q. It is necessary to keep that kind of implements in stock, is it? A. Sometimes it is necessary. I think I have telegraphed fifty dispatches, within the last three months, for agricultural goods.

Q. Now, you are necessarily required to keep them? A. Yes, sir; as I said before, we can start our agricultural goods in September or November, and get them here in time, around the Horn.

Q. Under the special contract with the company, do you have the privilege of bringing goods around the Horn if you desire? A. No, sir; our contract says all our freight shall go over the road.

Q. Is it the same in the case of other merchants in San Francisco; take, for instance, Murphy, Grant & Co.? A. I couldn't say; the most of their freight comes in the Spring of the year. I suppose they ship more in March and April than any other months, and perhaps in September.

Q. From the nature of the business, is it not a fact that they ship freight at all times, and that the goods come at no certain time? A. They ship every month in the year. Our freight bills will average from fifteen to twenty-five thousand dollars every month in the year.

Q. Do they not, on account of business principles, have to bring their freight through as quickly as possible? A. No, sir; sometimes they take six months to bring them here.

Q. For houses that deal in particular articles, is it not necessary for them to bring them from New York as quick as they can? A. I think so. I am not familiar with other classes of business. When they do, I suppose they pay open tariff.

Q. Isn't it a fact, that under those circumstances, not having the facility to ship at certain times of the year when their goods are most needed, they are obliged to have a special contract with the railroad company? A. No, sir; I don't think it is necessary on the part of any merchant in San Francisco to have a special contract with the railroad company. I am not so familiar with drygoods or groceries as I am with hardware.

Q. In your business, you can wait six months for the goods? A. Yes, sir.

Q. Therefore, you can bring them around Cape Horn without any trouble or detriment to your business? A. Yes, sir; there are a great many classes of goods that are needed to get here, that we get overland, within thirty days. If we were out of a contract, we should probably get by railroad, under open rates, from fifteen to thirty thousand dollars per year.

Q. But the bulk of your business could go around Cape Horn, without detriment to yourself? A. We could bring everything around the Horn, but we would have to contract six months in advance.

Q. Will you please state the nature of that special contract? A. The nature of the contract is, that we shall ship every pound of our goods that we receive or sell on this coast overland that comes from the United States. From Europe, we can ship by steamer to Panama, or around Cape Horn, but everything that we purchase by eastern lines, we are to ship by rail.

Q. Is there anything else in the contract? A. There are a dozen or more clauses in it.

Q. State any other? A. Another clause is, that we shall not purchase any goods except from those that are brought by rail to San Francisco. That is (something to that effect), I do not pretend to give you the exact language, but it amounts to this: you can't go into the San Francisco market and purchase any goods of any kind unless they come by rail, in any large amount.

Q. Suppose you did purchase differently from the stipulations of the contract, what is the effect of it? A. It violates it. They annul the contract.

Q. Who is the judge as to whether it should be annulled? A. The railroad company naturally would be, if they knew it.

Q. Suppose there is a difference of opinion between the railroad company and the shipper in regard to whether it has been violated, then who judges of the violation? A. The railroad company, and that is one of the troubles. It gives the interior merchants more latitude and San Francisco very little in that respect.

Q. Suppose you sign a contract with the railroad company and they say: "Mr. Hawley, you have violated your contract." You reply that in your opinion you are justifiable—you have a reason that may be sufficient—who judges between the railroad company and the shipper? A. They shut right down on you, and claim that you have violated the contract, and there is always a great many overcharges (it can't be helped) upon the goods. They refund the money to us. They claimed that we had violated the contract, and they locked up some twenty-five or thirty thousand dollars for several months, till we cleared the matter up.

Q. That was robbery, was it not? A. Yes, sir; but we did not object.

Q. Suppose there is a difference, then, between a shipper and a railroad company, and the shipper tells them that he is justified in the violation, who is the judge whether he is right or otherwise? The company there is the absolute judge as to whether the contract has been violated, is it not? A. No; we can go right into the Courts and say, " Here, they are keeping back some of my money." They are not the ultimate judge, as——

Q. The contract is held void by them? A. That is another matter. I can keep right on shipping my goods, and they can charge the open tariff, and not refund my money until I prove that I am right. If they should hold back my contract, and say I had violated it, and I can prove that, I might have shipped around the Horn, and fight it out with them. I think there are two sides to the question.

Q. You think it is for the best interests of the State that these special contracts shall exist? A. Yes, sir.

Q. Do you believe that a contract which stipulates that the person who holds it shall not deal in merchandise with any person except it has been brought overland by rail by such person, is according to the best policy? A. It can't be otherwise. They have to have that in. They don't hold to it with the interior merchants; they give them greater latitude. If they will give me the privilege of sorting up in San Francisco—— For instance, I want forty or fifty thousand kegs of nails. Now, I can send nails around Cape Horn, including freight and insurance, at forty cents a keg. We pay seventy, or eighty, or ninety, under our contract. Now, if they will give me the privilege of buying those nails in San Francisco, I can save $20,000 a year. If they don't draw the line pretty straight, I can go and buy a thousand kegs from one merchant one month, and more from others that ship round the Horn; and if I did, I might divide the contract and give them a portion. I could arrange it with the parties from whom I buy to say, " You send them out to Gilman," and in that way I could avoid my contract and pay him a small commission. But they draw it strong and say, " You shall purchase all." I say, " What do you mean by 'all?'" "I mean the great bulk of your freight." I am at liberty to buy a great many things to sort up with, but they want to stop you from getting goods around Cape Horn.

Q. Do you know any instance where the company has annulled the contract, upon the ground that the person has sold goods to a party who was not a contractor? A. No; they have no right to. If I have a contract, I may sell to whom I please.

Q. Suppose you bought goods, when under the contract, from a person who has no contract. Do you apprehend that your contract would be annulled for that reason? A. I think so. There have been a great many annulled. I know of many instances where men have violated contracts, because men holding them have bought goods that were shipped around the Horn. They have taken contracts in good faith and then bought goods shipped around the Horn, and it has been found out time and time again; and by doing that they injure men who stand up to their contract.

Q. You know there are cases where men, not under a contract, use the name of a contractor in getting goods? A. I think so. I know of a house that told me they have a great many goods out under contract, because they could get men to stretch their consciences and allow them to do it.

Q. Is there any clause in the contract which says that the books of the shipper may be examined by the company in case of the supposed violation? A. Not that I am aware of.

Q. Do you think that it is discrimination in favor of persons? A. It certainly is.

Q. Is it not discrimination against the shipping interests of the country? A. Not to any great extent; it is slightly so. It is also an injury to the farmer, to some extent, but the farmer injures himself when he ships his wheat by rail to New Orleans and from there by ship. That is detrimental to the shipping interests around Cape Horn.

SENATOR McCLURE—Your contract does not apply to sorting up or to filling a temporary order? A. No, sir; but if we did so for the purpose of filling up by purchasing goods shipped around the Horn, it would violate the contract. I could save on some goods from two and a half to five per cent by doing so.

Q. You said that if it was to your interest you could ship again around the Horn when your contract expires? A. Yes, sir.

Q. You are not forced to take it? A. We were running a contract for four years and then broke off and sent around the Horn; I may do so again on the first of July. It is a matter of figuring whether I do or not—whichever is the cheapest.

Q. Do you understand that merchants are coerced into these contracts? A. Not at all; it is at their option to take them or not, and whether it is to their interest.

Q. It would make a great difference to the railroad company? A. Yes, sir.

Q. Then it is in the interest of both the railroad company and the merchants? A. Yes, sir.

Q. You deal a great deal with farmers? A. Yes, sir. I believe that under the special contract system we are in a position to benefit the farmers at times more than if we were shipping around the Horn, because we are keeping on hand now a constant supply of agricultural implements, and this season the demand is going to be very large—twice what it was last year. The demand is great, and we could not ship it without advancing the price of goods. This season we would have to ship twice as much as before, and we cannot tell in advance in time to ship around the Horn.

Q. This does not affect goods that may be shipped from Europe? A. No, sir.

Q. The principal ships that come take wheat to Europe? A. The ships that come here are about nine tenths of them from the European markets and about one tenth from ours.

SENATOR DEL VALLE—Isn't the reason of that the fact that there is no freight for them on account of this special system? A. No; I made a careful estimate of it two or three years ago, and found that the New York, Boston, and Philadelphia ships, which brought us merchandise, was about one tenth of the whole; and as for grain, for two or three merchants to go in and make a contract, would not affect the rate on grain—not half as much injury to the shipping around the Horn as the shipping of grain to New Orleans.

Q. In your line of goods, how many classifications are there? A. Six or eight—one, two, three, four—A, B, C, D. I think that every article is classified under one of those heads.

Q. Does that classification take in all classes of goods in the State, or is there any other division? A. A, B, C, and D, takes in all the heavy class of goods of this State.

Q. You deal entirely in hardware? A. And agricultural goods for farmers.

Q. Don't you think the fact that you deal in that class of goods causes the railroad company to be more liberal with you because you can ship them around by water just as well? A. I have no different tariff than Huntington, Hopkins & Co., and other large houses. Every tariff is the same on the same line of goods.

Q. You mean people who deal in that class of goods? A. I think that every merchant in San Francisco, who deals in agricultural goods, gets exactly the same tariff under the special contract.

Q. Has the firm of Baker & Hamilton a contract? A. The same as ours.

Q. Wasn't Baker & Hamilton compelled to get one in order to compete with you? A. No, sir. It is a question to-day. They think they are making less money than they would by shipping around the Horn.

Q. Then they are conducting business at a loss? A. No, sir; I don't think that they are, but they have stated, time and again, that they are losing by it. Now, it is just the same way in other business in San Francisco. One of the largest houses has a contract, but it is not a question of freight alone; it is sorting goods and getting them here in time, and the carrying of a large amount of stock and a great many benefits that we derive under the special contract.

Q. Isn't it a fact, that you get out of a certain class of goods, and that it would take too long a time to get them here by water? A. We keep a man doing nothing else but buying goods for our house in the San Francisco market, and so do Huntington, Hopkins & Company.

SENATOR SULLIVAN—And, therefore, it is a matter of necessity to ship by rail? A. It is a matter of dollars and cents, and that is the only thing that we take into consideration; only we pay more by rail than by water. We probably could get goods here for one hundred thousand dollars that will cost us one hundred and five thousand dollars to get them here by rail.

Q. It frequently occurs that you have to send goods across the continent when you get out of them? A. We always get them, contract or no contract, ever since the railroad was opened.

Q. Suppose you were dealing in San Francisco, and that you got out of a certain line of reapers and mowers, you couldn't go to the railroad and get them sent at the same rate as if you had a special contract? A. No, sir.

Q. Neither could you go, if you had a contract, and buy from a man that did not have one, but shipped around the Horn? A. We could not.

Q. And you say that is not malicious? A. I do.

Q. Isn't it a matter of fact that it discriminates against the shipping interests of the State? A. Slightly so; but not to any great extent. Every ship stopped from coming here would bring some freight, and would get some return freight, but if we had twice as many ships in San Francisco to-day, freights would naturally come down.

Q. Assuming that the tendency of these contracts is to drive the shipping from the water, then it is prohibiting the shipping interests and depriving us of its advantages, is it not? A. Certainly it does; but on the same principle, if the railroad company goes to the farmer and tells him, " Your freight by water costs you forty shillings, I will take it to Liverpool for thirty-eight shillings," there is not a farmer in the State but what will ship by rail. And they will ship by rail to New Orleans, and by steamer from there to Liverpool. They would not stop to consider how it was going to affect other shipping interests. They would consider their profits.

Q. You think that the interests of the country would be advanced, and that it would be cheaper and better for them? A. Yes, sir.

Q. If you could sell the farmers mowers at twenty dollars apiece instead of fifty dollars apiece, do you think that would benefit them? A. Certainly it would.

Q. And anything that has a tendency to raise freights, damages the interests of this State? A. It does, sir.

Q. In making up a bill of goods, if only a few goods are needed to fill an order, you can go out and fill it by buying from a person who ships around the Horn? A. Yes, sir.

Q. Does your contract make that exception or is it a mere personal indulgence? A. It is.

Q. Then they can discriminate in favor of a man that they like, and against a man that they do not like? A. Yes, sir; but they have got to lay down some general rule.

Q. The rule is the measure of the contract, is it not? A. If you agree to a contract, you agree not to buy goods that are shipped around the Horn, and it is at their election to stop you if you violate the contract.

Q. If you go out and buy goods at all, technically you violate the contract? A. Yes; but it is understood verbally with the railroad company that we can buy to fill up any small order that we desire. Now, the merchants in the interior, at Marysville and Stockton, etc., have five times as many privileges as the merchants of San Francisco have.

Q. Then, they have one interpretation for the merchants in the interior, and another for the merchants of San Francisco? A. Yes, sir.

Q. What do you think of that? A. I call it a "necessity."

Q. That is a new word for it? A. I will explain it. They desired to make arrangements with the larger San Francisco firms, and, as I told you, they made arrangements with Hawley Brothers for one year to test this matter, and after that, they took in nearly every one of the large wholesale firms of San Francisco. They desired to have a special contract too. After that, they took in the interior merchants. They said: "I hear you have a special contract?" "Yes." "We want the same," and the railroad company said, "We will give you the special contract." Now, a house in Marysville can get the contract the same as we can. They agree that all the goods they import shall come by rail, and also that they will not buy any goods to any extent from merchants who ship goods around the Horn. When they are out of goods at Sacramento, or Marysville, or Stockton, perhaps they do not want but one or two articles. The merchant comes down here and he says, "Under the special contract I cannot buy from you men that ship round the Horn, but I want the goods, and I cannot get them from any other house in San Francisco; I can't get them in the East; I must have them to supply my customers at once; what am I to do; I want a certain kind of headers." Now, the railroad company say, "We do not make this contract to injure your business; we make it to benefit you. We will give you the privilege of buying them, even though they came round the Horn." They buy of Baker & Hamilton, or of other men who have shipped around the Horn; but I do not have that privilege.

Q. Do you know whether there is any difference between the Marysville rate and the city rate? A. I am told that there is.

Q. In favor of which one? A. I have never seen a contract with an interior merchant, and I only get it by hearsay; but I am told so positively that it is in favor of the San Francisco merchants.

Q. Do you pay a certain amount of freight and at the end of a month or such a matter have a portion of it returned to you? A. I do.

Q. How much do you pay in that way? A. Our freights are two hundred thousand dollars a year. We pay them as they come, and I think there is on an average from ten to twenty per cent of the money that we pay locked up by the railroad company for a short time. Well, it is getting down to about a week now, but it used to be sometimes two months; sometimes, for instance, we would get a shipment of agricultural goods over the road and it would get tied up and they could not adjust it until they could have time to find out where the trouble was, and where the overcharge had been made, and who was to forfeit the shipping. There is a bill made out in the San Francisco office at the rate of the contract, and that includes all contracts made by them with other companies east of the Missouri River.

Q. They adjust the mistakes? A. They adjust the overcharges made against us by the parties in the East. They do not know exactly the terms upon which these parties are shipping the goods, and sometimes they have to pay the rates of those who do not enter into the pool.

Q. What is the average freight on a carload of goods overland? A. The cost of the freight on a carload of goods is from five hundred dollars to eight hundred dollars. We have had ten thousand dollars of overcharges at one time awaiting adjustment.

Q. You pay all that money before you receive the goods? A. We pay our freight bills before the goods leave the depot.

Q. Upon what basis do you pay? A. We pay the freight bill just as it is made out, no matter what it is. In fact we do not pay the freight bills. The arrangement is to assist the merchants of San Francisco. They authorize a man to take the goods and pay the freight bills, and he gives his own check, and when he brings them to us we pay him. That is the way business is done in San Francisco. We are obliged to pay it, even if it were overcharged three times.

Q. In case of a difference between the consignee and the shipper, it is the invariable rule that any overcharge is to be paid first and adjusted afterwards? A. Yes, sir; we always pay the freight bill just as it is presented to us, no matter what the overcharge may be.

Q. Supposing that there is any dispute about the loss of any goods, suppose that a part of the goods do not come, are you obliged to pay for the whole? A. No, sir; we pay freight only on those received.

Q. There is no rule requiring the whole of the money to be paid for the whole amount of goods shipped? A. There is no rule. For instance, it may be that I ship a carload of wheels, and I am charged for the full carload, but it says on the bill, "Twenty wheels to follow;" I pay for the full carload, and the twenty wheels came in may be in a week or two afterwards.

Q. Suppose that there are five wheels gone, do you pay for the whole and correct the matter afterwards? A. Certainly they do; you frequently have five cases and only four would come in. You pay freight on the five, because you can't very well determine what freight is on the four; but it is very seldom that a case is lost—it is not one time in five hundred.

Q. Supposing that the open rates are ten dollars and the special contract is five, do I understand you that the merchant pays the ten dollars, and that the adjustment is made to give him the five dollars difference? A. No, sir.

Q. Has there been any rebate of that character? A. Not that I know of. They do not make the freights to us in that way.

Q. I suppose you have studied this freight question to some extent? A. I have endeavored to do so.

Q. Did you ever calculate how much money the Central Pacific Railroad Company had tied up on your advances? A. No, sir. It would be very easily calculated. If there was $10,000 to us, multiply it by the number of merchants.

Q. Do you not think that that is harsh on the merchants? A. Yes; it seems to be. But they say it is necessary; that they have good reasons for it.

Q. Do you know whether any of that money is kept back for fear that the merchants will violate their contract? A. I never supposed it to be. If they understand that he had, they would say to him, "I understand that you have violated your contract, and we will not pay you any rebate till this is adjusted." They may have done that with other merchants; I can't say. In our case, I know.

Q. Do you know of many firms in this State that have had the temerity to fight with the Central Pacific Railroad Company, concerning the compliance with this special contract? A. I don't know of a single firm but what have had some little grievances toward the railroad company. I think that Baker & Hamilton had a matter at one time, and that it was never satisfactorily fixed up.

Q. You have heard of the suit which the firm of Richards & Harrison have with the Central Pacific Railroad Company? A. No, sir. Well, I saw something in the paper about it, but I couldn't tell the origin of it. I know that they have several claims against the railroad company, upon several different occasions; whether they have started suits or not, I don't know.

Q. Do you not, as a merchant, dealing in agricultural goods, depend largely upon the country trade? A. I do, almost altogether.

Q. What is the effect, as far as country trade is concerned, upon the man who has no contract with the Central Pacific Railroad Company? A. If he is a man that is doing a small retail business it has very little effect, because he is supposed to buy all those goods in San Francisco; but the railroad men go to men at different points, and say to them, "You may have a special contract," and that is the fact at a good many places in the interior. Then they come to us. They buy a carload, and they can't dispose of them, then they come to us and ask us to carry them.

Q. Do not the merchants discriminate in favor of the man who has a special contract as against the man who has not, in San Francisco, in regard to the country trade? A. No, sir.

Q. There is no discrimination at all? A. No, sir.

Q. Isn't it a fact, that the Central Pacific Railroad Company have discriminated against the merchants who received their freight by water, in reference to the country trade? A. Not that I am aware of; I never heard of it.

Q. You have never known of any such discrimination being practiced? A. No, sir. We shipped around the Horn for two years, and we never knew that they discriminated against us.

Q. When a farmer has ordered goods, haven't they forwarded other goods in preference to those that were shipped around the Horn? A. I never have known them to fail to forward our goods as soon as any other freight.

Q. Assuming that the Central Pacific Railroad Company will not carry the goods at all of a firm that ships by water, do you not think that that would have an injurious effect upon the people of the State? A. It would.

Q. If that is the effect of the special contract, do you not think that it would be contrary to the best public policy? A. If it had that effect, certainly.

Q. I understood you to say that when Mr. Stubbs came to you, that you showed him that you had lost $60,000 by carrying your goods under special contract for that year. Is that correct? A. Not exactly. I told you that after we had been shipping a year that we stopped and went around the Horn, and that he came to us and asked us to make a new contract. He says to us, "We want to carry all your goods." I said to him, "Provided you give us satisfactory rates." He said, "What terms do you want?" Then we figured up and showed him that we had followed out the provisions of the contract and paid the prices then exacted; that we had lost on last year's goods $67,000; and upon that showing he offered a reduction of the special contract, which at that time was in force.

Q. What reason did he assign; you stated that he consulted with the Union Pacific Railroad Company? A. At first he said that my figures lied, but that he would see the railroad company and take three weeks to examine them; but he gradually yielded, and we also gave up a little, and made the contract.

Q. Do I understand you that the Central Pacific Railroad Company, as a special favor to Mr. Stubbs, reduced these rates? A. No, sir, not as a special favor to our firm at all; he was negotiating with another firm, and whilst he was negotiating with them we took it up, and Baker & Hamilton and other firms, and we got the rates satisfactory; but he showed us no favor more than to any other house in San Francisco, for he said, "If I make this contract with you, I shall have to make it with all;" and it takes in all the wholesale merchants.

Q. Do the smaller merchants, and those who do more of a retail business, have the same rates that you get? A. I do not understand that they have; I have never seen their contract; I don't believe that they do.

Q. They discriminate in your favor as against the retail dealers? A. So I understand it.

SENATOR McCLURE—Do I understand you to say that during the two years that you shipped round the Horn that they did not discriminate against you as to open rates? A. No, sir; they did not discriminate against us as to open rates.

Q. You had the same as others? A. Yes, sir.

Q. You are well acquainted with the merchants of San Francisco? A. Yes, sir.

Q. Do you know of anything arising out of the relationship between the merchants of San Francisco and the Central Pacific Railroad Company, with reference to this special contract system, that would cause any merchant of San Francisco to hesitate to make a truthful statement with reference to the special contract system? A. I know of no reason why a merchant should not come here and tell the truth, with regard to the special contract system, except one.

Q. State that? A. There seems to be an impression through the State that the merchants of San Francisco are getting special rates, under this special contract system, over and above the interior, and that their trade with the interior merchants and the farming community will be affected.

Q. You are honest in your statement, and feel no intimidation in making it? A. Not at all.

Q. As far as you are individually concerned, you know of no reason why everything should not be stated with reference to the system? A. No; if I understand your bill here, it gives discrimination to the San Francisco merchants, in their favor. Why should they not come here and tell you; if it is in their favor, they should favor that bill with slight modifications.

Q. Then you think if the bill should be passed that it would be in favor of the San Francisco merchants, and against the interior? A. The first two or three sections of this bill, with slight modifications, I would favor it.

Q. How is it with reference to discrimination between persons?
A. The bill states, as I understand it, that there shall be discrimination.

SENATOR SULLIVAN—I understood you to state that there was a special contract between you and the Central Pacific Railroad Company, and that afterwards, at the end of the year, you commenced shipping by water? A. Yes, sir.

Q. And that afterwards there was another arrangement made. Did you make mutual concessions in making that arrangement? A. Yes, sir.

Q. Until you arrived at the basis? A. Yes, sir.

Q. In that arrangement other large shippers in that line of business were consulted, were they not? A. Nearly every one of them. Yes, sir; they were all consulted, small and large, and asked a reduction, and it was fixed up.

Q. Has the tendency been to lower or raise the former price of goods since you entered into the system? A. There is a difference among merchants as to that. I may claim that under the special contract I can sell my goods cheaper than I could without. Another merchant may figure that the goods cost a trifle more and that therefore they ought to charge higher. I have felt that under the special contract I had an advantage in some respects over merchants that shipped around the Horn, and that I could compete with them successfully and sell the goods lower, and that I have made money by it in some years.

Q. You are familiar with the shipping interests of San Francisco? A. Somewhat so.

Q. Supposing that all of the merchants of this coast shipped their goods by rail, what would be the percentage of shipping that would be lost to this State? A. I couldn't tell you the percentage, but it is very easy to ascertain. If you take the Journal of Commerce you will find, say sixty ships, with general merchandise. If the goods were shipped around the Horn those would not come to San Francisco. I looked over the matter two years ago and I found that about one tenth of all the ships coming here were loaded with freight for San Francisco (general merchandise) not including ships that came from Europe. There are a great many ships that bring merchandise from Europe, but any one under a special contract can ship goods upon them.

Q. Is the carrying done principally by foreign ships? A. Four fifths of it.

Q. In loading a foreign ship for San Francisco, say from Liverpool, is it not customary for them to touch at some point on the Atlantic for a portion of their load? A. I never have known them to do so.

SENATOR WHITNEY—I understand you to state that you thought this bill, with some slight modifications, would be a good bill for San Francisco, for the reason that it recognizes and provides for discrimination? A. Yes, sir.

Q. Will you explain to the committee what you meant by that? A. It says that there shall be no discrimination, but on line ten of the first page, it says, "except as hereinafter provided." Now, if you will give us plenty of exceptions, we shall certainly be satisfied. Now, what are the exceptions? On page second of this bill, at line fourteen, "different rates may be made for express matter, for fast and slow freights." I wish to find out what slow freights are; I never heard of any such thing as slow freights, or fast freights, but it says so here. Supposing that a number of the merchants of San Francisco did not care particularly whether they got their goods here in a hurry, and that I can get them here in twenty-five days on an average, I will make a contract that they shall be delivered here in sixty days. Now, this bill calls for "fast" and "slow" freights; it calls for "carload lots, and lots under a carload." Then, the merchant of San Francisco can ship a large amount, and gets a chance to discriminate as between fast and slow freight. You propose to discriminate between large and small merchants, and one will take part of a carload, and another will take the remainder. Now, if you go still further and add this clause, "between merchants who ship one, two, three, four, and five hundred thousand dollars," probably there should be another rate. That is what I asked Mr. Stubbs to do a year and a half ago when the matter was brought up; I told him to discriminate in proportion to the amount of freight that went over the road. He took those facts and laid them before the eastern roads. I can see that it would affect the discrimination, and I should say that that bill is about what we want in that respect, if the amendment that I have suggested is put in. I have not consulted with others, but from what I know of those matters, I should presume so. It would be satisfactory to me, and I think it would be to the merchants of San Francisco.

Q. If the bill prohibits discrimination, they would not like it? A. No, sir; they would not like it.

Senator Vrooman—Your freight is how much? A. About $200,000 a year.

Q. At the beginning of the commercial year can you ascertain exactly what your freights would be for that year? A. Yes, sir; the year that our line of business really began commenced in September.

Q. Before you made a contract with the railroad company I understood you to state that you made a yearly contract around Cape Horn? A. Not for all of our goods, but for the great bulk of them.

Q. Would you be compelled to have your freight rate fixed for the commercial year, in shipping around the Horn? A. I would have to know what the rates were before I could make a contract.

Q. Wouldn't it be to your benefit to make a contract to ship round the Horn for a year? A. Yes, sir.

Q. Then, under a law which prevented you from making a contract with a railroad company for a year, and which did not prevent you making a contract with a shipowner, you would naturally be driven, under the financial pressure, to make a contract with the shipowner? A. Yes, sir; I should certainly do it.

Q. In that way it would deprive the railroad company of all freight? A. Yes, sir; nine tenths of it would go by ship.

Q. Who made the rate between you and the railroad company? A. It is mutually fixed up by both of us. They came partially to our terms, and we sided up to theirs.

Q. You got such a rate that it would pay you to ship overland?
A. We did.

Q. Did they come to your rate? A. They came to it where we could not give in, and we gave them a rate on seventy-five or eighty, and where they could give us a good reason they gave us one on perhaps twenty.

Q. Where they did not give you a good reason for departing from the tariff that you had settled yourself, they came to your terms? A. Yes, sir; they came to our terms.

Q. Some questions have been asked you, trying to draw a distinction between the merchants in your line of business and the merchants in the drygoods business, as going to show that the drygoods merchants were under obligation to the railroad company, because they had to ship goods every month; and Murphy, Grant & Co. were cited. I presume they could ship goods around the Horn, if they desired to wait six months for their goods? A. Yes, sir; but they would have to wait, and they would probably save something from what they pay under the tariff. Now we save on heavy goods, but on some goods we are willing to pay a heavier tariff, and pay twice as much on seasonable goods as on unseasonable goods. They know that they would have to get seasonable goods by rail, but the railroad company never advance above the open rate.

Q. I understood you to say that the railroad company discriminated in favor of certain classes of persons in San Francisco? A. That is my impression. I have never seen any of the contracts; but people tell me that there is a discrimination.

Q. People in your line of business? A. Yes, sir; in fact, the interior merchants know that the San Francisco merchants get an inside rate.

Q. How many merchants are there in San Francisco in your business? A. We claim about six wholesale merchants. There are four or five in the hardware, and six in hardware and agricultural.

Q. Do you understand that you are all to have the same rate? A. Our contract says, that if any man gets a lower rate, we all—six or eight or ten of us—have the same.

Q. Every man in the same line of business would get the same rate? A. All wholesale merchants, but not the retail merchants.

Q. Isn't it a fact that you large importers objected because the rate was open to the small importers the same as it was to you? A. They should object to that if they were.

Q. Is it a fact that the large importers of San Francisco protested against the special contracts because they gave the small importer the same chance that they did the larger ones? A. They gave them a better chance.

Q. Why? A. I will tell you why: Here is a merchant who is complaining that he has not got as good a contract as the San Francisco merchant—I was speaking to him this morning. He says: "You import forty carloads of plows a year, or about that. Why should I not get them as cheaply as you do." "Do you think that your customer at Marysville, and your customer at Chico, and your customer at Red Bluff, should join together and bring in one carload of plows and get them at the same rate that I do forty carloads?" "No, sir; I do not." "And yet you complain because a man can undersell you who outranks you in San Francisco, and who is at the tide water."

Q. You think that the man who is the largest shipper should have the best rate? A. Yes, sir; and your bill demands it.

Q. Why do you think the largest importer should have the best rates? A. Because he has always had that advantage by water, and unless he has it by rail he will go back to the water and have it there, and then the small retailers in the interior go together, and they can make up their orders and outsell the wholesale merchants in San Francisco, and that is driving the trade away from San Francisco. There are three or four houses there, and their trade has been thrown off by the eastern merchants at Chicago and St. Louis and Kansas City, who send their agents on to this coast, and their drummers, and they go to one hundred different points, and say, "We want you to buy your goods in St. Louis. We have special contracts with the railroad company, and we will give you the benefit of that. We will give you rates that undersell San Francisco. We don't have to pay a license, and we don't have to pay storage," and so they are getting our trade continuously. We have started men round through the country to say, "We want your trade. Give us your business on some terms, because we are here. If you do we will send men there to pack the goods, and send to the factory, and gather up the goods, and send them directly to Stockton, or anywhere else." I don't know but what we will go out of business entirely, and start a business in New York and solicit orders.

Q. One of the objections which you have to these special contracts is that it enables the merchant to get his goods delivered as cheaply in Sacramento, and other interior points, as he can get them in San Francisco? A. Yes, sir.

Q. You think, then, that these interior towns ought not to enjoy the same facilities for getting freight as the San Francisco merchants enjoy? A. No, sir; we cannot pay freight to Oroville and compete with a house that receives goods in Marysville.

Q. If we can sell the goods in Marysville cheaper than you can sell them in San Francisco, is that not a benefit to Marysville? A. It may be a benefit to the customers if he can do it, but it is breaking up the business of San Francisco, and discriminating largely against San Francisco and in favor of Marysville, and it will naturally force us to start branch houses in the interior towns.

SENATOR CROSS—Would you be able to furnish agricultural implements under the contract cheaper than without it? A. We will sell this year a thousand Buckeye mowers, and we could contract to have them laid down in San Francisco at four dollars and fifty cents or five dollars apiece freight, and we have a contract by which we pay really six or seven on the matter of Buckeye mowers; the farmer has got to pay more unless we take a smaller profit. They are made at New York, and cost us nothing except shipment around the Horn. But if he wants wagons which are made in St. Louis, he has got to pay more for them if we ship them around the Horn. One article will cost more and another less. Now, the question is, does the freight on the whole line of goods cost any less overland than by water? If it is a little less either way they get the benefit of it. On some few articles they pay more, and on others less, but on the average I think it is better for him to ship overland.

Q. What do you mean by "rebate" upon freight, in a commercial sense? A. The contract may be for three cents, and when they send him in a bill they may give him a rebate of the difference between three and two.

SENATOR SPENCER—Do you call overcharges a rebate? A. There is seldom a freight bill made out according to our contract; it is made out higher; and this rebate that we get is in one sense an overcharge and in another sense it is rebate; I can't distinguish it. Freight goes over four or five different roads, and some of them charge more than that road; it may have been correct, but it has to be divided up; the agent may not understand it; and on some goods the freight from Omaha is a regular tariff; there is no trouble about that; but at a great many points east of that on the roads freight is overcharged.

Q. Do you get this rebate for the purpose of giving you a lower rate than your contract, or for the purpose of bringing it down to what the contract is? A. For the purpose of bringing it down to what the contract is.

Q. If you shipped by open contract and paid more than the freight bill, when you got your money back, what would you call that? A. Overcharge; we have got no rebates at all; they are all overcharges that we have paid in.

SENATOR SULLIVAN—When your money is tied up by the railroad company for the purpose of adjusting differences, is it from the nature of the business or for the purpose of using it to control you in any way? A. It comes from the nature of the business. The railroad company have been seeking to avoid it all the time, and they are getting nearer and nearer to it, and the overcharge now will be only sometimes for a day or two and growing less all the time. It is a good deal of trouble to them on their part.

Q. It is not for the purpose of oppression? A. Not at all. I never looked at it in that light.

Q. Do the merchants of San Francisco so consider it? A. No, sir; the railroad company are a little slow sometimes in making up claims, and take a longer time than it ought to, but when we get an explanation of it it seems to be reasonably necessary. We have some trouble sometimes in trying to settle them ourselves. They have got to go over so many roads and find out the rates that it takes time.

Q. What difference would this bill practically make over the present system? A. With a slight modification I think it would be acceptable to the merchants of San Francisco. I would sign it on our part. It does give us much discrimination. It is a bill permitting discrimination, the way I look at it.

Q. You think that at the present time there is no discrimination but under this bill there would be? A. There is discrimination at this time, but I understand that a great many of the people of the State are crying out against it and this would seem to sanction it.

Q. This simply makes it worse? A. This seems to give the railroad company authority to make these discriminations. I only put in that amendment, that I suggested there, supposing it would be all right in that portion of it.

Q. You are in favor of it, then? A. As I understand it, I am.

Q. The railroad company ought to be in favor of it, then? A. I don't know whether they are or not.

SENATOR WHITNEY—I understand that you think there should be no discrimination in dispatch, speed, or accommodation of any kind. Do you know that any complaint has ever arisen at which that could be justly aimed? A. I do not, sir. I have never known of any discrimination.

Q. Either in dispatch, speed, or accommodation? A. No, sir; not on the overland. I have known of discrimination in other States.

SENATOR VROOMAN—Do you know whether or not the Central Pacific Railroad Company advances freight charges at Ogden when it receives goods from the eastern lines? A. Not to my knowledge. Freight from the east comes billed to them at the eastern tariff, and they add their own.

SENATOR TAYLOR—Do you know whether or not there is any rebate upon open rates? A. I never have heard of any.

Q. You are a member of the Chamber of Commerce in San Francisco? A. Yes, sir.

Q. What proportion of the merchants have these special contracts? A. The railroad company says about fourteen hundred. I don't know but what they have given them to every man in the State.

Q. That many in San Francisco? A. No; in the State. A large majority of the wholesale merchants have these contracts. I don't know how many.

SENATOR MURPHY—Would not the practical effect of this bill be to drive your business off if it should pass? A. As I interpret the bill, it gives us about the same discrimination; but if it allows no discrimination at all the wholesale merchants can go round Cape Horn shipping goods.

Q. Suppose that every merchant in the State would pay the same rate for shipping as under the special contract system, what effect would it have on the San Francisco merchants? A. I think they would go round Cape Horn. They would have to do so for self protection. The effect would be that the railroad would have to advance freights to the interior merchants. They could not live at it as at present.

Q. Why would they have to ship round Cape Horn if all parties were brought down to the same level? A. When you bring all parties down to the same level, you give the interior merchants an advantage over the larger merchants of San Francisco. They would have the advantage over us, and for self protection we would have to go round Cape Horn.

Q. In order to protect the merchants of San Francisco you have to give them a lower rate, and the merchants of the interior a higher rate? A. Yes, sir; as explained awhile ago. The interior merchants have more latitude than the San Francisco merchants.

Q. Wouldn't that have a tendency to build up the interior? A. No, sir; it would bankrupt the interior. You would have a man with three thousand dollars trying to build up a wholesale business; importing goods directly from the East, and trying to compete with others, and in six months it would bring disaster to the State.

Q. Suppose that he had a large capital that would be sufficient to transact the business. Of course it would not have that effect then? A. No, sir; you can ship the whole mercantile business of San Francisco to Sacramento. It might possibly be done. It would build up those interior towns, provided they had capital to do business. If the Marysville people bought goods in the East, I would have to pay freight from San Francisco to Marysville to compete with them.

Q. If that is true, isn't it also true that the interior merchants get the freight that goes by their door to San Francisco and back again, making a double freight? A. No, sir; the goods come from the East directly to him, and do not go to San Francisco under the present system.

Q. Even though the merchant in San Francisco is importing the articles? A. Yes, sir.

Q. Is that not a system where the railroad company permits every man in Marysville to have a special contract? A. An open contract. He would ship to the Town of Marysville direct.

Q. If the open contract was too high, the goods would be shipped past his door to San Francisco, and then brought back again, so that the Marysville merchant would have to pay twice? A. No, sir; the merchant in Marysville would be as he is at the present time. His goods would be delivered there. We could have forty carloads delivered there. We could ship our goods from the East, and have them delivered anywhere on the line of the railroad before reaching San Francisco. If they aim to build our interior merchants up and make them wholesale, and the San Francisco retailers, it will have that tendency, and will compel our San Francisco merchants to go east, and send out our agents, as Chicago and other places are doing at the present time.

SENATOR SPENCER—Don't you think it would be better if there was no such thing as special contracts, and that everybody shipping over the line of the road should pay their just proportion of freight, and a reasonable charge upon that freight, at any point to which it is shipped, either to San Francisco or anywhere else, and no discrimination between persons except a reasonable charge for transporting fast freight, and let them ship by water if they wanted to, or by rail if they wanted to, giving the merchants that privilege, and leaving out all considerations of special contract, or persons, or places? A. No, sir.

Q. Don't you think that the merchants would make just as much money if they had to ship upon the same terms as other persons similarly situated? A. That has been discussed by the railroad company and by the merchants whether it would drive the trade of San

Francisco, or the great bulk of it, around the Horn. The railroad company have had three or four different lines coming in. They must have that trade or go into bankruptcy. The Northern Pacific cut off the northern trade; and there is the Central and the Southern, and they cannot exist unless they have the trade of San Francisco; and if they have to put on a tariff the effect will be to drive the trade around Cape Horn. We are willing to try it that way; the San Francisco merchants will be satisfied.

Q. I understand you that if it were not for the special contracts all freight would be shipped around Cape Horn? A. The great bulk of them would be.

Q. That would be the most of the heavy bulky goods? A. It would, I judge, as long as it was in effect, cause certain classes of goods to go around the Horn. It would be cheaper to send goods by rail at four or five cents a pound, than to send them around the Horn at nine dollars a ton.

SENATOR WHITNEY—Do you think that if they got all the freight around the Horn, it would be just the same as if it were all brought by rail? A. To a certain extent.

Q. Do you think it would be advantageous for us to go back, as it was before railroad time, and for the benefit of this State? A. Not for the freight and passenger business. The railroad has brought a great many persons here, and the State is filling up very materially under it, for the State depends upon the population.

SENATOR SPENCER—I meant (and there may be a little doubt about my last question), if you, as a merchant of San Francisco, saw proper to transport goods across the continent by rail, that you should have the same privileges and charges granted to you as any other merchant, and the same in regard to all those places in the interior of the State, and that these respective merchants should have the same opportunities to ship by sea if they wanted to. Wouldn't that be the best regulation; wouldn't that regulate itself, as between the merchants with these respective contracts, so that the contracts could not have a tendency to change the rates of freights and fares, and the commerce of the State? A. It changes it in this respect; it takes it from the overland; to a certain extent it helps the interests of the State. They make more money from freights than from receipts of fares. The more freight the railroad company can take, the cheaper they can take fares, and thus they will build up the interest of the State. I don't think it would be fair to the merchants of San Francisco; I don't think they would find it to be much cheaper to ship around the Horn, than to ship overland. I understand that if, instead of five hundred, I only ship fifty carloads by rail, I should have a better freight than the merchant of the interior who went around among his friends and got up a carload of freight, and shipped it in the name of one of them and gets the same rate.

Q. Would the merchants of the State, and of San Francisco, make the same money every year if the rates were open to all alike, and they could ship in any manner they chose? A. I think they would.

SENATOR MURPHY—Why should a man who ships five hundred carloads over a road get a better rate than a man who only ships one?

A. Because it is the best men, and the men of clear intelligence and judgment, that have this rate, and a right that they have always had in the past.

Q. Why is it? It does not cost any more to operate a road with five hundred cars than it does with one? A. I differ with you there. You will understand that a railroad company look at it in a different light. If you apply to them at the Willows to take a carload of grain to San Francisco, and they have nothing else to take, they would have to charge you nearly as much for it as to take forty for me.

Q. That is true where you take an isolated case—where they have but few cars—but on a great overland route it ought not to cost any more? A. Yes, sir; they could take a full train of forty cars, and bring it through to San Francisco to one house cheaper than they could to forty houses.

Q. If the forty houses are all there at the same time? A. Yes, sir; because it is all divided out into forty houses, one at one place and one at another, and one at Marysville and one at Stockton, and they would have to break up a train, and stop forty times, and make out forty freight bills; and there is a great deal more trouble connected with shipping forty carloads to forty houses than to one house. They bring them all overland and divide them up after they get them over here. They switch them off at Marysville and back up and get one car there, and then come to Sacramento, and switch and delay there, and get one out for Sacramento, and then one at Stockton, and another to San José, and then to San Francisco. They ought to have a train come right straight through to San Francisco and not stop at those other places at all.

SENATOR VROOMAN—Has the tendency of the special contract system been to raise or lower the rates of freight for the State? A. To lower them.

SENATOR MURPHY—In holding back this money which they claim is a necessity, is it not done for the purpose of punishing the parties for a violation of their contract? A. I have never known them to do so.

Q. They don't hold it and then go out and hunt up these parties? A. No, sir; unless they think they have sufficient proof that the parties have violated their contract, and then they stop right there.

SENATOR SPENCER—Do you ship any class of goods by these special contracts upon which you sustain a loss? A. No, sir; I don't know as we have to sell goods at a loss because we ship them overland. Sometimes staple goods are sold at a loss whether shipped by railroad or by the Horn.

Q. Do you know whether the railroad ships that class of goods in order to stop competition? A. I don't believe that they do.

Q. If ships were encouraged to come here from New York they would be here to take freight back? A. Yes, sir.

Q. By their not being encouraged to come here it raises the prices of freight to Europe, does it not? A. The more ships there are in San Francisco to take the freight the less the rate would be.

SENATOR VROOMAN—I understood you to state that there were a great many more vessels there than there was freight for? A. Yes, sir, three to one.

Q. A great many waiting to get loads? A. They could get it but they will not accept the freight. They expected a rate of about twenty-five shillings and they can only get twenty. That arises from the fact that in 1881 they had a large amount of wheat to ship and freights went up, and in October and November, 1883, the San Francisco merchants were offering fifty shillings for vessels, and that attracted them from all parts of the world, and when they came they chartered them at thirty shillings.

Q. The amount of wheat was not so great as they supposed, and the market of Liverpool declined, and they could not afford to ship it at that rate? A. No, sir; nor at the present rates, either.

SENATOR VROOMAN—I suppose that 'those ships cannot afford to take the rates because they come here empty? A. It is very seldom that a vessel comes without a cargo, but when we send out word that a vessel can get fifty shillings, they will come here empty from China or Australia; but if they come here expecting fifty, and get twenty-five, they will not take it, and are laying up.

SENATOR SPENCER—The more freight they brought here by water, the less they could afford to take the freight that we export? A. There has been plenty of freight to bring them here. Any quantity of them come here without freight. There are fifty of them in San Francisco lying idle because the San Francisco merchants cannot afford to pay over thirty-five or forty and leave them a profit.

Q. A ship is very seldom here without a charter? A. No, sir; sometimes they are chartered before leaving Liverpool.

Q. Sometimes they have to come here without a load? A. Sometimes.

Q. If those ships had plenty of freight to bring here, then they could take freight back for less? A. Yes, sir.

Q. How do you reconcile your statements? A. These ships that are in San Francisco are staying there, not because there is no freight, but because they will not accept it at twenty-eight or thirty shillings. Now, will it help the freights and the farmers if another hundred ships were loaded to San Francisco. No; it would only depress the market and the price of grain.

SENATOR DEL VALLE—When those ships came without a charter they did so upon the assumption that there was going to be a great deal of wheat to be shipped? A. Yes, sir; and that they were going to get fifty shillings. But the most of them came here because they were chartered to come, and to get a certain rate of freight. The charter they received depended upon what they were going to get. They came here with coal, for instance, hoping that a fifty or sixty shilling freight would help them out.

STATEMENT OF HON. C. S. STEPHENS.

MR. CHAIRMAN: I don't know that I have any particular statement to make. Of course, I was in the other House, and worked for the passage of the bill, believing it to be a beneficial bill, for reasons that were satisfactory to me, among which was that I myself had some business with these railroad companies, and I will just relate the circumstance: I had shipped some freight from New York, and desired it to be left at Stockton; and when I got the shipping receipt, it was shipped to San Francisco, and I was told that they would not leave the freight at Stockton at all. It was a piano, and it went on to San Francisco and came back by the boat. I felt somewhat aggrieved, because they could have favored me by leaving it at Stockton. I would have been perfectly willing to have paid them for leaving it there, but instead of that they took it to San Francisco, which was against my wish. The instrument was damaged in consequence, by the boat, and that has influenced me in my action in regard to this bill; that these men would designedly carry that freight beyond a terminal point for the purpose of compelling me to pay back freight on it, and for that reason I preferred fetching it up by the boat. A gentleman in the City of Stockton told me that they were treated in the same way in regard to shipping a carload from Reno. They had to pay the full price from Reno to San Francisco, notwithstanding the car only goes to Stockton, and they have got to pay that price, and then pay eight dollars back freight besides. So that it costs them eight dollars more to ship a carload from Reno to Stockton than to San Francisco. That looks to me like it was not a fair business, and if men can't be persuaded to quit it, if there is any power in legislation, and I think it is in this bill, this thing should be stopped. That is the reason I worked for the bill, and another one is this, that came under my own notice: I refer to the Railroad Commissioners. When they were in Stockton I appeared before them, and asked them to inquire into it. My son-in-law purchased a piece of land up in Tulare County, and desired to ship up some lumber to build a little house. He was a poor man. He went first to the agent of the railroad company at Stockton, and asked him what they would charge him to ship about one thousand five hundred feet of lumber up to Tulare County, and they told him they would charge him just the price of a car; I think it was from forty-five to sixty dollars; and a car will carry eight thousand feet, and carries ten tons; he told them that he only wanted to carry one thousand five hundred feet of lumber, that there was not enough to load a car, but they wouldn't take it unless he paid the full price of a car, which would be forty-five dollars for eight thousand feet, sixty dollars for ten thousand feet. Then my son-in-law says to him, "Then I will take a car that will carry eight thousand feet at forty-five dollars, and I can put my household goods and kitchen furniture on it also, they won't weigh over a ton." "No, you can't do that, you will have to pay for the use of the car, but you can't put those things on it; you can put lumber on it and nothing else; the furniture you must put inside of a box car." He said, "Well, let me put my family on and take them up, and it will not make a load the whole of it." "No, your family must not be on an open car, they must go in the passenger car." "Well," he said, "I will haul the traps and family up there with my horses;" and he refused to do it; he would not ship at all. I think there is a better way of managing railroads in the interests of the people. The idea of making a poor man pay the same price for shipping one thousand five hundred feet of lumber that you would make a rich man pay for shipping eight thousand feet, I don't think is a proper method of conducting a railroad anywhere; and that is the reason I have been in favor of some bill (it don't make any difference whether it is the Barry bill or what bill it is), to regulate and control these interests, so that a poor man can have his rights the same as a rich one.

SENATOR DEL VALLE—When did this discrimination occur, with reference to the piano? A. About six years ago.

Q. That was before the new Constitution was passed? A. Yes, sir.

SENATOR SULLIVAN—Has anything of that kind ever happened since? A. No; because I have not shipped anything; but these parties told me a week ago Tuesday, that they generally charged that way still.

Q. How many years have you lived in Stockton? A. Twenty-two.

Q. During that time have you known the railroad company to remove its track for the purpose of discriminating against any locality? A. Nothing—only what I heard. Quite a number of merchants talked with me at the time the Railroad Commissioners were there, and they said they didn't care about creating hostile feeling with the railroad company that way, and they preferred not to go before the Commissioners, and one reason was that they had no confidence in the Commission anyhow.

SENATOR REDDY—I understand that in the conversation you had with the merchants at Stockton, they came to the conclusion not to prefer any charges before the Commissioners, for the reason that they thought the Commissioners would not afford them any relief? A. Yes, sir; that it would be liable to lead them into more trouble; that if the Railroad Commissioners did not interpose, the railroad company would come down on them.

Q. What do you mean by "coming down on them"—discriminating against them? A. Yes, sir.

Q. Then the merchants of Stockton seem to labor under more or less fear of the power vested in the railroad company of discriminating against them? A. Some of them do; some of them there don't seem to be much afraid of them.

Q. What proportion of the merchants that you talked with made that declaration or joined in it? A. Well, I don't remember as to the number, but then there were several of them.

STATEMENT OF HON. A. T. HATCH.

THE CHAIRMAN—Do you desire to make any statement? Answer—I will make this statement: That we are favorably located for shipping, and have no cause for complaint. There is water by which produce can be shipped from our stations. I will say that all the favors I have ever asked from the railroad company I have received;

so I am not the one to growl in this matter. If you want men to appear before you that the railroad company have harmed I do not think I am one of them. I have not been cinched by them, and I am not in favor of any cinch measures. [Objection.] I do not use the term "cinch" out of any disrespect to the legislators. I think that there is one thing in this bill that would work a hardship to us, unless there was an exception maintained. If it was left so that those who had large quantities of grain to ship could command the cars for too long a period, it would be well to allow those having live stock or fast freight, to ship it; but there is a good many little exceptions to that.

SENATOR DEL VALLE—Have you read the Barry bill carefully? A. Not as carefully as I would have done if I had known that I was going to be here.

Q. Don't you notice that that exception is made in the bill? A. Not in that way. Is that the only exception?

Q. Live stock is not excepted to in words as yet. You think that such an exception as live stock ought to be made? A. I do.

Q. What are your shipping points? A. Saucelito and Cordelia.

Q. Have you competition at both places? A. Possible competition at one place and actual competition at the other.

Q. What is the difference in freight, from the points where there is competition, between the railroad and the water? A. I do not really know what the water freight is; I never use it.

Q. Does not the water freight give as satisfactory accommodations as the railroad? A. No, sir.

Q. Have the benefits that you have enjoyed been based upon the water facilities that you have? A. It was supposed that they reduced all their prices there on account of water accommodations.

Q. You are a farmer? A. Yes, sir; a fruit grower.

Q. You ship fruit more than anything else? A. Yes, sir.

Q. By the carload? A. Sometimes, and sometimes less.

Q. Do you have any special rate? A. No, sir.

Q. I understood you to say that you received other benefits from them? A. It was mostly a reduction in times past. Freights are much less than they were. I asked a reduction and got them to the city on fruits. And I asked the carriage of full cars by passenger train to Sacramento, and I got it at reduced rates for eastern shipments.

Q. Was it a general request by all the farmers there that such a reduction should be made? A. Sometimes it was one farmer, and sometimes it was three or four; at times it has been made for all. I never asked a personal favor.

Q. Have you had any experience in the matter of special contracts with the railroad company? A. No, sir.

Q. Are you aware of the existence of such? A. Yes, sir.

Q. Have you ever seen a special contract? A. No, sir.

Q. Do you know the terms of one? A. I do not.

Q. If such a contract existed, by which the railroad company bound the signers to send their freight by no other means than the railroad, and not to purchase from any except those who did ship through them, do you think it would be advantageous to the best interests of the State? A. No, sir.

Q. If such a system as that did exist, would it not, in your judgment, be detrimental to the shipping interests of the State? A. It would.

Q. Have you been among the agriculturists of the State in any other section than your own? A. I have.

Q. Have you conversed with them in reference to this matter of transportation? A. Somewhat.

Q. Have you been through the San Joaquin Valley? A. I had no conversation with any one in that part. I was there about two years ago, and there was something said about such matters.

Q. You have talked with people in different portions of the State, in your capacity as President of the Horticultural Society? A. Yes, sir.

Q. Have you learned the general opinion of the people in regard to the transportation question? A. There are a great many people who are dissatisfied with the present system.

SENATOR REDDY—I understood you to state that you had no cause of complaint against the railroad company, or of the accommodations that have been afforded to you? A. I did.

Q. Where is your place? A. At Suisun, Solano County, and in Cordelia, Solano County.

Q. You have water communication with San Francisco? A. Yes, sir.

Q. Do you attribute your happy condition of things to the water communication, or to the railroad company? A. To both.

Q. Honors are equally divided; they are easy? A. Our freights would not be so cheap unless there were both. The water would probably be more expensive than it is if there was no railroad there, and vice versa.

Q. Do you know the rates that are paid by water from your place to the city? A. Not positively; I think it is less, though, than is paid by rail. I think that the rates by water are one dollar and fifty cents, and by rail it is one dollar and seventy-five cents.

Q. The people of your place are all at peace with the railroad? A. Yes, sir; well, there is one man that has not been at peace. He started a lawsuit for being put off the cars several times.

Q. I mean about rates of freights and passenger fares? A. I don't know of any dissatisfaction there very recently.

Q. How long is it that the rates of freights and fares have been satisfactory to the people? A. The rates were put down to the present status something like a year and a half ago.

Q. Before that time had there been any considerable complaint about freights and fares? A. It was tolerably high.

Q. What do you mean by "tolerably high?" Just as high as they could possibly stand it? A. Not quite; but when we asked a reduction we got it, and that was on one particular article of freight. We gave them a reason why it should be less, and they made it so.

Q. Was there any competition attached to that? A. No, sir.

Q. Isn't it a fact that the railroad company agreed with your shippers that they should ship all their freight of certain classes by rail and not by water? A. Nothing of the kind. I never heard of anything of the kind.

Q. Are the persons who ship by rail permitted to ship by water without any consequences? A. I have never shipped any other way and I do not know.

Q. Why have you not shipped by water if the rates were lower? A. Because the time was an object.

Q. Was that the only reason? A. And the regularity.

Q. Was there any other reason? A. No, sir.

Q. Isn't it a fact that you were informed and knew that if you shipped your stuff by water that you would have to pay higher rates when you wanted to ship by rail? A. I never knew that it was so.

Q. Have you ever tried it? A. I have never tried it; I never knew there was any such circumstance existing.

Q. What is the difference in time in delivering your freight by water and by rail? A. There is quite a great deal; I don't know how much; it is very irregular; there is no steam communication by water.

Q. Had there been before the advent of the railroad? A. There had.

Q. And that was the way that the fruit was moved? A. Yes.

Q. How many months was that kept up after the advent of the railroad? A. About ten months.

Q. At what time did it cease? A. Some few years ago.

Q. Do you remember how long ago? A. I do not. Sometimes, for a few months at a time, there would be communication by steamer, and then it would go off again directly.

Q. How long have you resided at that place? A. Thirteen years.

Q. In what business have you been engaged? A. Fruit growing exclusively.

Q. If there is any discrimination practiced by the railroad company, it is in favor of your place? A. If there is any, yes, sir.

Q. If the discrimination works your way, you are satisfied with it? A. We are satisfied.

Senator Johnson—Are you advised as to the sentiment of Sonoma County as to the Barry bill? A. No, sir.

Q. Do you think that there ought to be any discrimination as between persons and places in the matter of the shipment of freight? A. That can be construed for me to say "Yes," otherwise I would say "No." There are peculiarities here that might cause me to say "Yes." Different persons might in different places be so situated that there would have to be a difference in prices to make it right and just.

Q. Do you stand upon the San José platform? A. I am a Republican; but I am not much of a politician.

Q. Do you recollect that provision of the platform adopted by the Democracy that there ought to be no discrimination between persons or places as to freights? A. I don't know anything about it.

Q. Do you not think that the words "perishable articles" in that clause of the Barry bill will satisfy your community in the shipment of fruit? A. More exceptions than that would be necessary to my mind. I don't know what would satisfy them. I know that I might be so situated that I would not be satisfied with that.

Q. I am speaking more particularly of a fruit-growing section. Do you not think that ought to satisfy a fruit-growing section, as a general thing? A. There would be some stock raising, and live stock would not want to lie over till a large quantity of green fruit had been shipped, which might require several days to move it.

SENATOR McCLURE—Have you read this Barry bill? A. I have read it, but if 1 had known that I was going to be called here as a witness I should have read it more carefully than I did.

Q. What are your views as to section seven of the bill, and of that of your neighbors, if you know, in respect to that provision in the bill as to the effect that it might have upon your community? A. I think it would be rather damaging to a community where they had more than one line, if they had a water monopoly.

Q. That is to say, that if they dispatched one carload ahead of another out of its order, they would subject the property to forfeiture? A. Yes, sir.

Q. Do you think that would meet the approbation of the community in which you live? A. I don't think it would, of the thinking portion of them.

SENATOR SULLIVAN—If the Barry bill will have the effect of protecting the people by law from unjust exactions; if it will have the effect of preventing unjust discriminations as against individuals and localities; if it will have the effect of promoting equal services upon equal terms to all persons, would you not say that it-is a good and proper bill? A. With those several "ifs" in it I would say "Yes."

Q. Don't you think you could be more explicit? A. Yes, sir; I think by putting in a few words in the Barry bill I could make it do that.

Q. Let us hear what suggestions you have to make? A. In regard to discrimination between persons, I would say: "Who were similarly situated at the same places."

Q. Do you believe that there should be any discrimination made as between persons in the same locality—between man and man, and between persons who are in the same business? A. No, sir.

Q. Supposing you could send a certain quantity of freight to San Francisco for two hundred dollars, and that another man was charged four hundred dollars for sending the same quantity to the same place, do you not think that would be unjust and unfair? A. It would seem so to me.

Q. Now if it could be shown to you by testimony that such was the practice of the railroad company in other parts of California, do you not think that any law that could be passed for the purpose of remedying that defect in our laws would be a good and proper law? A. I do not see any reason why such things should be done. I can't see how it would be right; it may be right, but if it is I am too thick-headed to see it. I am satisfied, though, that it has been done.

SENATOR VROOMAN—I understood you to state that you were satisfied that discriminations between persons were made? A. I have been so informed by persons and papers, that they have special contracts by which they receive special rates upon entering into the contracts.

Q. Does your answer mean anything more than that there are such things as special contracts? A. Yes, sir.

Q. You think that special contracts are discriminations? A. It appears so to me.

Q. And you think that to that extent they are unjust? Would you consider that special contracts were discrimination if they were open to all similarly situated? A. No, sir.

SENATOR TAYLOR—You are a member of the State Horticultural Society and Vice-President of the society? A. Yes, sir.

Q. Do you ship a great deal of fruit? A. Yes, sir.

Q. Do you know what the rate is per ton upon that fruit from the place where you ship it to any point in San Francisco? A. Yes, sir; one dollar and seventy-five cents per ton. I think it is seventeen dollars for a car, and that a car holds ten tons.

Q. What is the distance from the point at which you ship to San Francisco? A. About fifty miles.

Q. Do you know what the rates are per ton for the same class of fruit from Folsom or Sacramento? A. No, sir.

Q. Do you know any other point from which fruit is shipped where you are acquainted with the rates? A. Vacaville.

Q. Do you know the rates that are charged from there? A. Just twice.

Q. Just twice the rates from Suisun? A. Yes, sir.

Q. What is the distance from Vacaville to San Francisco? A. About twelve miles. That is the difference between the two places.

Q. They charge you twice as much? A. Yes, sir.

Q. And your distance is twelve miles greater? A. Yes, sir.

Q. Do the points of Suisun and Cordelia have competition by water? A. Yes, sir.

Q. Is there any competition from Vacaville? A. No, sir.

Q. Do you know whether or not they charge the same price per ton for short distances that they do for long distances? A. I do not know.

SENATOR WHITNEY—Upon what line of road do you ship from Suisun to San Francisco? A. On the Central Pacific Railroad.

Q. Is Vacaville on that same line? A. No, sir; it is on another line of road terminating at Elmira.

SENATOR TAYLOR—About how long is the Vacaville road? A. I don't know; about four miles.

Q. Do you know whether or not the Auditor of the Vacaville road makes his report to the Central Pacific Railroad Company? A. I so understand it.

Q. Isn't it a fact that that road is under a contract to the Central Pacific Railroad Company? A. Yes, sir.

Q. Isn't it a fact that the freight is billed right through from Vacaville to San Francisco? A. I don't know.

SENATOR MURPHY—You live in Suisun? A. In Suisun Valley.

Q. Do you know of any discrimination in charges in the same classes of freight between different persons? A. I don't know such to be the case.

Q. Did you ever hear any complaint in your neighborhood in reference to the order in which freight is dispatched? A. I did not.

SENATOR TAYLOR—Did you ever know of an instance where they have made discrimination between persons living at the same place and shipping from the same point, as to the matter of the dispatch of freight? A. No, sir.

Q. Have you ever heard of any difference in price between persons similarly situated? A. They are the same, as far as I know.

Q. Are you in favor of a uniform rate per ton per mile? A. I am in favor of treating all just alike, as near as possible, without favor to any—that would be charging them all the same price.

Q. Per ton per mile? A. I don't know about that; I think there are places where there might be people benefited without harm to others.

Q. Would you consider this a just principle, that the longer the run the less the rate per ton per mile? A. I think that would be better than to have it uniform.

SENATOR REDDY—You know nothing about the views of your people; you are only speaking for yourself? A. Only for myself.

Q. Do you know anything about the rates for freight, except on fruit? A. Yes, sir.

Q. What classes of freight are you sending? A. Produce, only. Fruit manufactories are shipping out some.

Q. What other freights are you acquainted with? A. Green fruit. All products that come from there, except green fruit, are at a uniform rate. I believe from our locality, green fruit is lower.

SENATOR BROOKS—Do you think it would be in the interest of the fruit-growers to have a uniform rate per ton per mile? A. I don't know how to consider that. There are some points now that it would be hard upon under such a rule. Freights and fares are less in proportion than they would be if it was uniform. Some points nearer pay more in proportion to the distance, and, therefore, makes it easier on those that are at a distance, and although they pay more than the near ones, they do not pay so much per mile per ton.

Q. Do you think it would be in the interest of other fruit-growers who live round about you to have a uniform rate per mile per ton? A. Yes, sir.

Q. As against persons living in the mountains? A. Yes, sir.

SENATOR CROSS—Are there any instances within your knowledge which might make it desirable for the railroad company and in the interest of shippers to discriminate as to freights, as to which should be forwarded first? A. Yes, sir.

Q. Please state any such instances? A. I don't think of any particular instances, but circumstances would arise every day where it would be acts of justice to ship some goods in preference to others, although they had no priority of place.

Q. Could you make the matter any plainer to us? A. Well, a case of live stock, or a family moving their property from one locality to another, it might be sent first. It seems to me that is plain to any man.

Q. Would it be your idea that live stock should have preference over any other production, and what other production? A. I think all things perishable; all live stock.

Q. Why do you think live stock is preferable in the order of shipment over anything else that might be offered before them? A. Simply on account of its being alive, and requiring more care, and more liable to damage than dead freight by being longer on the cars, and the expenses and trouble of caring for them at the stations if they are not on the cars, would make it burdensome.

SENATOR REDDY—You spoke of families, in moving, being compelled to wait while grain might be forwarded. Did you ever know of an instance of that kind in this State? A. No; but it might occur under the provisions of this bill.

Q. How often would that occur in California? A. It would probably never occur unless under such provisions.

Q. The case that you imagined might never occur; it is simply within the range of possibilities? A. It is probable that it might occur a thousand times.

Q. In case the bill goes into effect you apprehend that some family will be delayed in getting their furniture carried? A. That was a mere simile to show where it might operate. There are a good many others.

Q. Are you in favor of allowing railroads to discriminate? A. I think there is a kind of discrimination that is necessary, and an unjust discrimination that is not necessary.

Q. Do you desire the railroad company to determine which is a just and which is an unjust discrimination? A. No, sir.

Q. Do you know of such a thing ever having been done in this State as an individual taking all the cars of a railroad for a week? A. They had no law like this.

Q. As it is there now, do you apprehend that it will be done? A. Those will be the rules of the railroad company.

Q. They have rules now against discrimination in that manner? A. Yes, sir; they do not allow it so much now as this law would.

Q. You would rather depend upon the rules of the company in this matter than upon the laws of the State? A. No, sir; there might be fifty small lots to go, and such a man as Dr. Glenn could, at one time, run a railroad for a few weeks.

Q. You speak about possibilities and probabilities, which do you mean? A. Actualities; if it is true that they forfeit their charter, if they don't do it as a penalty for not doing it. •

Q. Do you know of an instance in this State where any one has kept a railroad occupied for a week? A. No, I do not.

Q. Then why do you think it would happen if the Barry bill passes? A. Because the penalty is that they must do so, or forfeit their charter.

Q. You spoke about the rules of a railroad company; where have you seen any rules? A. At our station.

Q. Your experience is confined to Suisun? A. It is very limited.

Q. How near is Suisun to the Sacramento River? A. About fifteen miles.

Q. That has been the sum of your experience in these railroad matters? A. Yes, sir.

Q. And you give,.as your opinion from that experience, that the Barry bill is good for the State? A. No.

Q. You think that the Barry bill will not operate well on the affairs of the State? A. I don't say "yes" to that.

Q. Do you say "no?" A. I was asked for my opinion.

Q. Upon what do you base whatever opinion you have? A. On my judgment.

Q. And your experience at Suisun? A. No, sir; on my judgment of what the corporations would do where the penalty and the act to do, or to avoid the penalty, enter into consideration.

Q. As between shippers, would you have the first come first served? A. That is the way it always has been.

Q. It worked well? A. Yes.

Q. Have you big fruit growers been able to crowd out the little fruit growers? A. No, sir.

Q. Wouldn't it work the same way in other things and other farm products? A. Yes, sir.

Q. Don't you think, as a rule, that the first come should be first served? A. Yes, sir; but there may be exceptions. -

Q. Do you legislate for the rule or for the exceptions? A. I would avoid those exceptions as much as possible.

Q. You would not forego legislation altogether? A. No, sir.

Senator Sullivan—I desire to know if you have ever seen the book upon which the tariff is kept by which you shipped your freight at the railroad office? A. I have never looked into it.

Q. You went to the agent and asked him? A. That is all.

Q. Did he tell you without examining the book? A. Certainly; he was so used to it.

Q. Do you know if such a book is kept by the agent at Suisun? A. I suppose so. Of course they keep it. I am satisfied they do.

Q. Don't you think it would be a good thing to have a book of that kind, so that every shipper could know how much his freight was? A. Certainly it would.

Q. Do you think that a good provision? A. Yes, sir.

Q. Into how many classes is fruit divided for freight purposes? A. I think three, but ours all goes at the same rate.

Q. How do they estimate charges? A. By weight. They have different rates on fruit shipments east; I am not conversant with that.

Q. What distinction is made between dried fruit and canned fruit? A. None; I think there is no distinction made for shipment to the city.

Q. How in regard to shipments east? Q. I understand that green fruit pays the most; two or three times as much as dried fruit.

Q. What is the reason for that? A. There is no other way to get it there, while dried fruit can go another way, by water.

Q. On account of lack of competition they can charge you a higher price? A. I think so.

Q. The green fruit brings a higher price in the market? A. Not per ton. I don't know but it does in the East.

Q. That is one of the reasons for the extra charge, is it not? A. Because it depreciates, or because it brings a better price?

Q. Because the value is greater in the market; that enters into the charge also? A. It is possible.

SENATOR JOHNSON—If there is to be any classification of fruit with reference to its being forwarded with dispatch, don't you think it would be advisable to have it in the bill? A. It would be well, if the bill was right. I think it can be done properly; this body can do it.

Q. Who would you suggest to make the classification? A. I think this body is competent.

Q. As between the railroad and the Railroad Commissioners, which would you sooner trust with the classification? A. Well, I believe I would prefer to trust the railroad. I never was in favor of a Railroad Commission.

SENATOR CROSS—Is there any difference in the necessity for speed in the transportation of different kinds of fruit? A. Yes, sir.

Q. Which requires to be forwarded with the greater speed? A. Green fruit.

Q. Explain why? A. On account of its being more perishable.

Q. Which requires to be handled with the greater care? A. Fruit is not handled by the railroad company or its employés—not touched; it is loaded at the expense of the shipper, and unloaded at his expense.

Q. Do green, canned, and dried fruits have the same accommodations? A. Green fruit is sent by slow freight.

Q. When you speak of green fruit paying two or three times as much, do you mean that which goes as fast freight? A. Green fruit goes about the same rate of speed and pays twice as much as dried fruit or canned fruit, and it goes in a similar car.

Q. How is it, as between fruit that goes at the greatest speed, or as freight, and the ordinary rate? Q. That is about three times as much.

LETTER FROM JOHN T. DOYLE.

MENLO PARK, April 14, 1884.

MY DEAR SIR: I have said to you before that if any committee of the Legislature desires my presence in Sacramento for information or consultation, I will go there. But I object to being put in the position of a lobbyist, even for a public object, and have, therefore, replied to your letter and telegram that I decline to go as a private solicitor for legislation. I added my emphatic opinion that the Barry bill is a just, wise, and much-needed measure. What more could I say, unless asked·by authority?

I went over the bill, as it passed the House, carefully, section by section. It deals with and affirms general principles, the justice or injustice of which can be determined by plain people. These are:

1. That railroads constructed by authority of law are public highways.

2. That the corporations charged with the management of those highways are charged with the performance of a public duty.

3. That in the discharge of such duty they are to deal impartially with all applicants. There is to be no privileged class.

4. That corporations created by authority of State laws must live up to the law of their organization or cease to live under it.

These are the principles on which the bill is framed; and I think the people of this State will watch with interest the publication of the yeas and nays which will show which of their representatives ventures to deny any one of them.

I have read all the objections stated to have been urged to the bill before the Senate committee. They are all, so far as I observe, based on the supposition that most strange and improbable circumstances will occur, in which case inconvenience or evil might result from the rules laid down. One gentleman, for instance, apprehends that he may suddenly be called upon to transport thirty carloads of lumber in preference to an equal quantity of wheat arriving a few moments later. His road has been in operation now over sixteen years, and an equipment of two locomotives and eighteen freight cars, all told, has hitherto sufficed to do the whole business. Let us hope that the general rule of gradual growth of population and business will not be so grossly violated in his neighborhood as he apprehends. Another fears that for a casual error or misconduct of a Superintendent, or a local agent, the Attorney-General will be malicious enough to demand, and the Courts foolish enough to grant, a forfeiture of charter. The public will hardly share his apprehensions. The punishment of offenses against the public has never been, and is not likely to be, conspicuously severe in this State. No man who does his duty according to the law of the land need ever fear prosecution, much less conviction, for the unauthorized acts of his employés. A third gentleman suggests that the removal of a temporary trellis and substitution of a solid embankment may violate the requirement to maintain structures in a state of equal efficiency, etc., for the purposes for which they were designed. By and by he will realize that "the greater includes the less," and that in law what is superior to a trellis will be deemed by Courts equal to it.

These objections are simply puerile. The proof that they are not seriously thought of by those who urge them is that they offer no amendment to meet the supposed contingencies. The attempt to formulate such an amendment would expose the absurdity of the supposition. The rule of impartiality must either be affirmed or denied *in toto*. If denied, the railroad companies are left to practice such and so much discrimination as they please. If affirmed, and an isolated case of hardship should arise, we must trust, as we do in other cases, to the good sense of public officers, and Judges, and jurors, to meet the emergency. Equal rights over public highways, and in public conveyances, is doubtless the law now. Was any one ever prosecuted for giving preference to persons who were infirm and helpless? What chance would such a prosecution stand?

Mr. Hawley, I observe, puts his objections on other grounds. Practically, his objection is that if this bill passes it will break up the "special contract system," which he favors.

Mr. Hawley's house is one of the most extensive in the State. His importations amount to millions in the course of the year. He is of opinion, that for that reason, he ought to pay less rates for the same service than those charged to younger and less prosperous concerns. While I admire his frankness in this suggestion, I think he, and the few large houses similarly situated, will be alone in admitting its correctness. It exhibits forcibly the radical objection to the whole system of discrimination which finds expression in these special contracts, viz.: That it creates at once a class of privileged persons, distinct from the rest of the community. By the exercise of it, the railroad companies have power to select which men in a particular place may do business at a profit, and which may not, and thus reduce the whole trading community to a state of practical servitude. For obvious reasons, they prefer to build up one large concern to a dozen small ones, and the tendency and effect of their policy of discriminations, therefore, is to concentrate all commercial business in the hands of a few large houses. One monopoly thus draws round itself a dozen subordinate ones each tributary to it. The rest of the commercial community is relegated to the position of a body of petty traders, who pick up a precarious support by the permission of the great houses which enjoy the favor of the railroad companies.

Such a state of things may be found unobjectionable to those who possess large capital, and, therefore, fall within the privileged class, but it is destructive to the prosperity of the State; for the simple reason, that its tendency and effect are to make the rich richer and the poor poorer. There is but one safe principle to follow in relation to these public roads, the use of which is essential now in the daily life of all men, and that is absolute impartiality. The maxim that we are all equal before the law, is the cornerstone of our whole system of government. Why should it not apply to public highways? What reason can be rendered to the contrary?

Yours, very respectfully,

JOHN T. DOYLE.

HON. THOS. F. BARRY.

SECOND LETTER FROM JOHN T. DOYLE.

MENLO PARK, April 15, 1884.

MY DEAR SIR: In addition to what I then said, I would like to add a few words on certain sections of the bill:

The requirements of section three are leveled against such nefarious proceedings as the destruction of the wharf at Santa Monica. It was a magnificent structure, several hundred feet long, with a depth of water for the largest vessels, railroad laid on it extending direct to Los Angeles, stationary engines, and all facilities for unloading a large steamer in four hours. It was built by a railroad company organized under the laws of this State, and by authority of the same. The stock of the company was afterwards bought up by people controlling a rival line of transportation, having much inferior facilities (viz., lighters at Wilmington), and deliberately destroyed; not suffered to decay, but *willfully destroyed*. For the truth of this statement I refer to Governor Stoneman, from whom I had it. I learn recently, that a similar act of vandalism has occurred at Santa Cruz, and was perpetrated by another railroad concern. I think there is no other civilized country in the world where such an act would not send its perpetrator to prison. Such things are crimes against civilization. Richelieu's stone blockade of La Rochelle, though done by the authority of the sovereign, and as a war measure against armed rebels, has been condemned by all history as infamous. These acts were done in profound peace, and by corporations deriving their leave to exist from the laws of the very people against whose best interests they were directed. Should there or not be a law to forbid such infamies?

Section four is a provision necessary to keep the State's control of its own corporations. In various actions brought by the State against the Central Pacific and Southern Pacific Railroad Companies, they have pleaded that they have derived certain privileges from the General Government, and have been made Federal corporations, and thus exempt from State control and State taxation. Some months ago the Southern Pacific Company moved heaven and earth to get a Federal charter from Congress, which the Legislature remonstrated against. Lately, I see Connecticut has granted a charter, under which an attempt may be made to consolidate in some way all connecting roads, including the Southern Pacific. It is evident these companies intend to escape all State control, if possible, and the Legislature should be forehanded with them, and prohibit all such proceedings. From the moment the State gives up the absolute control of its own corporations, and its own highways, it loses its independence and its autonomy. Yours truly,

JOHN T. DOYLE.

Hon. Thos. F. Barry.

———

LETTER FROM JOHN F. KIDDER.

NEVADA COUNTY NARROW GAUGE RAILROAD, }
SUPERINTENDENT'S OFFICE, GRASS VALLEY, April 12, 1884. }

Hon. C. W. Cross, Sacramento, California:

DEAR SIR: As I am unable to personally appear before the Judiciary Committee of the Senate, in reference to the proposed legislation regarding the railroads of California, and as the "Barry bill" has been so thoroughly ventilated, that it would seem superfluous to give my opinion of the injury said bill would cause, not only to the railroads but to the general public, I therefore desire to give you, briefly, the facts in regard to our own narrow gauge railroad, as to its construction, value of the investment, and reasons why the State should not interfere with it.

The Nevada County Narrow Gauge Railroad Company was organized under a special charter of the State of California (a copy of which is hereby submitted), granting said company the right to charge certain rates of freights and fares, greater than those authorized by the general law of the State. Without such provision, it would have been impossible to procure the necessary capital to build said road, as no one would have been foolish enough to invest their money with a certainty that under the general law, or rather the rates allowed by that law, there would have been no return for their investment. The cost of the road and equipment has been to the present time, $608,559 88, as follows:

	1882.	1883.
Cost of construction and equipment	$595,522 02	$598,521 55
Value of material on hand	8,945 23	9,102 69
Investment in City Bank stock	935 64	935 64
Excess of cash items over audited accounts	1,823 22	
Total	$607,226 21	$608,559 88

The money to build the road was subscribed locally, and no donations of either State or county aid were asked or given. The enterprise has been a blessing to the people along the line of the road, and no complaints have ever been made or reductions asked in any of the charges made for passenger or freight traffic. There have been three (3) dividends, of three per cent each, on the capital stock, amounting to a sum total of twenty-one thousand seven hundred and ninety-eight dollars, since the opening of the road in April, eighteen hundred and seventy-six, which is all the return the stockholders have received. The gross receipts for each year of operating the road, as given below, show that the business is rapidly decreasing since eighteen hundred and eighty-one, with a probability that the present year will show a much larger decrease. This, as you well know, is owing to the suspension of hydraulic mining:

YEARS.	Mileage of Locomotives.	Gross Receipts.
1876 (April 17 to December 31)	33,957	$70,760 26
1877	49,444	90,518 60
1878	50,744	98,085 97
1879	52,261	101,949 24
1880	68,148	115,655 55
1881	75,052	116,465 81
1882	67,671	105,273 20
1883	61,612	100,978 07

At the same time, the expenses for operating are greatly on the increase, owing to the necessary renewals of bridges, superstructures, rails, cars, and motive power. I append the income account of 1883:

INCOME ACCOUNT, 1883.

Gross earnings	$100,978 07
Dividend, Citizens' Bank stock	18 72
Total	$100,996 79
Excess of expenses over income	574 97
Total	$101,571 76
Total operating expenses	$80,771 76
Interest, bonded debt	20,800 00
Total	$101,571 76

I scarcely deem it necessary to dilate on the facts as I have shown them, but I would ask, can the great State of California ignore its contract with us, and force us to suspend operating our road.

Your obedient servant,

JOHN F. KIDDER,
President and Manager.

LETTER FROM W. F. WHITTIER.

SAN FRANCISCO, April 15, 1884.

To the Judiciary Committee, Senate Chamber, Sacramento:

I duly received your letter of the tenth instant, inviting me to appear before your committee and give my views regarding the Barry bill. I am very sorry to say that not only pressing business, but the state of my health, will prevent my leaving home at present.

I have only given the bill a cursory examination, which, however, is sufficient to convince me that it is open to objections.

Perhaps it would be well for me to say that my firm—Whittier, Fuller & Co.—is not, nor has it ever been, under contract to ship any, or all, its goods by rail. We conduct our business in our own way, shipping such goods by rail as it seems to be to our interest to ship that way, and choosing any other route at pleasure.

Generally speaking, with regard to legislation on railroads, I will say that it seems to me that all discriminations between persons and places, which have for their object, or are likely to produce the effect of favoritism by the carrier, to create conditions which do not now exist, such as contracting their business into the hands of one, or of a few persons, as against the rest of the community, or as diverting the trade from one point to another point viewed with more favor by the persons operating railroads, should be prohibited, and the carriers so restrained as to make it impossible.

On the other hand, it is the result of my own experience in business that discriminations, *per se*, are not always unjust. The laws of trade recognize this. Indeed, I might say that discrimination may be regarded as second only to competition in its contribution to the life of trade. It should be recognized, too, that there are natural conditions which give one place, on account of its location, the advantage over another place, and it is also true that there are persons—merchants, producers—who by their tact, industry, and application, do possess advantages over their neighbors. Common carriers, while restrained from creating such conditions, it seems to me, should not be allowed to destroy them. My conclusions might, perhaps, be summed up in this: That having provided such legislation as will prevent, or punish, unjust discrimination in favor of persons or places, there should remain the greatest possible freedom to both carrier and shipper, for the purpose of the development and extension of trade.

It seems to me that the first section of the Barry bill is vague and indefinite, to the extent that it is likely to be mischievous. We have been large shippers for years over, perhaps, all the transportation lines in this State, and have never yet experienced partiality, discrimination, preference, or favor in the matter of dispatch, speed, or accommodation, or prices; nor have we ever had occasion to complain of these things being done against us in favor of others. I don't know that the section referred to goes any further in restraining these acts upon the part of the carriers than the Constitution. I doubt it materially.

I note a provision that all freight shall be dispatched and forwarded in the order in which it is received or tendered for transportation. So far as our firm is concerned we have never experienced the necessity for any such legislation. I can see, however, how it might be made an excuse by the carriers for putting the shipping public to a very great deal of inconvenience. In many cases it could concentrate the business of the State in the hands of a few, for a time, at least.

I doubt very much if the interest of the carriers, conceding that they proceed from a not altogether enlightened spirit of selfishness, would permit them to discriminate in the matter of forwarding freight. On the other hand, I can see where an ironclad rule of the nature provided in this section, would be, not only a cause of inconvenience to the public, but the source of much litigation. No rule should be established that would permit me, with a large tonnage to be moved, to engage the facilities of a carrier for my exclusive benefit, for even a short period. There are shippers who can, and often have, tonnage amounting to thousands of tons, that sometimes can be suddenly thrown upon the carrier, monopolizing its facilities for a time, long or short, to the exclusion of others.

The interests of the carrier are such as to prompt it to prevent this as much as possible. Under the law, as proposed, the carrier would have no option in the matter. I think that the bill would be improved by eliminating that portion altogether.

As to section second, I question very much the expediency of forbidding, absolutely, all discounts, rebates, special contracts, special rates, or other devices for charging more or less than the published rates. It seems to me that a prohibition of unjust discriminations, preferences, or favors in the interest of certain persons or places, would be sufficient.

In the matter of special contracts, as I have said before, my firm has not been under contract with any of the railroad companies in this State. I know that the contract plan enforced on through business has been the subject of a great deal of criticism. It has not been handled by the railroad company as, perhaps, I should have handled it. At the same time, perhaps every one of my fellow merchants would suggest a plan as different from mine as mine would be from that of the railroad company's.

I cannot see that these special contracts have been detrimental to the interests of the State. If they have worked a hardship in any sense, it has been against the interests of the merchants of San Francisco, in that it has given the interior merchants the facilities and advantages which were, before the opening of the railroad, enjoyed, wholly and exclusively, by the merchants of San Francisco, by reason of its seaport.

There is no question but that it has had a tendency to reduce freights. There is no doubt in my mind but that if the railroad companies had been able to offer me rates which I could see were, upon the whole, equal to those my firm enjoys by the use of all three routes, I should have been glad to have made a contract.

I should like to see the wholesale principle recognized by the carriers, as it is recognized by merchants and traders in their dealings with each other. It strikes me that a principle so universally recognized in trade ought to be observed in the conduct of such a potential factor in trade as the transportation interest has become. All the rates, privileges, and facilities offered by a carrier ought to be open to all persons upon the same terms, but it strikes me that the carrier is precisely in my position. It has transportation to sell, while I sell paints and oils. A customer who will buy an invoice running into the thousands, will certainly receive a discount from me, and from all of my competitors, from the rates that I would sell for to the purchaser of an invoice of a hundred dollars.

I am not prepared to say that it is practicable, and I do not know that your honorable committee will regard it as expedient, from the standpoint of public policy, but I cannot see why the carrier should not be allowed, or rather why it should not be obliged, to pursue the same principle, for, certainly, it can afford to do so. In other words, it appears to me that just as I can handle my goods and turn them over in large lots at a lower price, and make the same percentage of profit as in smaller lots at higher price, so the carrier can handle large lots of goods for one individual at a lower rate and yet make the same percentage of profit as by handling an equal amount in smaller lots for different persons at a higher price.

I don't know that the special contract system has ever been put in practice by any carrier in its local business in California. It seems to me that there might be cases where a special contract—that is, not a contract which shall be in the interest of an individual, or a community, as against some other individual, or some other community, but which shall be "special" in the sense that it shall be different from the usual and ordinary term of carriage by the railroad company—would be necessary in order to enable the carrier to properly serve the public. Our State is young. Our agricultural, horticultural, and manufacturing interests have still great room for growth and development. They may be, in large sense, dependent upon facilities for transportation for their success, and the carrier should not be forbidden to make terms and conditions essential to their success, provided such terms and conditions shall be equally available to all the public under similar circumstances.

With respect to section third I have nothing to say.

With respect to section four, it strikes me as a very unwise provision. We need railroads. We should be in the attitude of welcome continually, and instead of making laws which might be construed, whether justly or not, as hostile towards such enterprises, we should avoid even the appearance of discouraging them. I can see no great good end to be served by enacting that section into a law, while I can see that it might be the means of preventing the extension of railroads now touching our borders, which are incorporated under the laws of other Governments or States.

With respect to sections five and six my advice would be worth little to your honorable committee.

With respect to section seven, as a matter of opinion, I will say that it seems to me that a provision that will forfeit the charter of a corporation for the illegal act of an employé or an agent, which may have originated in malice towards the corporation, or in ignorance, or carelessness, is unnecessarily severe. Laws should be enforced. Corporations as well as individuals should be made to respect and obey the law, but a needlessly severe penalty more often works to defeat the end of the law than to secure it. It seems to me that this section can be amended so as to secure obedience to the law, and that, too, by modifying the penalty instead of enacting it as it now stands.

I have no criticism to offer regarding section eight.

I should have been pleased to meet your committee and to have given it an opportunity to question me as to my views relative to this bill if that were at all possible. Regard for my duty as a citizen has impelled me to give you, hastily, these criticisms, which I hope will be received in the kindly spirit in which they are tendered.

Yours very respectfully,

W. F. WHITTIER.

_____

Statement of J. B. Wheeler.

Mr. Chairman and Gentlemen—Senators: I make no pretensions to oratory or elocution. Like one of our notable fellowmen—and I base the remark upon one that he made—a platform is calculated, not to catch flies, but to catch men. But were I not to make a few remarks in regard to what brought me here (and I presume to say, for what you are here), I should be recreant to my duty at least. We are all here, I presume, for a purpose. There was a time when it was considered that you were called here in the interest of the Government established by our sires of the revolution in the interests of the people; but there is a great issue at stake, or seems to be now, between the Government and another power seeking to be the Government. I would not make these remarks did I not understand the jeers of some of the gentlemen. There was a time, I say, when we had what we supposed to be a government of the people; a purely coöperative democratic government—a government by and for the people, but there is a power that has grown up, a mighty power in our land, that bids defiance to that government. It is a coöperative government, too, as I understand by coöperative government, to be a government of interests, and as our forefathers intended it should be a government of coöperative interests.

[A point of order was raised, that the gentleman should address himself to the subject.]

All right. I can't very well speak of that first; I don't know how, unless I am allowed to give the two governments. There is a government of the people; a coöperative government.

SENATOR BROOKS—I would like to ask the gentleman if he has any objection to giving his ideas upon this bill? Answer—In a very few minutes I will answer your questions. I want to say to you that our forefathers intended to have a coöperative government, and now it is a coöperative government of incorporations. That is a power that is making itself apparent in this Government—the coöperative interests of the corporations.

SENATOR KELLOGG—I ask that the gentleman give us his ideas in regard to the bill.

[Senator McClure appointed to conduct the examination.]

Q. What is your name? A. Wheeler.

Q. Where do you reside? A. If I am permitted to make a further statement—I reside at Oakland.

Q. It has been the custom of this committee to first allow a gentleman to give a general statement with regard to his views of this bill No. 10. You will now have an opportunity to make such statement, and then I will ask you a question or two in reference to it. This is a question of discrimination and abuses by transportation companies? A. I suppose that any further statement of mine according to my ideas is shut off now?

Q. You have made a pretty full introductory statement. A. It is very short considering the cause and the importance——

Q. Well, we are limited now in time. A. Well now, I would like to ask you a question; I would like to ask why this change of procedure?

Q. There is no change of procedure? A. I have been before this committee for the last week, and I understand how it has been conducted.

Q. You will proceed and state your views with reference to this bill, laying aside for the present these questions of great public policy? A. That is what I intended to speak of.

Q. You have made the introductory remarks? A. It leaves them in a very bad condition.

Q. I think the Senators will understand your position ? A. Perhaps they do.

Q. I understand that the platform upon which you stand is a coöperative platform ? A. Yes, sir; coöperative—a platform of the interests of fifty millions of people, and the coöperative interests of a few corporations. Now in order to prevent "discrimination," it would be necessary for me to show that the cost of carrying freights and fares—that the rate per mile—is merely nominal. I have been before this committee for the last few days, and I have heard several of the railroad magnates upon this point. They pretend to say that it is impossible for them to carry freights and fares without discrimination.

Q. Are you stating the conclusions of the witnesses ? A. I pretend to say that you cannot treat the case correctly without making a statement of what freights and fares shall be, leaving to them a decent respectable profit for doing the business ; and all the railroad gentlemen which I heard make statements before this committee, have testified that it was impossible for them to do business unless they were allowed, both in time, place, and price and persons.

Q. Are you speaking of accommodations also ? A. Yes, sir. In order for me to show that they can, it is necessary for me first to show the cost of actually carrying freights and fares to be merely nominal. It amounts to simply nothing. I will give you a statement of the cost of carrying freights and fares, and prove why.

Q. Have you the statement prepared ? A. No, sir; not in full. I have stated to you that I could not treat the subject fairly and properly. I do not ask you to take my figures alone; I propose to show by their own statements; but I will first give you my own figures. They say I am a maniac, and that I am crazy; when I take their own statements to prove that my statements are correct, you will no longer have cause to say that I am crazy. I propose to show the cost of carrying a thousand passengers three thousand miles—the cost of taking a fifteen-car train to New York. Some might say it would be the fuel, but I will leave it to you whether it will be the fuel. The cost of coal for a fifteen-car load three thousand miles—coal per day three tons, cost from ninety cents to two dollars per ton ; that is what it costs Stanford and Crocker, the owners of these rights, across the plains. They have their own coal beds—they own them—and it costs them what it costs them to get the coal out of the mine. Any person knows the cost of excavating coal, and that only costs from forty-five to ninety cents a ton, after being conveyed on this same railroad for a thousand miles. We will take the highest rate, always giving them the advantage, for they are poor gentlemen, and I don't wish to take advantage of the poor. Three tons at two dollars per ton equals six dollars per day; for a six days' trip equals thirty-six dollars for coal; and that would be, at the price of Towne's statement, one hundred and eight dollars. Towne says that the coal costs him six dollars per ton ; two brakemen, at two dollars and twenty-five cents each, four dollars and fifty cents per day; one engineer, four dollars; one conductor, three dollars; the amount for hands on the train, fourteen dollars per day, six days—six times fourteen equals eighty-four dollars; cost of keeping the roadbed in repair for three:thousand miles at thirty men to the hundred miles, at a dollar and a half a day, eight thousand one hundred dollars to keep the entire line in repair for six days, allowing eight trains a day to pass over said roadbed per day—four trains each way. By dividing the cost, eight thousand three hundred dollars, by the number of trains passing over the road, six days, you have one hundred and seventy dollars to the one train. The cost of the one train portion of the keeping the roadbed in repair for the entire route, sum total up to date, two hundred and ninety dollars. We get at the wear and tear of the road by figuring the life of a car at thirty years, which is short. I will guarantee that a car can be kept in repair, if it is built like the one-horse shay that we all heard about when we were boys, for that will run fifty instead of thirty years. By figuring the life of a car at thirty years, I get the first cost of a train at sixty thousand dollars, and the cost of repairs of a train at sixty thousand dollars more; sum total, one hundred and twenty thousand dollars. The total number of trips we would make in thirty days, one thousand eight hundred and twenty-five; the cost of one trip would be as many times as one thousand eight hundred and twenty-five is contained in one hundred and twenty dollars, which is sixty-one dollars, for the cost of keeping one train in repair during a six days' trip.

Q. You have not charged anything for oil? A. I have not got to that yet. Oil is always an after consideration. Oil (putting his hand behind) sometimes is a previous consideration. We will add the oil and find the general cost. It would take about five dollars' worth of oil to run a train to New York City, but we will put it at seven dollars and fifty cents. We don't wish to take any advantage of the poor. For Superintendent's and incidental expenses, say, on an average, that it costs five hundred thousand dollars per annum, all told, and no more. That is to be divided by the entire business—and there is something like two thousand five hundred to three thousand trains pass across the continent every year, besides the other home business in the State. That would not make over ten dollars a train for these incidental expenses.

Q. I would suggest that you give us the results of your figures? A. The conclusion is that it is ten dollars. I have not the figures here, but I figured it out before I came here. Now, the sum total of taking that train to New York is three hundred and ninety dollars. Divide that by the number of persons; fifteen cars will seat one · thousand and five passengers—I mean in the emigrant cars. I am speaking of common people, and not of sixty thousand dollar cars.

SENATOR BROOKS—I want to ask a question? A. I would like to finish the statement.

Q. Do you know, of your own knowledge, any discrimination that has been practiced by the railroad company in this State; if you do, the committee will hear you on those matters of facts? A. I have seen some facts of discrimination. I know of some.

[Senator Spencer appointed to finish the examination.]

MR. WHEELER—Am I permitted to go on and finish?

SENATOR SPENCER—Is it material to you whether you go home now or in the morning? A. I will answer the question. As long as you will hear the truth from me I will stay with you.

Q. I was about to outline an examination, and I did not know but you were in a hurry to get home. Do you know anything about the transportation of goods in its order? A. Well, I made a proposition, as I understand, to answer your question.

Q. Have you any objection to section one of this bill? A. I have it here. I will read it to you.

Q. Go on. A. (Reading)—This is a coöperative; that is corporation—no coöperation. Going by rail, are you, or by telegraph?

Q. I suppose you have read this bill. Shall I read it to you (reading the bill quite rapidly)? A. You needn't read it in that style.

Q. Have you any objection to section one of it? A. Provided it is built on the coöperative plan and operated under the coöperative system.

Q. Do you see any objection to section two? A. I will have to see and read it myself. You are not a good reader. It is strange that you American people that are sent here cannot read well. If you ask me questions properly I will answer if I am permitted to go ahead and make my statement.

Q. I simply want to ask if you have any objection to section two? A. This is a farce that has been perpetrated here against me. If you think I am not capable of seeing these things, you are very much mistaken.

Q. Have you read this bill? A. I have, sir.

Q. Have you any objections? A. If it is your intention——

SENATOR TAYLOR—I object to the witness scolding and intimidating the Senator.

SENATOR SPENCER—Have you read the bill? A. Yes, sir.

Q. Do you see any objection to this bill? A. Yes, sir.

Q. What are your objections to it? A. If you will allow me to go on, and in my regular way, I will come to it and point them out.

Q. I only desire to call your attention to the bill under consideration? A. In the first place, a portion of it does not allow discrimination.

Q. Have you read section two of this bill? A. I have read it all.

Q. Is there any objection to section two? A. If this is the line of questioning that you are going to present I will read it very carefully again, as I intended. I was here, and saw your proceedings for the last four or five days, and in spite of the best evidence that the railroad can produce, by the magnates of the railroad company—and this is a matter of discrimination, I propose to show.

Q. Well, I will thank you on behalf of the committee, and we will now adjourn. A. Just wait a minute.

SENATOR BROOKS—You have been engaged in politics for some time? A. What has that to do with discrimination?

SENATOR KELLOGG—I understand that you have given this subject a good deal of time and attention? A. I have, I think, more than any other man.

Q. You have put nearly all your time in upon it? A. Yes, sir.

Q. You have done nothing else during the last seven years. Have you ever shipped or received a ton of goods over these roads? A. I don't know what that would have to do with the cost.

Q. But your study has been a benefit to the people? A. Yes, sir.

Q. You were at one time a candidate for Governor? A. That don't make any difference.

Q. Do you agree with the statements made here that there ought to be no discrimination as to rates per ton per mile? A. I do; there should be no discrimination.

Q. Do you say that the rates ought to be the same on long hauls as on short hauls? A. I do not.

Q. Explain your views on that proposition? A. There ought to be no discrimination in persons—in proportion to the distance.

Q. Then, you are in favor of discrimination thus far? A. Yes, sir; it should be a fixed thing. I could not answer that without bringing in this coöperative government, if we were trying to arrive at justice at all. If a man lived less than two hundred miles away, his freight should not be more than two cents per ton per mile.

Q. Have you a schedule of the rates which ought to be charged? A. Yes, sir.

Q. Read it? A. We are figuring on a basis purely coöperative; a purely coöperative democratic government, by and for the people, to do the greatest good to the greatest number. The first one hundred miles, two and a half cents a mile; call it three and a half; twelve tons to the car, forty-two cents per ton to the car; fifty cars on one train; forty-two times fifty is two thousand one hundred dollars for taking a train one hundred miles. The first two hundred miles, one and three fourth cents per ton per mile; the first three hundred miles, one sixth of a cent per ton per mile; four hundred miles, seven eighths of a cent; six hundred miles, seven tenths of a cent.

Q. Do you make it anywhere on your schedule that the distance is so far that they can haul for nothing? A. No, sir; it never goes down to that. A half cent is as low as it goes.

Q. Do you think that there ought to be discrimination made in prices or classes? A. Different classes should be; yes, sir. It would be impossible to carry some goods by the ton.

Q. Do you think that a cargo of wheat ought to be shipped at the same price as a cargo of tea? A. No.

Q. How about live stock as to discrimination in shipping? A. I think live stock is perishable; it is possible for them to eat themselves up paying expenses. That is——

Q. Would they perish? A. The man might perish.

Q. Is there any other facts that you desire to bring before this committee? A. All that I ask to state further is just this, I wanted to show you that the men who testified here——

Q. That would be the business of the committee? A. My statement here is, that you should go a thousand miles for four bits a ton. I want to corroborate that.

The Chairman—Do you desire to make any correction to what you have stated? A. I want to ask that the railroad deal fairly by the people who have built the road. The measures they adopt to carry their principles are such as should not be used by a railroad representing a capital of seven millions of dollars. We find that they can protect themselves against legislation, and against the control of the Government. These are the big points of this subject, irrespective of the mere matter of money, which I conceive is of small moment compared to the degradation of the country, which we all admit. Therefore it must be controlled, and I understand that is what you are here to do. Your duty is found in an article in the Constitution upon corporations; that the Legislature shall pass all laws necessary for the enforcement of the article. You wish to take up this subject, and pass such laws as are required to control these matters, and the receipts of the railroad company, over which you have reasonable control. The difficulties are twofold.

STATEMENT OF GENERAL NAGLEE.

GENTLEMEN: I appear before you in answer to your request. I would like to state in regard to these railroad matters, that I like to look at a locomotive of a thousand tons passing over the country at a rate that only a bird can fly. It seems a most extraordinary thing, that we should have such facilities of transportation. In the olden times any one could put his boat upon the waters; anybody could build his boat; anybody could carry transports, and the result was, that there was no such complaint, and there ought to be no complaint in the matter of mere railroad transportation, and there ought to be no difficulty. I look upon difficulties encountered in this subject as coming from the fact that railroads go out of their sphere altogether and interfere with the polities of the country. They should not interfere with politics, but should let the parties alone. Another thing in that matter of politics, we find that the one in relation to this matter of discrimination, and the other in relation to over-charges. These are the most important of all outside of the interference of politics.

They are entitled to a certain consideration, and a limited consideration. As far as the railroad is concerned, it is the law of the land, and they should be entitled, first, to their expenses legitimately, honestly, and economically made; and they are only entitled to a fair consideration for their investment. Now, it is a big point to determine how much they shall have. I don't think there is any difficulty in that, for the simple reason that we have the reports of experts as to what has been received, showing that they have charged unfairly, and three or four times as much as they should. The reports of Mr. Towne show that the expenses of these roads is about eleven or twelve millions of dollars. That they are entitled too. Now, if eleven millions of dollars is a reasonable expense of the road, I will allow two millions more, and a million for contingencies, say fifteen million dollars, and no more. Now, they are receiving twenty-five millions; they are not entitled to it under the decision of the Courts, but only to a reasonable consideration. This ten million dollars over and above what they should receive, should be left with the people of the country. There should be means taken by which it should be done—by which the facts should be ascertained—and then the power should be prevented from charging heavy freights, dragging out money to which they are not entitled. They break down manufactures. We should encourage manufactures. With our new State, we should do a great deal of manufacturing at home. These things are done in the most extraordinary way, and the methods taken to prevent interference are most ingenious.

One illustration is the paper business. We were being successful in the manufacture of paper, and there were incentives for the establishment of a large number of paper mills, and we were making it successful. The railroad company said, "You shall not do it, because we want to bring all the paper over the continent. We will introduce the paper so low that it will be worth almost nothing, and will put a double price on wood pulp, and increase the cost by which paper can be made, and we will put the price of transportation so low that they can afford to send all the rags east." Now, in regard to the farmer: They had to pay so much for carrying wheat that they could not afford to send it to New York, and so much for carrying flour that they could not afford to send the flour. The matter of raising wheat has become material; we will raise fifty million bushels this year. We know that ships are coming here, and that this wheat can be shipped around the Horn at from two pounds to two pounds and a half; but the railroad company, by their special contract system, are preventing the ships from bringing freights to this coast. They should be prevented from any such interference. The ship must have double freight to take it back if they have to come here empty. Thus they break down the raising of wheat. There ought to be one million of tons surplus this year, which, at a loss to the farmer of five to ten dollars per ton, would make a loss in the aggregate to our farmers of from five to ten millions of dollars. My share of the crops this year in San Joaquin County will be fifteen hundred to two thousand tons. At the above figures it will make to me a loss on this crop of from seven thousand five hundred to fifteen thousand dollars. Another large interest of this State is that of fruits. Fruits ripen here much earlier than they do in the East, and if the shipper could get them into the markets there they could get the best prices for them; and with any reasonable prices for freights, we could have our whole country raising fruit. Instead of charging eight hundred dollars for a carload of fruit, it should be brought down to a reasonable figure—something like two or three hundred dollars. The result would be, that everybody would be encouraged in fruit raising, and instead of sending carloads, as we now do, we would have trains of cars loaded with fruit crossing the continent. I was in business in San Francisco, and had worked there for a long time, and wanted to retire. I had made a sum of money that I thought was sufficient for me, and it was suggested that I should go into the grape business. People from the old country told me, "This is the best country in the world for raising grapes." The people of France and Germany, and Hungary and of Italy, and all other wine countries, brought their vines and planted them here, and the result is, that a cluster of our grapes is four times as large as when grown in Europe, with superior qualities. These gentlemen said: "Here is the place to make wine and brandy, and you can develop a fine industry." They said: "General Naglee, have you any idea of the extent of the wine country of France?" "No; tell me about it." "Why, they produce twenty-two hundred millions of gallons," which, at twenty cents per gallon, produces four hundred and fifty millions of dollars per year—three times as much as the entire cotton crop of the United States. The wine crop of France paid the enormous penalties placed upon France by Prussia in two years. This great industry seems not to be appreciated by the railroad company, for without a special contract, the freight charge is six cents per pound, or forty-five cents per gallon, making no allowance for tare, which is fully in weight equal to that of the wine, thus doubling the regular rate, and making an absolute prohibition. If allowed to use the ocean, the freight would be at the rate of six tenths of a cent per pound to New York—about one tenth of that charged by rail. The excuse made for the above excessive charge, was because of the liability of leakage and breakage. The simple manner of disposing of this question of risk and insurance, is to ascertain from the books of the railroad company the actual amount paid for loss in an entire year, divide it by the gross receipts of the year, and add the fraction to the freight, which would dispose of the question of loss and risk for all the future. Now there should be a limit to the amount of charges that they are allowed to make. If there is not, if they can charge fifty millions they can charge one hundred millions. They should be limited, and they are entitled, as I said, to a limited consideration; and I think, that under their showing, about thirteen millions would be reasonable. You should say, " We will allow you so much money; you shall do as you ought to do; you shall bring your classification down to a half dozen classes; say dry goods so much, hardware and agricultural implements, so much."

SENATOR CROSS—We were in hopes that some of that good brandy would come this way? A. You shall not be disappointed. It seems to me that we should fix the amount that they shall have, and then make reductions in favor of the people of everything beyond that. Now, these special contracts are all wrong, and they should be stopped. They have more complications than in the tariff of the Government of the United States. What did they do in times of old with ships? A ship was to sail for San Francisco, and everything that comes along was taken at the same figure. It didn't make any difference; stone, wheat, or anything else; they didn't stand upon the order of taking freight, but took all that was offered, and found a place to put it on board ships of three or four decks—a great deal more difficult matter than to put it in a box-car—and there were no questions about a half or a whole ton. The heavy material must go to the bottom of a ship, and the lighter to the top, but there was no trouble. What does it cost to load a car? Why, seven men can load a car in a half an hour, which at one dollar and fifty cents per day would be just fifty cents for loading the car. Now, where is there any sense in this matter of a car, or a half a car, or in an extra charge for loading and unloading? Now, there is another point in the Barry bill. Why not just simply make provision for a half a dozen classes, and everybody can comprehend it in that way? Another thing is the matter of fares. In New York State, they are two cents a mile. Here they double it up, and then double it up again. Our relations with the railroad allows us to demand of them reasonable charges, and there are decisions which say that you shall not charge one man one price and another a different one. A few days afterwards I sent to San José for a carload of slabs for fuel. I was charged twenty-two dollars the carload to Bethany, one hundred and twenty-three miles. The car, by my direction, was taken to Tracy, from Bethany, seven miles, and the charge was eleven dollars. A gentleman told me that he sent two two-year old stallions to Arizona. Said he, "When I asked for my freight bill, I found that I was charged at the rate of four thousand pounds each." He supposed there must be some mistake, but the agent showed his printed regulations from Fourth and Townsend Streets, and that he was allowed no discretion in the premises, and, although the stallions weighed but eight hundred pounds each, he was compelled to pay on eight thousand. Another friend of mine had been sending sheep to New Mexico, and the rate had been invariably at one hundred and sixty dollars per carload. He wanted to send a car of Merino sheep to New Mexico, of superior quality, and applied to the railroad company for terms. They requested him to return in three or four days. The railroad company telegraphed to New Mexico and found that there was a demand at a good price for the Merino sheep, and charged him five hundred and sixty dollars for the carload. Two gentlemen of my acquaintance wanted a special contract to ship, one tin, and the other wheelwright material, from New York. The answer of the railroad company was, "Send a list of the persons with whom you deal in San Francisco." The names were found on the black list at Fourth and Townsend Streets, and any contract was refused. A firm with whom I am dealing in San José, applied for transfer by freight of goods from San Francisco. The answer was, "You have patronized the narrow guage railroad," and his application was refused. Still another gentleman of my acquaintance, engaged as the agent of an agricutural implement manufactory in or near Chicago, had a special contract. He found after his arrival here that the terms were greater than he would pay to send his goods to New York, and thence by Cape Horn, twenty-five thousand miles, to San Francisco. He complained to his friends of the outrageously unreasonable charges. The railroad detectives reported him at Fourth and Townsend Streets, and his contract was shut off on the ground that he talked too much. A friend shipped some mules from Livermore to Visalia, and the carload was charged at sixty-nine dollars. A few days afterwards he sent a carload of barley to feed the mules, and the charge was two hundred and twenty-seven dollars. A friend living in Stockton shipped fruit to the East. This brought him in contact with others shipping fruit from the Sacramento Valley, who were favored by the railroad company, and his venture failed, he losing four thousand dollars. Lately, in San José, the San José Times made itself obnoxious to the railroad company by exposing their outrageous practices. The railroad company determined to suppress the paper, and it so resulted by combining with a ring under the control of the Board of Education, who required the teachers to subscribe one hundred dollars apiece, under threat of losing their positions, to purchase the paper. The purchase was effected.

SENATOR McCLURE—I understand that you think we should first ascertain generally the cost of building and constructing the road, then the expenses, and then allow them a reasonable compensation for the use of their money, and that they should be limited to that as a compensation; and that a bill fixing freights and fares should be passed; and that a maximum rate should be fixed, and that all beyond that should be used to cheapen and regulate matters naturally? A. I should allow the railroad company the actual expenses honestly and economically made in running the road. I should allow them two millions of dollars for the use of their capital invested, this to include all personal service. To these I should allow them to hold back one million five hundred thousand dollars to meet extraordinary contingencies, but the balance unexpended should be carried forward to the next year, and all of the remainder should be paid into the State Treasury. I should require the railroad company to make sworn monthly statements to the Controller, who should be required to examine the books and vouchers of the railroad company and verify their reports.

Q. Your proposition is, that they are making too much money? A. Yes, sir.

Q. You think that they are entitled to a reasonable compensation for the money invested? A. Yes, sir.

Q. Your idea is that there should be a maximum rate? A. You have Railroad Commissioners who should attend to that matter, in the interest of the people. When you go into the experience of this State and of New York, and other States, and examine the matter, you will find that our railroad companies are overcharging, and charge three times as much as they should. The average of all freights in New York State is only seventy-six one hundredths of a cent, while the average in this State is two and one fourth. By the statistical returns made at Washington for the year ending June 30, 1883, the rate for the transportation of grain from all the Western States to the Atlantic, was but twenty-seven one hundredths of a cent—a little over one quarter of a cent. In all moneyed transactions there are a payer and payee, and both should be equally represented. In transactions with the railroad company the Railroad Commissioners were intended to represent the payer and guard their interests, which they have failed to do; but allow the payee to charge and collect at his pleasure, with no protest against any extortions, overcharges, discriminations, special contracts, or rebates.

Q. These are matters which you have investigated, which lead you to the conclusion that there should be a bill providing for a maximum rate of freights and fares. Were these facts the result of your own personal research? A. In regard to the subject of a maximum I have fixed three cents per mile as that of fares, and two cents as the maximum of freights per ton per mile. Taking then the figures furnished by Mr. Stanford in his open letter published in the Argonaut, which were five hundred and fifty millions of tons of freight carried one mile, and one hundred and eighty millions of passengers carried one mile, and apply the above figures, the result will be as follows:

550,000,000 tons at two cents	$11,000,000
180,000,000 passengers at three cents	5,400,000
	$16,400,000

In connection with the above I have asserted that the expenses of the Central Pacific were for the year eleven millions of dollars. I would then allow two millions five hundred thousand dollars to the company to compensate them for the use of their capital, including their personal services. I would add one million and a half to provide for extraordinary contingencies, which would in all amount to fifteen millions of dollars; the balance between this and the gross receipts should be paid into the State Treasury; and the rates of freight and fares for the following year should be reduced that no surplus above the allowances made to the company could longer accrue. The gross receipts of the company for the last year were twenty-five millions of dollars; all of which, above fifteen millions, should either remain with the people or be paid into the State Treasury.

SENATOR TAYLOR—Have you read the provisions of section one of the Barry bill? A. Yes, sir.

Q. Do you think the provisions of that section are in the interest of the shipper? A. I make no objection to the bill; I think it would meet the requirements intended.

Q. You make no objection to the bill as a whole? A. I don't object to that section. It is merely a repetition, to some extent, of section two, of article twelve, requiring the Legislature to make penalties.

SENATOR DEL VALLE—It is claimed by some of the opponents of this bill that if it be adopted, it will have the effect of driving capital out of the State, and prevent competition in railroads? A. I don't see that it can affect capital. I see no difficulty; anybody can get a charter.

Q. Do you know anything about the special contract system? A. The company fixes certain arbitrary rates, two or three times a reasonable one, which is called an open rate, and which is charged and collected, unless you enter into a special contract, and by which you are required to release the company from certain risks that they incur as common carriers. The special rates thus obtained are largely beyond those prescribed for the same service on other roads. I object to the special contract system, inasmuch as it tends to drive off ships. Then they pay $100,000 a month to the Panama steamship company as a subsidy for not competing with them. It works a great wrong. They can, under it, make or break individuals or places. You are well aware that Huntington, Hopkins & Company have been doing about one half of the entire hardware business of the State. Why? Because they have better rates. I warrant you they don't pay as much as anybody else, or not any more, if any thing at all. Through the means of these contracts, favoritism can be extended and a community be increased or broken down. They can break anybody down. If they want to favor a man in Arizona in business, they can allow him to sell goods cheaper than anybody else. It ought not to be permitted.

SENATOR McCLURE—That is, the whole system; that is, not confined to this State? A. I have one of the special contracts. I do not care to have it go out of my possession, or that the names should be made public. The names must not be read. The Clerk may read all except the names:

Contract between the Union Pacific Railroad Company, the Atchison, Topeka, and Santa Fé Railroad Company, and the Missouri Pacific Railway Company, and others.

This agreement, made and entered into this ———— day of ————, A. D. one thousand eight hundred and eighty, by and between the Union Pacific Railroad Company; the Atchison, Topeka, and Santa Fé Railroad Company; and the Missouri Pacific Railway Company, for itself; and the St. Louis, Iron Mountain, and Southern Railway Company; the International and Great Northern Railroad Company, and the Texas and Pacific Railway Company, first parties, and the firm of ————, of the City of ————, second party. Witnesseth: That in consideration of the agreement made by the second party as hereinafter described, to be by said second party fully performed, maintained, and fulfilled, said first parties have covenanted and agreed, and do hereby covenant and agree that upon all the goods, wares, and merchandise shipped from the eastern points hereinafter named, all or any of them, and consigned to said second party at ————, during the term of this contract, the freight charges shall not exceed the following rates, in United States currency, per one hundred pounds, gross weight, namely:

ARTICLES.	FROM—				ARTICLES.	FROM—			
	New York	Pittsburg	Cincinnati	Chicago		New York	Pittsburg	Cincinnati	Chicago

Upon freight not herein specially provided for, the rates shall not exceed those provided by the freight tariff published by the first parties, which may be in effect between the cities named at the time such freight is shipped.

Freight from the points hereinafter named shall be transported as follows, i. e.: At New York rates—From Boston, Philadelphia, Baltimore, Richmond, Petersburg, Lynchburg, Gordonsville, Charlottesville, and Staunton, Va.; Charleston, W. Va.; New Orleans, La.; Harrisburg, Pa.; Newark and Trenton, N. J.; Albany, Troy, and all stations on the Hudson River Division of the N. Y. C. & H. R. R. R.; Port Jervis, and all stations east thereof, on the N. Y., L. E. & U. R. R.; Brookville, Chaudiere Junction, Coaticooke, Cornwall, Coteau Landing, Montreal, Prescott, Pt. Levi, Quebec, Riviere du Loup, Sherbrooke, St. Hyacinthe, and St. Johns, Canada; Rouses Point, N. Y.; Rutland, Vt.; and all stations on line of Boston and Albany R. R.; and stations on Hoosac Tunnel Line in Massachusetts.

At Pittsburgh rates—From Buffalo and Suspension Bridge, N. Y.; Wheeling, W. Va.; Greenville, Sharon, and Sharpsville, Pa.; Guelph, Hamilton, London, Paris, Rockwood, and Toronto, Canada; Bellaire, Cleveland, East Liverpool, Leetonia, Niles, Portsmouth, Steubenville, and Youngstown, O.; and all stations on L. S. & M. S. R'y, between Buffalo and Cleveland; also all stations on P., Ft. W. and C. R'y, East Massillon.

At Cincinnati rates—From Columbus, Dayton, Defiance, Deshler, Delphos, Fostoria, Hamilton, Junction City, Lima, Lockland, Mansfield, Middleton, Monroeville, Mt. Vernon, Newark, Sandusky, Shelby, Springfield, Tiffin, Toledo, and Zanesville, O.; Detroit, Mich.; Auburn, Connersville, Fort Wayne, Indianapolis, Jeffersonville, Lafayette, Logansport, Peru, Richmond, and Wabash, Ind.; Danville, Ill.; and from Louisville, Ky., with Ohio River, transfer charges added.

At Chicago rates—From St. Paul and Minneapolis, Minn.; Bement, Crystal Lake, Decatur, Delevan, Elgin, Freeport, Lincoln, Pekin, Peoria, Quincy, Rockford, Springfield, Taylorville, and Tolono, Ill.; Beloit, Kenosha, Milwaukee, and Racine, Wis.; Leavensworth, Kans.; Hannibal, Kansas City, St. Joseph, and St. Louis, Mo.; Clinton, Ia.; and all points on and east of the Mississippi River on the main lines of C., R. I. & P., C. & N. W., and C., B. & Q. Railroads.

Said first parties also agree that in case they, or either of them, any time during the continuance of this agreement, shall print and publish a regular freight tariff from the eastern cities hereinbefore referred to, to California points, which names lower rates upon any or all articles than the rates herein provided for upon such articles, said second party shall have the benefit of such tariff rates upon such articles during the time that such tariff may remain in force.

And said first parties furthermore agree to protect said second party from any "cut" or lower rates than those hereinbefore provided that may be published or charged by any other railroad company or companies, which may operate a through or all-rail line from any or all of the eastern cities hereinbefore named, for the purpose of diverting freight from the lines of the first parties. The intent and purpose of the foregoing being to guarantee to the second party rates which shall be as low as those charged and collected upon the same articles, between same points, by any other all-rail route which may now or at any time during the term of this contract compete for the traffic of California.

Said first parties further agree that in the event of active competition with the Pacific Mail Steamship Company for the traffic between New York and San Francisco, the rates to be charged the said second party during the period of such excessive competition, within the term of this contract, shall not exceed those current by the Pacific Mail Steamship Company's vessels, at the time of shipment, by more than the following figures, i. e.:

For goods hereinbefore named at following rates for transportation from New York:	Excess of rail rates above current rates by Pacific Mail steamers not to exceed:
All goods named at rates not exceeding one dollar and fifty cents per hundred pounds	Fifty cents per hundred pounds.
Rates exceeding one dollar and fifty cents, not exceeding two dollars and fifty cents, per hundred pounds	Seventy-five cents per hundred pounds.
Rates exceeding two dollars and fifty cents, not exceeding four dollars, per hundred pounds	One dollar per hundred pounds.
Rates exceeding four dollars, not exceeding six dollars, per hundred pounds	One dollar and fifty cents per hundred pounds.
Rates exceeding six dollars per hundred pounds	Three dollars per hundred pounds.

It being agreed that by the term "current rates" is to be understood the average rates actually charged and obtained by the Pacific Mail Steamship Company upon goods of each specific kind transported by it upon the steamer receiving freight in New York for San Francisco, at the time that the shipment is made by rail as to which a claim for reduced rate is made by the second party.

It is also understood and agreed, that the above named guaranty as to excess of rates above Pacific Mail Steamship rates shall not apply during any portion of the term of this contract, when the rates of the Pacific Mail Steamship Company from New York to San Francisco are subject to the control of the first parties, or either of them. The said first parties further agree that the freight of the said second party shall be transported without unfavorable discrimination in the matters of time and attention, as compared with goods of the same class consigned to other parties.

In consideration of the guarantee of the foregoing special rates of freight, the second party has covenanted and agreed, and does hereby covenant and agree to ship, or cause to be shipped, by way of the railroads owned or operated by the first parties, and such other connecting railroads as may be designated from time to time by the said first parties, all the goods, wares, and merchandise handled by said second party, which may or shall be purchased in or obtained from any point in the United States or Canadas east of the meridian of Omaha, during the term of this contract, for sale or use on the Pacific Coast, whether such goods are shipped in the name, or for account of said second party, or otherwise.

It is mutually understood and declared that the object of this agreement is to secure for and give to the first parties the transportation of all goods handled by said second party, which may be shipped from the Eastern States and Canadas to San Francisco, or other port or point of distribution on the Pacific Coast, during the term of this contract. Also, that said second party is able to control the matter, and direct the manner of shipping said goods, and that in the event of any portion of said goods being diverted from the routes by which it is herein agreed they shall be shipped, such conversion shall be construed as, and held to be, prima facie evidence of default in the performance of this agreement by said second party; and it shall then be optional with said first parties to annul the agreement, or to collect, as liquidated

13 b

damages, a sum equivalent to the charges said goods would have been subject to if shipped by rail in accordance with the terms of this agreement.

It is also mutually understood and particularly agreed that the special rates of freight herein provided are for the sole use and benefit of the second party; and that said second party shall not allow the use of its name or shipping marks in any way, or by any other party or parties, which shall procure for said other party or parties the benefit of said special rates of freight; and it is expressly stipulated that in case said second party shall apply, by sale or otherwise, any party or parties who are known to handle goods which have been shipped via any route not herein designated, from the territory east of the meridian of Omaha to any point or points on the Pacific Coast of the United States, or to British Columbia, during the term of this agreement, said second party shall pay or cause to be paid to said first parties freight at the regular tariff rates on the goods so supplied; in default of which said first parties shall have the right, at their option, to cancel and annul this agreement.

For the present and until further notice shipments made by the following routes:

From New York, via either the New York Central and Hudson River Railroad; the New York, Lake Erie and Western Railroad (formerly called the Erie Railway); the Pennsylvania Railroad, or the Baltimore and Ohio Railroad, as may be designated by the General Agents of the first parties, to whom shippers should apply for information as the route via which the Commissioner of the trunk line wishes that shipments should be made from New York, and from whom bills of lading for New York shipments should be obtained.

From Boston, via either the Boston and Albany Railroad, the Hoosac Tunnel Line, or the steamers of the Baltimore and Ohio Line.

From stations on the Boston and Albany Railroad, and stations on the Hoosac Tunnel Line, via those lines, respectively.

From Philadelphia and Harrisburg, Pa., and Trenton, N. J., via the Pennsylvania R. R.

From Baltimore, via the Baltimore and Ohio Railroad.

From Richmond, Petersburg, Lynchburg, Gordonsville, Charlottesville, and Staunton, Va., and Charleston, W. Va., via the Chesapeake and Ohio Railroad.

From Albany or Troy, N. Y., Rutland, Vt., and all stations on Hudson River Division of the N. Y. C. and H. R. R. R., via the New York Central and Hudson River Railroad.

From Buffalo and Suspension Bridge, via any railroad line leading westerly from those points.

From Cleveland, O., and local stations upon the line of said road, via the Lake Shore and Michigan Southern Railway.

From Newark, N. J., via either the Pennsylvania Railroad, or the New York, Lake Erie, and Western Road.

From Pittsburgh, via the Pittsburgh, Fort Wayne, and Chicago Railway, or the Pittsburgh and Lake Erie Railroad.

From Alleghany, Pa., via the Pittsburgh, Fort Wayne, and Chicago Railway.

From Portsmouth, O., via the Scioto Valley R. R., or the Baltimore and Ohio Railroad.

From Wheeling and Bellaire, via the Baltimore and Ohio Railroad and the Cleveland and Pittsburgh Railroad.

From Steubenville and East Liverpool, O., via the Cleveland and Pittsburgh Railroad.

From Montreal, Quebec, Reviere du Loup, Pt. Levi, Coaticooke, Rockwood, Sherbrooke, St. Johns, Coteau Landing, Toronto, Chandiere Junct., St. Hyacinthe, and Rouses Point, via the Grand Trunk Railway.

From Cornwall, Prescott, Brockville, Toronto, Hamilton, Guelph, Paris, and London, Ont., via the Great Western Railway of Canada.

From Cincinnati, via either the Cincinnati, Hamilton, and Dayton Railroad; the Indianapolis, Cincinnati, and Lafayette Railroad, or the Ohio and Mississippi Railway.

From Dayton, Hamilton, Lima, Lockland, and Middletown, O., Richmond and Connersville, Ind., via the Cincinnati, Hamilton, and Dayton Railroad.

From Toledo, O., via either the Wabash, St. Louis, and Pacific Railroad, or the Lake Shore and Michigan Southern Railway.

From Chicago, via either the Chicago and Northwestern Railway; the Chicago, Rock Island, and Pacific Railroad; the Chicago, Burlington, and Quincy Railroad; the Wabash, St. Louis, and Pacific Railway, or the Chicago and Alton Railroad.

From St. Louis, via either the Wabash, St. Louis, and Pacific Railway, the Missouri Pacific Railway, or the Chicago and Alton Railroad.

From New Orleans, via the Chicago, St. Louis, and New Orleans Railway, or New Orleans and Mobile and Ohio Railroads.

From Sharon, Greenville, and Sharpsville, Pa., Delphos, Youngstown, Niles, and Leetonia, O., via the Pittsburg, Fort Wayne, and Chicago Railway.

From Detroit, Mich., via the Michigan Central Railroad.

From Sandusky and Defiance, Junction City, Zanesville, Newark, Mount Vernon, Mansfield, Shelby, Monroeville, Tiflin, Fostoria, Deshler, O., and Auburn, Ind., via the Baltimore and Ohio Railroad.

From Fort Wayne, Ind., via either Wabash, St. Louis and Pacific Railway, or the Pittsburg, Fort Wayne, and Chicago Railway.

From Peru, Wabash, Logansport, Lafayette, Ind., and Danville, Ill., via the Wabash, St. Louis, and Pacific Railway.

From Columbus, Dayton, Springfield, O., and Richmond, Ind., via the Pittsburg, Cincinnati, and St. Louis Railway, by way of Chicago only.

From Jeffersonville, Ind., and Louisville, Ky., via J., M. and I. R. R.

From Bement, Tolono, Decatur, Springfield, Taylorville, Lincoln, Delevan, Pekin, and Peoria, Ill., via the Wabash, St. Louis, and Pacific Railway, and from points upon the main line of the Chicago and Northwestern Railway, the Chicago, Rock Island and Pacific Railroad, or the Chicago, Burlington, and Quincy Railroad, via such roads respectively.

From Milwaukee, Kenosha, Racine, and Beloit, Wis., via either the Chicago and Northwestern Railway or the Western Union Division of the Chicago, Milwaukee, and St. Paul Railroad.

From Whitewater, Wis., via the Chicago, Milwaukee, and St. Paul, and the Chicago, Rock Island, and Pacific Railroads.

From Hannibal, Mo., via the Hannibal and St. Joseph Railroad.

From St. Joseph and Leavenworth, via the Union Pacific Railway, (Kansas Division).

From Kansas City, via the Union Pacific Railway, (Kansas Division), or the Atchison, Topeka, and Santa Fé Railroad.

From all stations in Missouri on the main line of the Missouri Pacific, or the Wabash, St. Louis, and Pacific Railway, via those lines, respectively.

It is further mutually understood and agreed, that in case the first parties shall at any time have reason to believe that the second party has violated or disregarded the terms of this agreement, said first parties shall have the right to examine the books and papers of the second party, in so far as may be necessary to determine the truth of the matter in question.

It is further mutually understood and agreed, by and between the parties thereto, that all the freight covered by this agreement shall be shipped via such routes as may be designated from time to time by the first parties; and that said first parties shall not be deemed or held responsible for any overcharge in the rates of freight which may be made upon goods that shall not have been shipped by the carriers so designated.

It is further mutually understood and agreed, that all freight shipped under or covered by this agreement shall be truly and accurately described by the use of definite, not general, terms, and as far as true and practicable, by terms used in the tariff of the first parties hereto, so that the proper rate to be applied may be determined without inspection of the contents of the packages by the carrier; and that, in cases of doubt as to the exact nature of the contents of any package of freight consigned to said second party, the carriers shall have and are hereby accorded the right either to open said packages or to inspect the original invoices of purchase for the contents of said packages, in order to determine the proper rate to be charged thereon; and that in case it shall be found that any such package or packages contain freight of a higher class than that specified by shippers of same—the nature of the goods having been willfully misrepresented for the purpose of obtaining a lower rate upon the same than which would have been obtained under this agreement had the goods been truly described—the carriers shall have and are hereby accorded the right to charge upon such package or packages so misdescribed, double the regular tariff rate upon same.

It is further mutually understood and agreed that all freight shipped under this agreement is to be shipped subject to the rules, regulations, and conditions named in the regular freight tariffs of the first parties in effect at the time of shipment, and that the first parties and all other carriers which may transport the freight have been released or are hereby released from all liability for chafage of goods packed in bales, and other injury or loss arising from imperfect packages, and all other liabilities as insurers of any and all goods for which said tariff provides a "released" rate, or provides two rates, the lower of which is conditioned upon the signing by the shipper of a release of the form furnished by the company.

It is further mutually understood and agreed, that at the option of the first parties, all or any of the freight referred to in or covered by this agreement, may be waybilled at the special rates herein named, or at the tariff rates current at the time of shipment. In the latter case, the charges as waybilled shall be paid by the second party, upon the delivery of the freight, and at the end of each calendar month, upon the presentation of the bills for charges paid to the general freight agent of the Central Pacific Railroad Company, at San Francisco, together with the bills of lading for such freight (provided that such bills of lading have not previously been surrendered to the Central Pacific Railroad Company), or within a reasonable time thereafter, in which to adjust and audit the bills, the difference between the charges collected upon the delivery of the freight and the amount to be paid under this agreement shall be refunded to the said second party.

This agreement to take effect ————, 18—, (provided that no goods are then afloat from any city upon the American Atlantic seaboard for said second party), and is to remain in force until December 31, 1882, unless sooner canceled by the first parties, as and for the causes hereinafter named.

In witness whereof, the first parties have caused these presents to be subscribed by their general freight agents, and the second party has hereunto set its hand, upon the day and year first above written.

The Union Pacific Railway Company, by ———, General Freight Agent.

The Atchison, Topeka, and Santa Fé Railroad Company, by———, General Freight Agent.

The Missouri Pacific Railway Company, for itself and the St. Louis, Iron Mountain, and Southern Railway Company: the International and Great Northern Railroad Company, and the Texas and Pacific Railway Company, by ———, General Freight Agent.

Q. What effect has that special contract system upon the shippers of this State? A. The effect is to drive the ships from the San Francisco trade, and consequently to relieve the railroad company of competition, its effect falling heavily upon our farmers—causing a loss to them of from five to ten millions of dollars per year—it further results in favoritism, or coercion, at the pleasure of the company. Here is another special contract:

[The Clerk read as follows:]

"THE RAILROAD AND THE WINE INTEREST.

"The general rates adopted by the railroad monopoly compel the payment of a freight charge sometimes from double to treble that to which it will agree by special contract. The result of this is, that no one in California, out of a population of eight hundred thousand, can get a comparatively reasonable charge for transportation, unless by a special interview and a written contract with the company. A correspondent of the Examiner writes that he desired to send some wine to New York, and asked the charge, and was told: 'It will be six dollars per hundred pounds, but, by signing a contract, we will take your wine to New York at two dollars and a half per hundred.' Here is the contract. It shows how far such contracts are reluctantly accepted by shippers:

" SEASON FREIGHT RELEASE.

" WHEREAS, The undersigned ———, in the constant practice of shipping goods, wares, and merchandise on the railroad lines of the Central Pacific Railroad Company and its connecting transportation companies from San José to divers parties at divers places on said lines;

" And whereas said railroad company and its connections propose to ship all such goods, wares, and merchandise at *special rates*, which are less than the usual and customary rates, in consideration of ——— releasing them from all liability as insurers of such goods, wares, and merchandise:

" And whereas the undersigned desire to secure the benefit of such special rates, and to avoid the trouble and inconvenience of executing a separate contract for each shipment;

" Now, therefore, in consideration of the premises, and the further consideration of one dollar, to me in hand paid, the receipt whereof is hereby acknowledged and confessed, I do hereby release the said Central Pacific Railroad Company, and all other transportation companies over whose lines said goods may pass to destination, from all liability as insurers of any and all goods, wares, and merchandise, which may be shipped by me at such special rates on any or either of the railroad lines of said company or companies between the date of this instrument and the thirty-first day of December, eighteen hundred and eighty-two.

" In testimony whereof, I have hereunto set my hand and affixed my seal on this thirtieth day of August, A. D. eighteen hundred and eighty-two."

[General Naglee resumed:]

I think I said that the charges made on freights were very high. Gould started in business in Santa Clara. He went to the railroad company, and said: "I want to send some fruit to the East. What will it cost?" They said: "We will take a carload through for

$350," and a carload was shipped. When the returns came in, Gould says: "I did pretty well on that. I made over a thousand dollars on it." In a short time he went to the company again and said: "I want to send two carloads East. What will you charge?" "Five hundred dollars a car." Well, he sent that, and then wanted three carloads sent; but they increased the price till they charged him as high as $600 a carload. Now, if our fruit could be shipped at reasonable prices, I have no doubt in the world but we could sell all the early fruit in Boston, New York, Chicago, and Philadelphia markets. The railroad company make hundreds of thousands of dollars, and the whole thing is crowded down by their exactions.

Q. Do you know of any other circumstances of this character? A. I hear somebody almost every day making some complaint.

Q. Do you know of an instance connected with some pomegranates? A. I heard of an instance of some promegranates, which a friend of mine sent with some oranges to the city. Some of his people put them into the same boxes with the oranges. When they discovered the pomegranates, the railroad made them pay two or three times as much. They charged sixty cents a box for oranges, and $1 80 for pomegranates, although they did not occupy any more space, but it is a rule they have that everything shall pay all it will bear.

SENATOR SULLIVAN—Do you know, as a matter of fact, whether there is a contract besides the one to which we have just listened, which is called the "Pink Tariff?" A. No, sir; there was a contract which was made with some eight or ten wine men in San Francisco, who were associated together, on very extraordinary terms, and was rated very much in their favor, but I believe it has been abandoned.

Q. You don't know, as a matter of fact, that any special rates have been granted in addition to the special contract? A. No, sir.

Q. Would you be kind enough to give the committee a further statement in regard to the effect of the special contracts upon the shipping interests of the State? A. I conceive that the great object of the special contract was to cut off the shipping and to compel the merchants to bring the greater part of their goods across the continent, and they will require a much larger charge than if shipped by vessel. Freights have varied from four and five pounds down to two pound ten.

Q. Under which interest would the farmers of the State receive the most benefit? A. I estimate that the farmers of the country, by excluding the ships, would lose from five to ten million a year. From five to ten dollars a ton. I think that my loss in that direction was from five to ten dollars a ton this year. But I do not care so much about that as I do that the interest of wines and fruit are being kept back, and they have tried to interfere with the manufacturing interests of this State in such a way as to discourage those seeking to establish manufactories here.

Q. Do you know, as a matter of fact, that this committee received a letter from one of the manufacturing industries of this State—a sugar refinery at Alameda County—as to the effect of the Barry bill, and that if it was passed they would have to shut up their works? A. This is the first that I have heard of the letter.

Q. It was from a beet sugar refinery at Alvarado? A. As far as the beet sugar business is concerned, I have yet to learn that it has been a success. On the contrary, the information that I have had was to the effect that it was doubtful if the people making beet sugar were likely to succeed. If it had been a very great success I think I would have heard of it.

Q. In explanation it was said that they intended to make a beet sugar manufactory there, and also to import the cane, and make a sugar refinery. The proposition was to ship the cane from the Islands, and then transport it over a narrow gauge road to Alvarado, where they are now manufacturing. They shipped it to San Francisco, and then back again to San Francisco, by the South Pacific Coast Railroad? A. There were three or four companies in San Francisco, and they were till lately subsidized by Claus Spreckels.

Q. They were going to compete with Claus Spreckels, and in order to do that they had to have their rate lowered for sugar and coal from San Francisco to Alvarado and back again to San Francisco, and that if they were not permitted to discriminate in that direction the enterprise could not be started? A. It was a question of but a few miles and I don't see how that could affect the matter of an interest of that kind. My impression is that there is water communication there.

Q. Not for iron steamers. They would have to land at the wharf in San Francisco and then put their material on the cars and take it to Alvarado. The parties made the proposition that they would carry it so low as to make it a loss, and they hoped to build it up by running a factory there and charging for other business at the regular rates? A. I have heard nothing of that matter at all.

Senator Del Valle—You were asked this morning whether if the maximum of freight was fixed that the railroad company could discriminate beyond it? A. It only limits them to the maximum.

Q. Do you mean by that to say that they could discriminate as between persons? A. No, sir.

Q. But they could between classes? A. Yes, sir; but within the maximum.

Q. In shipping wines do you get your kegs back? A. No; not in shipping east.

Q. Have you any knowledge as to whether other industries, such as beer, have their kegs shipped back? A. Yes, sir.

Q. Do you know the weight of a barrel of beer? A. I estimate it by the weight of water. Seven and a half pounds to the gallon; and in addition to the beer you must take into consideration the heavy hoops and the thickness and weight of the staves.

Q. Isn't it a fact that in shipping those return packages, although they may not weigh more than forty-five pounds, yet they have to pay the regular rate of one hundred pounds for each? A. If you come down to a small proposition like that it amounts to nothing, for the simple reason that when you come to the matter of freight they carry five hundred and fifty million tons one mile and it is useless to come down to a matter of a few cents. They may have a great many rules and different rates; for instance, the bull ˜or the stallion which are counted at four thousand pounds each. Most persons are not familiar with these facts. The simple question, and it seems the more reasonable rule, would be to put them upon the ground that they are a company, and that they should be allowed a reasonable per cent upon the money invested. It is no use coming down to those small matters when the big item is˜the result. I don't think that the object of the people is to get down to the trifles, but to prevent the railroad company from cinching people.

Q. Do you know of any special contract made by the railroad company with Claus Spreckels? A. Only by general report.

Q. Do you not know as a matter of fact that the Central Pacific, by its tariff, actually prevents eastern shippers sending sugar to California? A. Only from hearsay.

Q. Do you know a case where a special contract has been given which has not been given to other merchants in the same business? A. I only know about all these matters from hearsay. I heard of a report of a contract between the railroad company and Coleman, by which Coleman——

[Objection.]

Q. Do you know of a case where the railroad company refused to give a contract? A. Yes, sir; this was told to me by the parties themselves; the facts were that they applied to the railroad company for a special contract, and the answer was: "Give us the names of the parties that you are dealing with." The names of the persons with whom they dealt were on their black list in the office, and they replied: "We won't give you a contract."

Q. Do you know of an instance where they have annulled a special contract, upon the ground that a person having dealt with one who brought goods by sea? A. I know of an instance where they had put a penalty on for his having bought agricultural implements which were brought over the water, and his contract was taken from him, and afterwards he was charged the full price.

Q. Do you know anything about the question of "rebate?" A. "Rebate" is where there is an understanding between the parties that they shall charge a man the open rates on his freight, and afterwards allow him a "rebate" or subtraction, which brings it down to the special rate.

Q. Are these overcharges? A. There are always two charges on everything. There is a special contract, which means a lower figure than the open rates, only the open rates are two or three times as great. The principle upon which the thing rests is, that you are forced to go into the special contract, for the reason that you cannot afford to do business and pay double or triple what other people do.

Q. Have you ever known the Central Pacific Railroad Company or the Southern Pacific Railroad Company to remove their tracks from any place which they wished to discriminate against? A. There was a notorious case occurred a few years ago, in which Senator J. P. Jones was interested. He built a railroad from Los Angeles to Santa Monica, and a wharf out to deep water was built at the latter place. Jones became involved and sold his railroad to Stanford & Crocker, and they destroyed the wharf, so that further competition should not be possible.

Q. Do you know of any other instance? A. No, sir; I don't know any of destroying property.

Q. Do you know of any that occurred at Santa Cruz? A. They made a wide gauge there, and took up the narrow gauge.

SENATOR KELLOGG (Chairman)—What is the usual weight allowed to a carload? A. Usually, about ten tons. And if they are in a hurry in the harvest time, they will allow you about fifteen. Sometimes they will let you put in more than the regular allowance, and then charge you double price; but the capacity is about ten tons.

Q. How many stallions can be shipped at one carload, with the proper conveniences for protection for that sort of animals? A. That depends a good deal upon the character of the animals—whether you use a whole box-car, or whether you divide the car into stalls.

Q. When a single stallion is shipped, does it not necessitate the sending of a single car? A. I suppose there is seldom more than one offered at a time.

Q. It would require about a half a car to ship a stallion? A. A partition could be put in, so that you could ship other stock—so that you could ship several.

Q. The handling of a stallion would be very different from the handling of other stock? A. Yes, sir.

Q. It would require more care and more labor? A. Yes, sir.

Q. Do you think that would be any reason for a discrimination in charging? A. I think, as I told you awhile ago, that the business is so large that it would hardly pay to notice these small items, because when you take them all they don't amount to anything.

Q. Your supposition is there should be so much paid for a stallion instead of so many pounds? A. The question is, whether you would put it in that way. Where there is risk, of course they should be allowed to charge a little more.

Q. The company would be bound to transport it safely? A. Of course; and they take the risks on everything else.

Q. They have to use the necessary precautions? A. They have to use proper diligence.

Q. And a greater amount of diligence in case of a stallion than in other things? A. Well, you come back at last to where I left you. When you come to look over it at the end of the year and find the entire amount, it don't amount to anything. Put in all losses by accident at fifty thousand dollars, and then divide it by twenty-five millions, add this portion to the freight, and you dispose of this whole subject of risk.

Q. In the shipment of a stallion does it require any more than ordinary care in handling? A. I suppose some of them do.

Q. It requires more care and attention than ordinary freight? A. Yes, sir.

Q. Do you think that would be any reason for charging more for the shipping? A. I think so.

Q. In your judgment, do you think that each article ought to be

charged for the services required to ship that particular freight?
A. I think that in all matters of this kind you could simplify the
matter very much, and it should be to the greatest possible extent.
If you do charge more in one instance you credit in the other. You
charge on both sides of the ledger, and when you want the results at
the end of the year it may be that in striking the balance you will
strike both off again. Adopt the plan suggested by me, and allow
the company, in this settlement with the State, all of their just and
economical expenses, and the cost and trouble of loading the trouble-
some vicious stallions would be returned to the company.

Q. I understood you to say that in your judgment the builder of
a railroad ought to be allowed a reasonable interest on the investment. What, in your judgment, would be a reasonable interest on
the investment? A. I should allow them five per cent, which would
be two per cent more than ordinary interest received at the present
time on large sums of money. If, on the contrary, you think it
unreasonable, give them six or seven.

Q. In your best judgment, what are the profits realized from an
ordinary business here in the State? A. Well, as far as money
investments are concerned, four per cent; and if you have to pay
taxes, five per cent. As far as business is concerned, at the present
time I do not think that it pays more than five or six per cent.
Now, in other business there is more or less risk, but as far as railroading is concerned, there is no loss at all; they are all compelled
to pay in advance. I do not know that they ever lost any money.
The instructions are not to deliver the goods until paid for. They
refused my check the other day for seventeen dollars, requiring the
cash.

Q. Do you think that there should be any discrimination between
persons in shipping goods, the classes of goods and all the circumstances being equal? A. I should say that there should be no discrimination between persons, or places, as far as that is concerned.
I cannot see any necessity for it.

Q. You spoke about the railroad company requiring a bond. Was
there any reason why they should do it in any case? A. If it was a
stranger to them.

Q. You would not discriminate between persons ordinarily? A.
When you have been dealing with a man for a long time, and you
know that he is a responsible person in every respect, then there is
no risk there. If, on the contrary, a new person came along, they
should take his case subject to rule and to reason. The company
relieve themselves of all responsibility by the terms of their special
contract, and in the single exception of perishable goods they might
secure themselves against loss of freight. With an irresponsible person they might exact security.

Q. Do you think that it would be reasonable to require one class
of persons to give a bond while other persons of the same class should
not be required to do so? A. That is a matter that the railroad company should judge, as to whether there would be a probable loss or
not.

Q. What is the reason why they require a bond for freight in the
case of the shipment of green fruit? A. It might become rotted.

Q. The fruit if not in good condition when shipped might deteriorate some? A. I have no doubt in the world but what it might under some circumstances, or there might be an accident upon the road, in which it might be delayed.

Q. Is that any reason why a bond should be required in the shipment of green fruit? A. Not if it was shipped by a responsible person.

Q. Do you think that a railroad company should take a bond from one party and be allowed to discriminate, and not take a bond from another? A. I think that the better way would be to make some rule for everybody.

Q. There are business reasons why a bond should be required in cases of shipment of green fruit? A. I don't object to that.

Q. Is it your judgment that there should be any discrimination in the prices charged for different kinds or classes of freight? A. Not to the extent it goes now.

Q. In your judgment, ought there to be any? A. I think there might be some discrimination under the maximum the State should establish; but there should be classification, and similar kinds of material should all be put into one class and at one rate. All agricultural product might be put into one class and at one price; live stock could be put in one class and at one rate; hardware in one class and at one rate. I should adopt the rule that the weight or measurement and the distance per mile should determine the amount of fare or freight, with no discriminations for persons or places Limit the amount you will allow the company to retain of the gross receipts—turn the remainder into the State Treasury, and the company will no longer desire any discriminations, special contracts, or rebates, and will willingly make none of these; for their business would be vastly simplified, both to themselves and the shipper.

Q. You think that in the fixing of rates both the shipper and the carrier ought to be consulted? A. I think it should be done in that way. In all other cases there is a payer and a payee, and the agreement is made between the parties.

Q. Do you believe that would be the best system which made a uniform rate for freights of all kinds? A. With only a very few classifications.

Q. You think there should be some classifications, and the rate should in some degree depend upon the classification? A. There is another point to take into consideration, and that is that they carry goods in both directions. 'If cars go east they have got to come west, and goods go in both directions, therefore a less rate with increased traffic. Another reason is, that as your rates decrease, your business increases, and your whole community increases, so that we all are encouraged by it.

Q. Then there are circumstances under which a railroad company ought to be encouraged in charging lower rates in one direction than in another? A. I do; and I think that this morning I gave the results of a twelve months' experience, terminating on the thirtieth of June last, referring to the transportation of the wheat crop from the Western States to the seaboard, showing that the average freight was but twenty-seven one hundredths of a cent per ton per mile, and for the whole freight carried it was but one and two fifths cents per ton per mile, whilst we find that on the New York Central, the average was only sixty-seven one hundredths.

Q. Isn't it seventy-nine one hundredths? A. No, it is sixty-seven one hundredths. The eastern roads drew their earnings from a population of fourteen millions, whilst ours, from a population of eight hundred thousand, carried only one third the amount of freight and received fifty per cent more money than the eastern roads.

Q. In the localities of which you speak in the East there are a large number of roads? A. Yes, sir.

Q. Is not that the aggregate, then? The proportion between the West and the East is very different? A. We carry much more wheat than any other road in the United States.

Q. Do you know any eastern road which has to incur the expense of maintaining miles of snowsheds? A. No, I do not; but then, there is another question we don't take into consideration, that the East is an exceedingly cold country, and ice and frost require a large expenditure, both in making the road and in the repairs thereafter.

Q. Are not wages of employés on railroads in California—on the Central Pacific Railroad—very much higher than in the East? A. I can't tell you precisely; probably they are fifteen or twenty per cent.

Q. Isn't it about double? A. I don't think it is a great deal more; the most of the labor that they have is done by Chinamen, and he labors at about seventy-five cents a day and boards himself; I do not think it is much greater, if not less.

Q. Were you correct in stating that a majority of the labor is performed by Chinese on the Central Pacific Railroad? A. I asked Mr. Wright, the Superintendent of six or seven roads in this State, and he told me there were seven thousand people on his payrolls; that the average to the mile was six or eight; on the three thousand miles of road there are twenty thousand people in the service, the most of whom are on the tracks.

Q. Could you give us some idea of the relative expense of the Central Pacific Railroad Company, as compared with some of those in the East of which you speak? A. I have not the statistics with me.

Q. Isn't there a greater difference in the cost of wages than there is in the price of freights? A. There is another view of the subject, which I think would meet what you are looking after, and which, I think, is far more satisfactory; take the gross receipts and the gross expenditures, and you will find the difference vastly in favor of the California companies. The expenses of the road here amount to about twelve million dollars, whilst the receipts are nearly double as much, of which the company receive ten millions more than they are legally entitled to. On the other side they divide three or four millions and are satisfied with it.

Q. Do you know a line of those roads called the Northwestern? A. I know something about it. If you refer to Poor's Manual, you will find the receipts, and all these matters.

Q. Does it not vary more than a million or two of dollars in a season? A. I could not tell you. I have been so much occupied in other directions that I have lost the run of them.

Q. I will ask you whether, in comparing rates between the eastern roads and the Central Pacific Railroad, you have taken into consideration in your estimates the difference in wages? A. I have taken the whole thing into consideration in taking the results, and I know that they must charge a great deal more than they are entitled to, because you have taken the gross receipts and the gross expenditures, and you find that they are all larger than they should be.

Q. Do you know anything about the relative cost of coal on the eastern roads and on the Central Pacific Railroad? A. No, I do not.

Q. Do you know whether there is a difference or not? A. I presume there is some difference.

Q. Have you taken that difference into consideration in figuring the relative cost, and what would be a reasonable rate of freights? A. I have taken the other view of the subject. You should take the gross receipts and the gross expenditures, and by that means you can get at it, and that is a more comprehensive view of the subject.

Q. But you have not gone into the details, I understand? A. I have by the other calculation.

Q. Do you know what the greatest elevation is in transporting wheat from St. Louis to the seaboard? A. No, sir.

Q. Have you taken into consideration the fact that the Central Pacific Railroad drag freights up steep grades, greater than those on the eastern roads? A. Yes, sir; but for the same reason, if you take a train up a grade, it has to come down when it comes back. These are circumstances you do not find in the railroad accounts. Besides the up grades are eastward, and the west grades are descending, and two thirds of the freight carried in California descends to San Francisco. And then, in relation to the matter, there are no more employés or engines, and the only circumstance would be that they would consume more coal, more power—and that is produced by the coal.

Q. Have you taken into consideration the wear and tear of rolling stock in going up and down heavy grades? A. Yes, sir; that is in. I will tell you a circumstance in connection with your friend, Huntington, a little while ago.

Q. Mr. Huntington is not my friend; I have never seen the gentleman? A. I beg your pardon.

Q. I should be glad to have his friendship, or that of any other person, if I could have it. A. Well, he and I were sitting together, talking about various subjects, and I thought I would get a point from him, and I said to him: "Huntington, one of the most extraordinary inventions that has ever been made was this matter of making the steel rail. It has only been in use eight or ten years; what has been your experience in relation to the matter?" "Our experience has been, that where our rails were wearing out, and the whole rail destroyed in six or seven years, the steel rail does not wear out at all. The other rails used to put us to from nine to fifteen thousand dollars' expense per mile once in every six years, and now we find that they are the best rail in the world; there is no apparent wear upon the rail." So there was a proposition brought in which works a material advantage, but only to the advantage of the railroad company.

Q. Upon the eastern roads how many loaded cars will an engine haul? A. That goes into the matter of the power of the engine—the character of the road.

Q. I am speaking of the ordinary freight engine? A. It is a matter of grade altogether. I think you are going in the wrong direction, and I will tell you why.

Q. I would be glad to be straightened out. A. You have been over the road ?

Q. I have traveled some. A. And you know that when you get on the other side of the mountains, all along in that section that comes up from the east, that it runs for hundreds of miles over a country that is level. Then you come on to the mountains. There you have rough work, but it does not begin to be as rough as you have in Pennsylvania. In this State you can go in the San Joaquin Valley for four hundred miles without grade, and over the most favorable country; and as you come up from San Francisco there is no grade till you go beyond Sacramento. Now, if you take the whole level road in connection with the other, you have more favorable country for a road than you have in Pennsylvania.

Q. Have you any idea how many loaded cars an engine will draw in ordinary work in the State of New York? A. I have not.

Q. One engine will draw forty loaded cars? A. I have seen an engine draw a great many cars, but it was under peculiar circumstances—simply to carry empty ones back.

Q. Every engine has got to go up to cross the mountains? A. Yes, sir.

Q. Do you know that starting from Rocklin and going on up over the mountains, that it requires two triple driving wheel engines to drag a train of fourteen cars? A. When I was an engineer a good while ago, they did not allow any grade on a road of over sixty feet to the mile. Now, if the grade is increased to one hundred and sixteen feet to the mile, it requires a heavier power to go up, as a matter of course, but the power of engines has also been correspondingly increased.

Q. What figures do you put as the basis of profits for the California roads? I understood you to state it at forty millions. Now, in addition to that, I ask you whether those values were estimated in this State in proportion to the entire value of the road or to the assessed value? A. They were made upon the basis applied in making the value of other roads.

Q. Can you give us some idea of the proportion of the entire value of the road, and of the assessed value? A. The company claimed in my county seven thousand dollars as a proper assessment per mile.

Q. Give me an answer to the questions as near as you can? A. I was called to testify what it cost in the case which was brought before the Board of Equalization.

Q. I would like to know some of these things. I live in an obscure country locality, and am not informed of all these matters, and I am trying to get information? A. I will give you a great deal of credit for practical intelligence, though you may live in an obscure country locality.

Q. Thank you for your compliment, but now what do you think was the difference between the assessed value and the real? A. I will refer you to your friend Crocker.

Q. I am not acquainted with Mr. Crocker? A. He swore, on one occasion, that it was one hundred and seventy-eight thousand dollars per mile, and on another occasion that it was sixteen thousand dollars. Here you have the assessment on one side and the real on the other, I suppose.

Q. I do not propose to act on any such statement, if I can get more reliable information. Can you not give us more reliable information? A. I don't know where you could look for more reliable information, except in the office of the company.

Q. You have been an engineer and you understand these questions. Could you give us some idea? A. If you will take the reports you will find that they make it about sixty thousand dollars a mile, but I think that that represents the capital after they have watered it up. The probability is that the road cost about thirty or forty thousand dollars a mile.

Q. Do you think that would be a fair estimate for assessment? A. I saw not long ago an assessment of a railroad in Illinois that was assessed at thirty-six thousand dollars a mile.

Q. Those roads do not cost as much as the California roads? A. More.

Q. How do you get at that? A. Don't forget that three fourths of the roads in California are over level grades and are cheaply made. Do you know a Mr. Gray? He was the Chief Engineer on this road for a time. I met him at Salt Lake, when the road was under construction, on the other side of the mountains, where it goes for hundreds of miles on an even grade, and he said that much of it ought to be made at a cost of from twelve to eighteen thousand dollars a mile.

Q. That was the grading? A. No, sir; that was the cost of the road.

Q. Do you mean on the slope included in the Union Pacific and the Central Pacific? A. I mean all the level line and up to the foot of the mountains there is little or no grade.

Q. Where was this; on the Union Pacific Railroad or on the other? A. This was on the Central Pacific.

Q. I was speaking about the Central Pacific? A. Yes, sir. The most expensive mile of road that they had to make was at Cape Horn, and that mile cost them one hundred thousand dollars.

Q. Including the high trestle? A. Yes, sir; that was noted as the Cape Horn mile.

Q. Have you any idea of what a mile of road costs in the Sierra Nevadas? A. That was the most expensive; they had never anything like it.

Q. There never was anything as difficult in all the history of railroading? A. One of the most extraordinary things in the world that ever occurred was on the road below here—you all know about it. They found a hole there in the road. They had been running right along, year after year, and one night, between daylight and sunrise, the whole thing went in, and they put a force on and went to filling it up. They put in piles and brought, not carloads, but hundreds of trains of cars, and dumped the gravel in, but they could not fill it. Then they tried to pile it, but they couldn't, so they gave it up.

Q. Taking into consideration the reasonable value of the construction of such a road as that in California, isn't the percentage of profits less than on some of the eastern roads of which you have been speaking? A. No, sir.

Q. Have you examined the official reports to determine that matter? A. I have examined so far as I desired to make the comparison of the receipts and expenditures. Then we must take into consideration the fact that this road runs through a population of seven or eight hundred thousand, while the eastern road runs through a population of fourteen millions.

Q. Other roads are running parallel with it at short distances? A. Yes, sir.

Q. So that would speak of the rate it would bear to the whole population? A. The profits depend upon the entire receipts; it represents the difference between the receipts and the expenditures.

Q. Have you any idea of the number of miles of railroad in California? A. About four thousand.

Q. Have you any idea of the number of miles in the State of Illinois? A. Something like three times as many.

Q. Have you any idea of the population? A. About four or five millions.

Q. Have you any idea of the relative profits of the railroad business in Illinois in a population of four millions, and in California with a population of eight hundred thousand? A. I suppose there is no railroad in the world that receives so much money, in proportion to the population, as the Central Pacific Railroad.

Q. The Northwestern at Chicago receives two millions more than the Central Pacific? A. I think they receive less.

Q. Do you know anything about the Chicago, Burlington, and Quincy road? A. I do not know much about that country, because I have been living in California.'

Q. Do you know anything about the receipts of the Pennsylvania Central system? A. Only from the reports.

Q. Or of the Pennsylvania Central combination? A. I had a comparison (I cannot lay my hand upon the paper), and a very satisfactory one.

Q. I will waive the question. You said something about the paper manufactory? At what points were those you spoke of? A. One in Santa Cruz County, and one in San José.

Q. How do you say they were broken down? A. By putting a very low price on paper brought from New York, and by a combination by which an extra price was put upon wood pulp, and a low price upon rags, by which they could ship them to New York. The paper and pulp came in this direction, and the rags went in the other.

Q. Do you think the low prices upon freights from the East here would tend to injure the manufactories of this State? A. Unquestionably.

Q. Do you think that would be worth taking into consideration?
A. Certainly.

Q. Which disburses in the State the more moneys, the freight carried by rail or by sea? A. The disbursements made by sea are merely at the seaboard. Any disbursements made by the railroad shipper, of course, would remain in the State. I should suppose there would be more disbursed by rail.

Q. Is not the disbursement a benefit to all the people of the State?
A. Yes, sir.

Q. Could you give any method by which we could ascertain the value of railroad property in this State? A. I don't know any better way than to elect some Railroad Commissioners who would devote themselves to the interests of the people, and allow them to make a reasonable estimate.

Q. Do you think that they would be able to do so? A. I would lay down a mile of track as a basis, and take everything connected with it—add to that the extra for grading the road, and I believe that any competent engineer would get at it, and go over the whole road and make up the estimate from that as a basis.

Q. Do you think that the value of the property would depend in any degree upon the profits realized? A. There you bring up a subject which is a very extraordinary one, because you cover the whole question of what they are entitled to and the gross receipts and expenditures.

Q. In fixing the profits of a railroad, or any other corporation, do you think it would be proper to take into consideration the risks involved in the investment at the time it was made? A. No; I think the risk at the time it was made has nothing to do with its present value.

Q. I am speaking of the reasonable profits? A. I stated the only connection that it has with it.

Q. Supposing that one business enterprise was a very risky one, and that another was a very certain one—do you think that there should be any difference in the profits allowed to the one investment over the other if the profits are to be controlled by law? A. The risk should be taken into consideration, but as far as the railroad is concerned I don't think they have taken any, or that it should be taken into account.

Q. I am speaking of the risks of an ordinary undertaking? A. I don't see that there is any extraordinary risk taken by the company.

Q. There is not now, but you know that when the Central Pacific Railroad was constructed there was a question as to whether it would pay interest on the investment? A. You are working into a very extraordinary history. Don't you remember that Gorham said that it took eleven thousand five hundred dollars, that they had to take out of their pockets, to construct the road. That is all they put in for all the dividends that they ever took out.

Q. Do you believe that there is any connection between the risk taken in an ordinary business enterprise and the profits that should be reasonably allowed? A. That risk was taken twenty years ago. I would take the whole bearing upon the subject in every way in which money is concerned.

Q. Do you believe that there are any engineers in the State who could go before the Commission and form a reasonable estimate of the value of the railroads in the State? A. I do. They make those statements every day. The engineers know the cost of everything that goes to make up a mile of road. Hundreds of miles of grading. on these roads do not cost three hundred dollars per mile. After you get the grading done, and there is very little to do, except in a mountainous country (where, of course, you have heavy expenses), the making of a mile of road is, according to the best rates, very light. The engineer understands the cost of each tie and the number of ties and rails necessary, and the cost of putting it together. Take a mile of road, then, at Oakland, for instance, as a basis, and add the cost for transferring the material as the road extends, include the cost of grading, and then multiply by the number of miles, and you have got it.

Q. Have you any idea of how many miles of tunnel there are on the Central Pacific Railroad in the Sierra Nevadas, between Sacramento and Reno? A. No, sir.

Q. Have you any idea of how many tunnels there are? A. No, sir.

Q. Have you any idea of the cost of excavating those tunnels? A. It depends a great deal upon the amount of material in them. If you go to the reports upon the subject you will get the results.

Q. Do you think that a mile of roadbed at Oakland would be a correct basis for the estimate of the running of a mile of tunnel through solid rock? A. That is probably another proposition. I brought that in under the cost of the construction of a single mile of road as a basis, because you would add the extra cost of all that character of work.

Q. Have you any idea of what the cost is of a mile of tunnel in the Sierra Nevadas? A. I know that the tunnels are a very expensive matter, but at the same time a matter of a few miles, compared with the whole cost.

Q. Do you know anything about the cost of running a tunnel for ordinary mining purposes, as compared with the cost of running a large railroad tunnel? A. The cost would not be in proportion to the section by any means:

Q. You think there would be some difference? A. There would be some, but it would be in favor of the larger one.

Q. You do not mean to say that it would cost more to construct the smaller tunnel than the larger one? A. No, sir; but all that is a matter of detail. You have got that all included in the cost of the original, the forty millions. I take that from the estimates of the engineers.

Q. Supposing that a mile of such tunnel as the North Bloomfield Mining Company made in their mine should cost upwards of a million of dollars, would that, in your judgment, be a fair basis from which to judge of the cost of a tunnel for a railroad in the Sierra Nevada Mountains, being in the same formation? A. Excuse me, if I do not confine myself to these categorical questions.

Q. You are only requested to answer the question in your own way; anything that answers it, is all that I care for? A. If you take the

14*

reports and find that this forty millions covers the whole cost, I do not see any need of going into all this detail. It does not give any result or any information to you or to any one else.

Q. I think that it gives me information. Have you any idea of where the trestles are on the Central Pacific Railroad? A. The highest are at Cape Horn.

Q. You do not know whether they have filled in all the places above Newcastle? A. No, sir.

Q. Have you any idea of how much that has cost per mile? A. It is a matter I have not kept in mind.

Q. Have you any idea of what the additional cost would be to the building of a mile of road in Oakland? A. The reason that I said that I would take a mile at Oakland was that the road, so far as the mere iron and wood is concerned, would be the same. All these other matters would come in and be added as additional, and would make the difference in the totals. There is no grading at all at Oakland. There are places there that the grading would not cost fifty dollars a mile.

Q. They would have to cover the ties with gravel? A. Ballast.

Q. That is, part of the roadbed? A. Yes, sir; but not the grading. It is put on for the purpose of stopping the dust and to keep the ties in place at the same time.

Q. You spoke about "watering" railroad stock; do you know that there has been any "watering" in the State of California? A. I think it is about all "water;" it is like a man owning a farm worth five thousand dollars, with a twenty thousand dollars mortgage on it.

Q. Suppose that the narrow-gauge railroad in Nevada and Placer Counties cost five hundred and ninety-eight thousand dollars in hard money, and that none of it whatever was a subsidy, would you call that water? A. That depends upon whether there are any mortgages upon it, or whether that is the value of the stock.

Q. [Question repeated.] A. No; I would not.

Q. Would you think that there was any water about? A. Not if it was honestly appropriated for the building of the road.

Q. Supposing that in the construction of the South Pacific Railroad there was about four millions of dollars expended, and that there was no subsidy at all or any bonded indebtedness upon the road, would you say that was water? A. Not if it was the legitimate cost of the road, and there was no issuing of stock afterwards which was watered. I was merely referring to the manipulation of such matters. Gould, when he found himself in possession of a line of telegraph stock of thirty-eight millions put the whole at eighty-two millions, and that difference represented the water.

Q. I am talking about the watering of any stock issued by the railroads of California? A. Whenever the public is made to believe that a stock is worth more than it is, that stock has been watered.

Q. That is what you meant when you said that the railroad stock was watered? A. I don't know that I did. I know that the railroad stock was watered.

Q. Do you think that the fact that slabs were of little value should be taken into account in fixing the rate? A. That is not what I was referring to. I think, as far as the value is concerned, you will find that you cannot charge one man more than another. The point I wanted to make was, that it costs to transport them one hundred and twenty-three miles twenty-two dollars, and when I ordered a car to be taken seven miles further they charged eleven dollars.

Q. Do you think that the fact that the slabs were of little value should be taken into consideration in fixing the rate? A. There you are getting into the same difficulty. It involves the question of classification, and I think that there should not be more than four or five classifications. But if you are going to allow discrimination, the slabs ought to be put in at the smallest value.

Q. Do you believe that there should be any difference between the transportation of the poorest and best quality of sugar-pine lumber and slabs? A. As far as that is concerned, I think that the people and the railroad ought to agree together as to the classifications. You should make your different classifications, and then put your different items in.

Q. I wanted, if I could, being young and green, to get the benefit of your experience as a business man, as to whether it would be well for the Legislature to adopt an iron-bound rule that such things as sugar-pine lumber should be charged at the same rate per ton as slabs? A. There is no reason for it. You should make but very few distinctions between one thing and another.

Q. Would you make as many as a dozen? A. It would be no matter, one way or the other.

Q. It might to a man who wanted to frame a law, and wanted to get the best judgment and experience of wise men? A. I do not care to go into these matters of detail.

Q. You would not care to answer that question any more directly? A. No, sir.

Q. Have you any idea of what proportion of the freights received by the Central Pacific Railroad Company come from the citizens of California? A. I know that the greater portion is received from the citizens of California, and that their local freight outnumbers largely the amount brought from the States.

Q. Which is the higher, on the whole, the freight on imports or the freight on the local traffic, including the farm products? A. The local freight.

Q. Isn't it a fact that it is only one third as much on the wheat crop? A. They charge two and a quarter cents per ton per mile, and on the other side they charge twenty-seven one hundredths of one cent.

Q. How many years ago was that estimate made? A. On the thirtieth of June last.

Q. Do you know whose statement that was? A. No, sir.

Q. The information that you have was that it was two and a quarter cents per ton per mile? A. Yes, sir.

Q. Do you believe that the railroad company, for the purpose of building up an industry in the interior, should be allowed to discriminate in favor of that industry? A. If there is any discrimination it ought to be for lawful purposes, and a reasonable one, and not one by which they can be permitted to break down the interests and industries of the country. Now the eastern merchant gets his goods transported into the towns of Los Angeles and San José at the same rates that the local merchants get theirs. There isn't any discrimination there, but it is certainly wrong and against the interests of the vessels coming to this State, and against the merchants of San Francisco. Now, isn't that a most extraordinary thing; how do you reconcile it? Now, a party wanted some machinery left at Virginia City, and made a contract to have it left there at a certain time. They telegraphed to know why the machinery was not delivered, and the first thing they found out about it was that it had been sent to Oakland. He wanted it sent back to him, but they said that they couldn't send it back; it had to be sent to San Francisco. And that machinery was absolutely taken across the bay and then sent to Virginia City.

Q. Do you know it, as a fact, that the Central Pacific Railroad Company has made such rates upon heavy machinery as has enabled California to manufacture and ship to Nevada, Idaho, and Utah all the heavy machinery used for mining purposes, at less rates than they can be procured from eastern dealers? A. I know that in transporting heavy mining machinery from San Francisco to those places, it ought not to cost as much, for the reason that they are five or six times the distance from those places as San Francisco.

Q. Do you know that the railroad company, by discriminating, has enabled the California foundries to manufacture all the heavy machinery used in mining in Utah, Idaho, and other States on this coast? A. I do not see where the railroad company are entitled to any particular credit there. It certainly is less distance, and then we understand the making of mining machinery on this coast. They have not had our experience in making mining machinery in New York. We have more ingenious people here, and we understand the requirements, and have the skilled workmen. New York has no workmen skilled in making mining machinery.

Q. Do you think it would be wise to allow specially low rates in order to maintain a sugar factory at Alvarado? A. There are not more than ten miles of country there, and the cost of transportation over that is not going to make or break a manufactory.

Q. Might it not? A. No; it could be hauled by teams for that distance. I understand that it is only about six or seven miles.

Q. Have you any idea what it would cost to haul it by teams? A. It ought to be about half a cent per ton per mile by railroad.

Q. Mr. Davis testified that certain parties were about to establish a sugar factory at Alvarado; that they had a certain amount of business already upon the road; that he could transport some additional freights at a very low rate, and that he would give that company a very low rate in order that they might manufacture sugar at Alvarado and make a profit; that if he was to charge them a uniform rate, it could not be done. Do you think that for such a purpose it would be reasonable to allow a lower rate? A. I think that a reasonable distinction in these matters is justifiable, if not done for the purpose of annoyance.

Q. Do you think it would be wise to pass a law which would prevent all discrimination? A. The trouble with the matter is, that if you are going into discrimination you do not know where to stop. There should be no distinction between one man and another.

Q. Do you think that there should be a reasonable distinction allowed? A. Not between individuals.

Q. Supposing that the railroad company could assist the manufacture of paper within the State by fixing a different rate of freight, do you think it would be wise to allow such a law as would enable them to do so? A. I think there ought to be no objection, providing it were done for an honest purpose, and then the people of California would not object to it. The people are largely influenced by the press of the State, and the railroad company have shown their influence over the press in the State.

Q. You do not mean the Chronicle? A. I refer particularly to a little paper in our own county, and they do attempt to influence some of the papers, and own some of the big papers of the State, and I think that is a subject of more importance to legislate about than the carrying of freight three miles. I think they ought to be made responsible to the people of the State. The people want redress; they want to be protected.

Q. Do you think that there should be any discrimination shown in favor of building up the manufactories of the State? A. I think the better way would be to allow it to none. Then they would have a common rule, and there would be no misunderstanding. The consumer has to pay it all in the end.

Q. The rich have to stand their share? A. The merchant does not pay for any of these things. He will sell his goods at a profit, whatever they may cost, and the consumer has to pay for it all in the end.

Q. Supposing that the cost of transporting by rail and by water were approximately the same, who would suffer in that event? A. It would not make any difference to the consumer; he has to pay it; he has got to foot the bills.

Q. If the railroad company should disburse a million of money in the State, that would be a benefit to the people of the State? A. While they were disbursing more or less, they are taking from the farmer the difference, between five and ten millions, from his wheat crop.

Q. Does it cost any more to navigate the high seas than it did before the railroad was built? A. A short time ago it was down to nearly two pounds on account of some corner which was attempted and which failed, but I think that all of our freights are higher now than they used to be. For the last five years, and the five years preceding, I have not been paying so much attention to the relative cost.

Q. Do you know about what year the Central Pacific was completed? A. About 1869.

Q. Have you any idea of what the tonnage of wheat was at that time? A. We did not have much wheat at that time.

Q. Have you compared the rates with the rates on wheat for the last five years? A. I have for the last ten or twenty years. The point is, that if you keep the ships away it is to our disadvantage.

Q. Was there ever a time, except when Friedlander was making a corner, that vessels could not be chartered at San Francisco to carry wheat to New York? A. I think there were always some ships here.

Q. Then the railroad company has not driven off all the shipping from San Francisco? A. I cannot tell you whether there are few or more. I do not know, but I do know that the effect naturally must be that when they are deprived of the freight in one direction they will charge more in the other. They could not bring freight here satisfactorily if they did not get freight the other way.

Q. Why do the Central Pacific Railroad make freights on some goods cheaper than they do on others? A. In order to put freights up after they have driven the ships off.

Q. Have you ever seen the figures showing the relative value of freight brought into the San Francisco market during the last few years by the Central Pacific Railroad? A. No, sir.

Q. Could you give the committee any idea of the relative increase in the value of the imports brought into San Francisco within the last few years? A. No, sir.

Q. You stated that if the rates of freights and fares were lowered it would tend to increase the population of the State? A. Certainly; I recommended that all rates should be so low that the population would be increased.

Q. Any system which would tend to increase the population of the State would be a benefit to the State? A. Of course it would.

A. Isn't it a fact that the Central Pacific Railroad, and its connecting lines, have increased the population more rapidly than it ever increased before? A. If there was anything I was disappointed about it is the fact that with our resources the development of California has been retarded by the rates charged. We should have had two or three million of people more in the State by this time.

Q. Would it cost an emigrant any more to go from New York to San Francisco by water before the Central Pacific Railroad was completed than it does now? A. They should have come a great deal cheaper.

Q. What did it cost to come by way of the Isthmus? A. There was a time when a man could come for twenty or thirty dollars.

Q. In 1864 and 1865? A. Everything was in an advanced stage at that time. They were willing to give almost anything to get here.

Q. What broke that down? A. The giving out of the placer mines. At the time of discovery of gold I came out here with the United States troops, and men would start for the mines and take nothing with them but a jack-knife, and they would come back with a sack containing five or six thousand dollars round their waists in about five or six weeks.

Q. Was it one of the main causes that money was not made here as easily as it was before? A. No; nobody comes here now with that expectation.

Q. Do you know what it cost an emigrant to go from New York to San Francisco before the Central Pacific Railroad was completed? A. No, sir.

Q. Wasn't it four times as much as it is now? A. I do not know.

I don't think the matter of a railroad is going to bring people here; it is only under the impulse of the moving spirit that they desire to come, and a natural desire to better their condition. I don't think the railroad is entitled to any credit on that score.

Q. What is the cost to an emigrant from New York to San Francisco? A. I do not know the price they charge. I know that it is so great that a great many of them have told me that the prices charged by the railroad company were so heavy that they could not afford to go across again.

Q. Do you know of any place in the world where a passenger can ride three hundred miles continuosly for the same price? A. Fares on eastern railroads are much less than here.

Q. What is the length of the Central Pacific Railroad from here to Ogden? A. Eight hundred miles.

Q. Eight hundred and ninety-one? A. Call it nine hundred.

Q. What is the length of the Union Pacific Railroad? A. The distance to New York is three thousand miles. I think the charge ought to be in proportion to the distance.

Q. Then the railroad which carries one train a day should charge the same rate as the road that carries four trains? A. They don't carry men in this instance. But the whole thing depends upon competition; a small proportion of the emigrants come to this place.

Q. How many people travel over the Union Pacific Railroad, as compared with the number that travel over the Central Pacific line, do you think? A. That has nothing to do with it in the world; you may think so, but I do not.

Q. Does not the Pennsylvania Central carry ten passengers for every one that is carried on the Central Pacific? A. I don't know. The whole road is a monopoly. On the other side competition limits it. The Central Pacific Railroad, as shown by the reports, ship the less number of people, and take the most money.

Q. That is where they nail the Central Pacific, ain't it? A. That is where the Central Pacific nail them.

Q. In your judgment, the road which carries one passenger per day, should not charge any more than the road which carries a hundred? A. I do not think, that because I am the one man, they should charge me a hundred times as much.

Q. It would require the same investment to construct a road to carry one, that it would a hundred? A. The parties who started this never invested but eleven thousand five hundred dollars of their own money.

Q. You do not answer my question? A. I do not think you are asking questions that are material.

Q. You refuse to answer that question? A. For the simple reason that I have answered it.

Q. Do you think that the quantity of freight transported over the road should have anything to do with the charges? A. I think so; I think that the whole matter should be determined by fixing the amount that the company should receive, and then fix the prices to make that amount. It would be the matter of quantity that would largely regulate the rate, and that should fix the sum by which the railroad should be worked.

Q. Supposing that the rates to this State should be reduced one half, would it in two years increase the quantity in proportion? A. You could not get at the proportion, because, while it would not increase the quantity on some classes of goods materially, it would increase it on others.

Q. What proportion of our land is planted to wheat? A. I cannot tell.

Q. Are the places where it is planted nearer the railroad lines or otherwise? A. The probability is that they are where they can transport it.

Q. Supposing that groceries were decreased in price two thirds, would it have a material effect upon the consumption—would it be increased? A. That is a question of whether they have got it to eat?

Q. If people have it they eat about all they need? A. It would be surprising if they didn't.

Q. Then, the lowering of freight would not increase the amount imported? A. I don't know that it would.

Q. Would it not be the same with regard to hardware? A. I suppose they would simply bring sufficient to supply the demand.

Q. What class of freights would be increased in this State by reducing the rate on them? A. The lowering of the freights would be a lowering of the money going into the pockets of the railroad, and the people would be benefited by having it left in their own pockets.

Q. Then, you do not mean to say that the lowering of freights would thereby increase the amount imported? A. I don't think it would, for the simple reason that we don't want them increased.

Q. Have you any idea of the population of the State for the five years immediately preceding the completion, as compared with the population for the last five years? A. No, sir.

Q. Do you know whether the number of ships in the harbor of San Francisco has approximately kept pace with the increase in the population in the State? A. I do not think that has any relative connection one with the other. I don't think that is the proposition at all. This is a matter of carrying goods.

Q. You do not think that the cost of transportation has anything to do with the number who come? A. I do not think that it has.

Q. Do you not think that a great many of the emigrants who come to New York have barely money enough to pay the cost of transportation to San Francisco? A. I understand that a great many of the emigrants now have a good deal of money with them.

Q. Is that your idea of them as a whole? A. I speak of them as a whole. There is a class of emigrants that bring a great deal of money with them to the United States.

Q. Have you any idea as to whether California gets its quota of immigrants as compared to the other States? A. I know it does not.

Q. Do you know whether the Chinese immigration has had anything to do with that result? A. There is some prejudice against the Chinese; I know that Kansas and other neighboring States have built up within the last few years, while we still have only about eight hundred thousand ; while they have got three times as many. I·don't see that the Central Pacific Railroad is entitled to any credit. We are more than five times as large as some of these States, and capable of supporting a population of twenty millions, and we have only about eight hundred thousand. I don't see that we have anything to boast of.

Q. Have you any idea of the relative value of the imports to the State of California within the last few years, as compared with the years just preceding the completion of the Central Pacific Railroad? A. You had better ask these questions of some merchant in San Francisco.

SENATOR WHITNEY—It has been stated here that lumber was brought from the Santa Cruz Mountains by rail for four dollars a thousand; that they had a great deal more than they could sell, and asked Mr. Davis to give them the privilege of sending it to Oakland at an additional fifty cents per thousand. Do you think that is a discrimination which is wise or that it ought to be prohibited? A. I think in all these cases, that if the motive is a good and proper one, that should determine it. Of course there might be consequences which we could not foresee.

Q. Do you think a law would be wise which would prevent Mr. Davis from making that distinction? A. There is a distinction which may be proper, provided it could be properly and honestly made, and from correct motives.

Q. Would you think it a wise law which would forbid such distinction? A. Only in this respect, that when you undertake to control men you have got to do it positively. If you leave a loophole open, they are certain to take advantage of it.

Q. Do you think that a law preventing all discrimination would be wise as an iron rule generally? A. I think so; I don't see how you can adopt any other principle.

SENATOR MURPHY—Do you believe that a reduction of freight and fares by rail would increase the quantity of shipping by water? A. It would reduce the shipping by water, because the greater the reduction, the more would go by rail.

Q. Then a reduction in rates would tend to drive shipping from the high seas? A. If they could say, "Your ships shall not come here," of course they would do so, and then they could increase their rates on all the freights. It is a mere matter of money.

SENATOR BROOKS—The wheat that is shipped out of this State goes to Liverpool mainly? A. Yes, sir.

Q. Do you think that the railroad would be compelled to carry wheat at any price that we may adopt by rule? A. They could carry it in the State as cheaply as they do on the other side, twenty-seven one hundredths of a cent; that would be to New York seven dollars and fifty cents, and then they would have other freight in this direction.

Q. Do you think it would be possible for a railroad company to move five hundred thousand tons of wheat from San Francisco? A. If they can't it would be necessary to send it by vessels.

Q. Then all this talk about driving the ships from the sea is talking about something that they cannot do? A. Well, I spoke of the motive; they require the merchants to sign a contract that they will not trade with those who bring these goods there, so, if they succeeded or not, they are entitled to no credit for what they have done.

STATEMENT OF MR. BARRY.

MR. CHAIRMAN AND GENTLEMEN: What I may have to say about this bill is rather in the nature of an argument than otherwise, because I had expected that questions might be asked by the committee. The object of the bill is to prevent discrimination on the part of railroad corporations, between persons or places, either by rebates on the part of the railroad companies, or in any other manner, and to fix uniform rates of charges between places in the transportation of freight, as well as to do away with the present system of special contracts, by prescribing a system by which the railroad companies will remain entirely within the control of the State. I take it as a fundamental principle that in its regulation of the railroad corporations, the State must, necessarily, have complete control over them, and, therefore, the passage of any such Acts as will tend to this object, and to prevent the abuses of the present system, are entirely proper. The State has the right to prescribe a system of laws for the control of railroad transportation, and as corollary to that it may enact laws for the government of railroad companies and corporations, that will prevent the adoption by them of rules of discrimination, such as the present special contract system. The bill being framed upon that basis, or with a view to those ideas, and for the purpose of preventing discrimination, it is made general in its terms, that all railroads built or owned by corporations organized under the laws of this State are public highways.

In regard to that, I would say that it is not proper to approach this subject with the view that railroads are simply common carriers, because they are subject to legislative control, differing from other classes of common carriers who are not subject to the same control, where the same reason does not arise. The railroad is controlled in its use as a public highway, just as a toll road owner collecting tolls is subject to the control of the Boards of Supervisors in whatever he does in reference to those roads. A common carrier who is a public agent, using a public highway, or a corporation of like character, is to be regulated and controlled because it is such agent. Therefore, I think that it should be laid down as a leading proposition, and a fundamental principle, that railroad corporations are not to be considered simply as common carriers, but as public agents, using the public highway. Then, as a natural consequence, "all roadway and right of way acquired by them, is for public use," etc. (reading the first section). Now, the object of that section is to make operative the twenty-first section of the Constitution, which refers to discrimination. It is true that there is a provision in the statutes which is supposed to be the governing law of the Board of Railroad Commissioners, and that there is a provision there in general terms, conveying simply the idea that freight shall be forwarded upon the same terms for all to all places; but I take it, that when the Board of Commissioners found that they had to take this section of the Constitution, which prescribes that there shall be no discrimination, they found that it was not possible to prevent it under this statute. Therefore, I have incorporated a provision going directly to this point of discrimination, which takes it up with more particularity, and prescribes a punishment, which to my mind will be efficacious. Laying down the principle that the railroads are subject to the control of the State, as embodied in the present Constitution upon this point, we have those principles in the bill, and the first step has been taken to prevent discrimination by railroad companies.

Now, in regard to section two. I presume that gentlemen of the committee are more or less familiar with it. Its object is to afford information to shippers, or other persons who may be more or less connected with railroad transportation in forwarding or receiving freight, by prescribing the posting schedules of the rates in all railroad companies' offices. In the bill, as first drafted, there was a proposition that they should be required to furnish copies of such schedules. The object was this: In all systems of railroads outside of this State, under the control of Railroad Commissioners, like the State of Georgia, or Illinois, there were schedules printed on the basis of uniform charges per mile, and instead of being a book of two hundred and eighty-two pages, as in this State for a few staple articles, was only about six or eight pages. The adoption of the bill, as it originally stood, would have compelled the railroad corporations to have adopted a system of charges which would have been rational, clear, and brief, so that any person in a trifling space of time could have ascertained exactly the system under which the charges were made for any distance; and a double result would have been obtained: First, the information sought would have been accessible to every person in California; and secondly, the means or mode of information would have been supplied which would enable shippers to protect themselves, and enable the general public to understand this subject, without being compelled to use a confused and involved mass of figures, such as the railroad company have inserted in this book of two hundred and eighty-two pages. In the bill now, that has been altered so that the railroad companies are compelled to furnish the schedule only for examination. Even then it is better than any rule regulating it at the present time. It is absolutely impossible for people to obtain any information whatever on this subject of freight rates. The railroad agents do not know it themselves. They are frequently compelled to telegraph to headquarters to ascertain what they shall charge upon certain articles. I say that the system is designedly involved and intricate, with all due deference to the committee, and I believe that some redress should be offered to the public, so that their rights may be maintained. Now, supposing that such schedules shall be furnished to the public in this manner, the section continues, "Such rates shall be equally available," etc., (reading remainder of section two). Now, Mr. Chairman, it seems to me that under any intelligent system of railroading there should be no objections raised to the provisions of this section. Why is it not right, that if the railroad company make a distinction for freight purposes of fast and slow freights, that those terms should be equally available to everybody? That if my neighbor gets a discount on his freight I should be denied the same? If my neighbor pays cash and gets a discount, why should I be denied the right and opportunity to the same? If he pays more for sending goods by fast freight than for slow freight, why should I not have the same privilege on the same terms? Besides that, there should be no distinction between him and me. When a freight bill is sent to my neighbor, and he pays it, he should not be able at the end of thirty days to go down to the treasury of the railroad company and draw the amount of money which represents the difference in charges, which he enjoys as a special favor, and which I do not enjoy, unless I, too, make a special contract. My neighbor, who is engaged in the same class of business that I am, should not be permitted under the special contract system to get special rates on the very articles that I am bringing here, and which the railroad company has said he shall be permitted to bring upon more favorable terms than myself. In other words, the railroad companies should not, and shall not, be permitted to make themselves a partner with every man engaged in business in this State, if they chose, and determine how much his receipts shall be. They should not, and shall not, determine, where his receipts are large, how much that business will bear, and then make such arrangements by special contract and special tariffs as to take the control of the receipts. Thus they could go through the whole line of business and put on their tariff here and there, to make a revenue of profit from every source, until they will hardly allow a business man to exist or to maintain themselves.

Now, if the system of special contracts is to be allowed in this State, and if no means are adopted by this Legislature, or by the Board of Railroad Commissioners, to prevent it, the mercantile community of California will be reduced to a condition of servitude, under which I believe no industrial or mercantile community in the history of the globe has ever existed. The principal reason why our business enterprises are slumbering to-day results from the condition of debasement and slavery under which business men are at the present time existing. Our business men have no enterprise. Why has eastern capital sought out adjoining territory to California? Is it not because we are restricted and bound within narrow limits by this corporation. They have lost all desire to extend business enterprises, knowing full well that every dollar of profit and every cent of gain is so much upon which the railroad corporations may base a further charge. What object has the business man of San Francisco to swell his trade or increase his business when he knows that down at the junction of Fourth and Townsend Streets the railroad company are ready to figure on how much more they can extract from him in the way of charges and in the way of toll. Now, I believe, that here in the State of California there is a complete and thorough knowledge of the far reaching effects of the system of special contracts, and of the necessity for a change, and I believe that in the mind of every just and fair man there is a comprehension of the principle that all men ought to be charged the same price for the same services. I think I need say nothing further on that subject, but will leave it entirely to your judgment.

(Reading section third.) I deem that section three is entirely within the purview of this bill for the reason that, in order to prevent railroad abuses, I believe that it is within the limits of wise legislation to prescribe a system for railroad corporations that will render them subject to State control in such manner that the result will be beneficial to shippers, and to prevent the abuses of railroad transportation. What redress have we if railroad companies are permitted to absolutely destroy and tear up and remove facilities for transportation which they have used? What system of railroad transportation would be complete that would permit railroad companies to tear up and remove all means of transportation? I would say, then, that it is a hypercritical objection to come in here and state that that section is not within the province of the Legislature of the State of California, or that it does not in any manner relate to the other sections of the bill. A further objection was raised here last March, when I had the honor of appearing before the committee in reference to circumstances of this character: What is the effect of the bill when a railroad company runs a side track, either for some one else or for its own purposes, to quarries or gravel beds or other things of that character belonging to itself? I believe I am within the limits when I say there are very few occasions when the railroad company will run side tracks for anybody but itself for such purposes. But suppose it does. This section states that the track must be maintained for the purposes for which it was constructed. When a quarry was worked out, what Court would say that it ought to be maintained? Are we to presume that a Court in carrying out this section to the letter would violate it in the spirit? It is to prevent such things as have been done by the railroads within this State, as when the Central Pacific Railroad Company destroyed that magnificent wharf at Santa Monica, at which the largest ships could float which come to the Pacific coast; a place at which vessels might anchor, and where great industries were growing up by which that whole section of country was becoming populous. The railroad company in a few hours destroyed that wharf, or destroyed the connection by which it existed. I believe that a railroad corporation that would do such a thing as that must be controlled within narrow limits; that it must be held under such control that hereafter the people shall not be liable to outrages or acts of vandalism of that character. If they can destroy a structure of that character whenever in their belief a road is growing up that promises competition, whenever anything is done by any individual by building a wharf in connection with a railroad by establishing facilities for public use on or near a system of railroads, unless some check is placed upon these corporations they will step in and either compel him to sell at a reduced price or render it comparatively worthless by a repetition of such acts as I have mentioned. I ask if it is right for the people of the State of California to be subjected to such acts of injustice, and such gross outrages? and whether it is true that under the provisions of this section any injustice can be done to the railroad corporations by any suggestion that it would affect the side tracks, or temporary tracks, or tracks built for the purpose of carrying passengers or freight while repairs are being made on the main line? I ask if, under the provisions of this bill, acts of that character are prohibited at the expense of or under the penalty of a loss of their charter? I ask the lawyers on this committee whether, from consideration of cases of this character, they would omit the penalty for cases plainly within the provisions of this bill? As it is, the bill is in its nature quasi penal; it imposes penalties of the gravest character, and I presume that any Court in construing it would not give any different rule of construction or interpretation than what is implied, for the purpose of doing an injustice.

As to section four, the object of that section was merely to restrain the railroad corporations in the State of California, whether they came from the outside or proceeded from the inside, and keep them entirely within the State control. It is hardly necessary to recall to gentlemen of this committee that only a short time ago, at the last session of Congress, a bill was introduced permitting the Southern Pacific Railroad system in California, Arizona, and New Mexico to consolidate. A resolution was passed through both Houses protesting against it. In regard to this matter, I have to say, that if a corporation comes into the State it is a foreign corporation, and the Board of Railroad Commissioners, being in their character somewhat of a judicial body, should they assume jurisdiction of that corporation, a question might arise as to whether or not any judicial body, even if qualified with extraordinary powers, would have the right to prescribe the rates of fares and freights of such foreign corporation. Now, it might be that, under the extraordinary powers of the Board of Railroad Commissioners, the question might be decided in favor of the State of California; but do the people of the State want to see the power taken from the Board of Railroad Commissioners by raising a question of constitutional power? Whether this body, being such a body, could exercise functions somewhat judicial in their character over a foreign corporation? And being non-residents of the State of California, would they, in a proceeding of that character, have the right to go into the Federal Courts? While it may be true that the Federal Courts are just as fair, and dispense the same justice, as the State Courts, still, the sovereignty of the State of California is vindicated in your own Courts, and it is to her interest, when she bestows favors on anybody, to ask that they have their differences and difficulties settled in her State Courts. Why should we permit a railroad corporation to enjoy privileges not given to other citizens, or permit them to derive an advantage of great investments and corresponding profits in the State of California, and at the same time be independent and free from the control of her Courts? Is that the policy, or is it the statesmanship, which should govern the legislators of the State of California, looking out for the best interests of their State? A corporation of that kind, continuous in its extent, owning properties in two or more States or Territories, and making contracts, or entering into mortgages affecting that property or being furnished with a system of mortgages or obligations extending beyond the State, would be a source of confusion under our system of taxation.

I will give an instance: Suppose that a system of mortgages covers a railroad from the City of San Francisco to the Rio Grande; suppose that it is a continuous line of railroad, forming a unit, in assessing it we should become involved in the complications of its connections in different places of its system of properties, mortgages, and rolling stock running into different States. Would all this line running in the different States have to be segregated into parts in order to determine how much the great State of California is to receive by taxation? Why should we do that? Why should we subject ourselves to those difficulties? Why should a corporation in the State of California be permitted to extend its power outside of the State, and to take a charter from another State? When it has a charter in this State and forfeits it, what right and how could that forfeiture affect the corporation beyond the line? What control would we have over our corporation when beyond our borders? The question would come up in any ordinary difficulty; it is a question of the gravest magnitude and one that has never been determined in our Courts. We can have this matter in such a condition under this section, that we can have such property and roadbed subjected to the same control as the property of private individuals in this State. These are but a few of the difficulties that present themselves to me. At the present time there is no provision in the laws of the State of California for any mode of forming a corporation except by incorporating within the State, and the only way in which this question can be raised would be when some of the Federal corporations came into the State, or some of our own roads should merge with roads from the outside, acting under a Federal charter. Under such circumstances, to what extent could we tax the Federal corporation, and to what extent could we control it? The result, to my mind, of all these questions is simply this, that insomuch as the people of the State permit these public agents to derive the benefit and a profit by the investment of their means for the public use in operating a road for the public benefit, and when the people of the State permit them to take toll for transportation of freight and passengers over the highway thus established, we should insist that these roads shall remain entirely within the control of the State of California. We have a right to do it, and I believe that we should never surrender that right. We have a right to say to any corporation within the State of California: "You have organized under our laws as an agent of the State of California, and now if you attempt to go beyond our borders and to consolidate with other roads receiving benefits from foreign corporations, either from the United States, or from any of the States, you shall not exist under the laws of this State. You shall no longer enjoy the profits and benefits which we gave to you. You are a creature of the State of California, and you shall not escape our control and set our laws at defiance." Is it possible to legislate upon this subject? I claim that it is. It is claimed that it is defeating competition. I believe that it will encourage competition and competition based upon principles of firmness and equity—a competition which is within the control of the State of California, which should derive the benefit from the competition. Who is most entitled to those benefits, the railroad people or the State of California? Who will derive the profit? And what competition will be of any avail if the competing parties are to pay nothing towards the burdens of the people of the State? Are they to enjoy these rights from the people of the State and yet be beyond her control? I say that it is the better policy that any body of men who desire to incorporate under our laws should comply with the provisions of our Code, and so locate their lines as to begin at the borders and connect there with others; and in that way we would have a complete chain of roads, affording competition in every particular, and based upon the laws of supply and demand. Whenever the people of the State can supply competing roads they will be built upon the conditions I have named—and they will be built. There is a widespread misconception as to the effect of this matter. I do not think it necessary to express my views further before this body of lawyers as to how a corporation beyond the State control should be managed with reference to this State.

As to the next section. Section four hundred and one of the Civil Code, provides, in connection with another section, that railroads in this State may consolidate and become corporations, etc. There is no statute determining how long a railroad corporation shall last.

If it be true that a corporation commences its existence from the time it files the original papers, and that it continues its life by consolidating with other corporations, we might as well strike that provision from our Constitution, so far as it says that the Legislature shall not have the power to extend the corporate franchise, because it would only be necessary for a body of men to organize a small road to last for fifty years, and when it is about to expire to consolidate with another which is younger, and thus its existence would never be brought to a close. Why should we permit that? That was not the intent of that system of consolidation, and I do not believe that it is now, under the provisions of the Constitution, to enact laws which contemplate the existence of a corporation for more than fifty years; and I believe every road, or corporation which enters into the consolidation should terminate with the existence of the oldest. Why should the Central Pacific Railroad consolidate with any other road in 1871, and thus continue its existence ten years longer than the time provided by law, thus existing for sixty instead of fifty years. If the principle is correct, that a corporation shall exist in this manner, if it is never ending, what protection will the people of the State of California ever have when it swells and grows till it overreaches the whole of the State? I believe that it is essential that any system of transportation should give justice between the railroad and the people, and if it is incorporated here, or consolidated here, subject to this section, I believe that there will be no objection made to it, such as would be were it incorporated outside of the State, or extended by consolidation beyond the control of the State.

In regard to section six. Any turnpike, or toll road, or public highway of that character, for a public use, is under the control of our laws, so that if the public desire to use the road no Court can deprive them of it. No Court or Legislature can do it. I think it is a fundamental principle that they belong to the people. Now what does this provision accomplish? (Reading section six.) No lawyer would ever give that any other construction in the world, except that it is the roadway and right of way which remain and are for the public use. And the other property is to be distributed among the stockholders. It is no new principle, it is as well settled and established as the right of the State to a reversionary interest in the public lands after the railroads shall have abandoned them. What is the difference, in principle, between calling a railroad a public highway and a turnpike a public highway? Wherein is the distinction? I believe that this provision of the bill simply announces the law, and is put in here because it is only necessary to provide what shall be done with the property of the railroad, after its rights shall determine how these penalties shall affect them, and for the reason that it interjects in this system a provision that must be made for the disposition of the property. It makes complete and carries out the system and accomplishes every object which could be asked for the control of the railroads, without in any way inflicting upon them the penalty which the Legislature might impose upon them at the termination of their charter.

Section seven—I believe that it is proper that a penalty should be fixed which would be most efficacious. I believe that a penal fine or imprisonment would be perfectly useless. I believe that a corporation which is powerful and wealthy would protect its employés if they were brought into a Court of justice, and pay fines if imposed, and that a fine would fail to reach and correct the violation of the laws. I do not believe that if the Directors of the Central Pacific Railroad Company found themselves in danger of incarceration in a jail that they would permit any such violation. I think that they would seriously hesitate and long deliberate before they would enter upon any system of practical discrimination or extortion. The penalty is severe and for that reason it is merciful. It will accomplish the object and prevent the crime, and if it does so I believe that it should be retained in this section.

As to the final provision of this bill, it is only prescribing under the provisions of article twelve, section twenty-two, the mode of enforcing the rates of freights and fares that the railroad company has prescribed, and I believe that it will insure a compliance by the railroad corporations with those rates. Article twelve, section twenty-two, of the Constitution, says that the Legislature may pass such laws as will insure a compliance, etc. I believe that the Attorney-General should sue out a writ of mandate in case the Board should fail to obey the Railroad Commissioners, to compel a compliance with their directions. Why ought they to be permitted to evade these provisions which the law and the Constitution say are right and just? Why should the whole people of the State of California for three or four years be kept waiting for a decis-

15ᵇ

226

ion of the Supreme Court, when the matter ought to be settled at once as to whether or not the Railroad Commissioners should fix those rates? The rates are conclusive, and the only question should be, do the railroads comply with them? What objection ought to be urged to the right of the State to proceed without stay? Under the criminal law a man would have to go to the State Prison pending an appeal, unless he has a certificate of probable cause. Under the common law, not only stay on appeal was usually denied, but even the right of appeal itself. There is no stay in case of judgment against defendant for unlawfully holding public office. It is said that the right of stay on appeal is common to every one under the common law, and when the railroad desire to appeal a sufficient bond should be given for the protection of the people who are the respondent. What bond should be given to protect the State of California? To whom should the bond run? What would be the benefit of that bond? I say that to give a bond in such a case would be child's play; it would be trifling with the principles upon which the Board of Railroad Commissioners acts and upon which it was established. The rates of the railroads should be established, and they should be compelled to abide by them. I say that it is a gross injustice to permit them to take an appeal from a writ of mandate. They should comply with the law made by the people of the State of California or forfeit their charter. Those are the provisions of the bill as I understand them, and the objects which it seeks to accomplish; and I do not know that I care to say anything further in regard to it.

I thank the committee for its kind attention.

The following is a copy of the bill as amended in the Judiciary Committee, after discussion by the members thereof. Whereupon, upon motion of Senator Johnson, the same was reported back, and its adoption, as amended, recommended, by the following vote:

AYES—Messrs. Taylor, Spencer of Napa, Reddy, Baldwin, Johnson, Kelley of Solano, Kellogg, Sullivan, McClure, Del Valle, Brooks, Murphy, and Cross.

NOES—Messrs. Vrooman, Perry, and Whitney.

[Amended by Judiciary Committee.]

ASSEMBLY BILL No. 10.

[Introduced by MR BARRY, March 25, 1884—Referred to Committee on Corporations.]

AN ACT TO PREVENT DISCRIMINATIONS AND ABUSES BY RAILROAD CORPORATIONS.

The People of the State of California, represented in Senate and Assembly, do enact as follows:

SECTION 1. All railroads built or owned by corporations organized under the laws of the State are public highways, over which all persons are entitled to transportation for persons and property on equal and impartial terms. All roadway and right of way acquired by such companies is for public use. All persons and companies engaged in operating any such road, or in transporting freight or passengers over the same, or which shall hereafter operate or engage as aforesaid, shall forward, move, and carry impartially for all persons offering freight to be transported or moved, without discrimination, preference, or favor to one over another, in price, dispatch, speed, or accommodation of any kind, [as to freight of the same kind or class, from the same station and in the same direction, except as herein provided. All freight [of the same kind or class] shall be dispatched and forwarded in the order in which it is received or tendered for transportation, except that a preference must be given to perishable articles, live stock, household goods, express matter and first freight. Provided, that in the transportation of persons and things, preference shall be given to the United States and the State of California,] and [facilities similar to those in use January first, eighteen hundred and eighty-four, and sufficient for the accommodation of the public, and all connecting transportation lines, shall be extended on like terms to all connecting transportation lines, whether by land or water, in the receipt and delivery of goods, exchanging cars, making connections by rail, and all other arrangements for expediting and facilitating the receipt, transfer, transportation, and delivery of freight.

Sec. 2. All persons and companies mentioned in the first section of this Act, shall at all times keep posted in a conspicuous place accessible to the public, at each of their stations and offices, a printed or written tariff or schedule, of all the rates of freight and charges in force for transportation [from that particular station] and points and stations to or from which they carry or transport, which shall be observed as a penalty of the same toll or freight charges to all persons doing, including the same. Such rates shall be equally available to all persons demanding transportation over said road, or any part thereof, without discrimination or favor to any, as provided, or section one hereof. All discounts, rebates, special contracts, special rates, and other devices for charging more or less than such published rates, are forbidden: provided, that a uniform discount (to be established and published as aforesaid) for payment in advance, or for prompt payment, may be made, and different rates may be charged for express matter, fast and slow freights, and for carload lots, and for lots under a carload; [and a less rate per mile may be charged for long distances than is charged per mile for short distances for the same kind or class of freights;] all such rates and discounts to be available to all applicants on equal terms.

Sec. 3. All railroad corporations must at all times maintain all their track and other structures [devoted to a public use] in good and sufficient repair and in a state of complete efficiency for the purpose for which they were constructed or adopted. Any such track or structure decayed, destroyed, or removed must be diligently replaced or restored to as good or better condition of usefulness and efficiency as before such decay or removal, [if necessary or convenient to the public use.]

Sec. 4. No railroad corporation authorized under the laws of this State is permitted to accept any charter or corporate franchise from any other Government, State, or sovereignty; and no corporation organized under the laws of any other Government, State, or sovereignty is permitted to operate any railroad or carry by rail within this State.

Sec. 5. Section four hundred and one of the Civil Code does not apply to railroad corporations formed by the consolidation of two or more companies previously existing; but the term of the existence of corporations so formed shall not extend beyond that of any of the corporations entering into the consolidation.

Sec. 6. On the expiration or forfeiture of the charter of any railroad corporation, its road and right of way acquired by it remain vested in the people of the State for public use. Its other property shall be sold, and the proceeds, after payment of its debts and liabilities, divided among its stockholders.

Sec. 7. Any railroad corporation violating the provisions of sections one, three, or four of this Act shall forfeit its charter and corporate privileges and shall be adjudged to have incurred such forfeiture and to be dissolved, in an action on behalf of the people of this State, to be instituted by the Attorney-General: [provided, no act of any agent of such corporation violating the provisions of this Act shall be construed to be the act of the corporation, unless authorized or ratified by the Board of Directors thereof.] Any officer, agent, or servant of any railroad company, who shall [knowingly] take part in the making, carrying out, or enforcing of any contract or agreement for railroad transportation in violation of the provisions of this Act, or in collecting charges, or paying or allowing discounts or rebates forbidden thereby, or who [knowingly and willingly] shall, directly or indirectly, enter into any agreement or undertaking, or give any orders or directions for, or consent or ratification to, the carrying of freight on terms in any respect different from those prescribed in this Act, or further making of any discount or rebate hereby forbidden, or for violating the provisions of this Act in any particular, shall be deemed guilty of a misdemeanor.

Sec. 8. Rates of freight or fare adopted by the Board of Railroad Commissioners, if not put in force and complied with by the railroad companies affected, may be enforced by writ of mandate on behalf of the people, to be sued out by the Attorney-General. Any company failing or refusing to comply with a peremptory mandate issued in such action shall forfeit its charter and be dissolved. On appeal from judgment awarding a peremptory mandate in such cases there shall be no stay of proceedings on appeal.

I certify the foregoing to be a correct copy of the statements and exhibits considered by the Judiciary Committee of the Senate of California, as shown by the phonographic reporter's notes, as transcribed by him for the committee.

C. W. CROSS,
Chairman.